RAKE AT THE GATES OF HELL

SHANE MACGOWAN IN CONTEXT

Robert Mamrak

ISBN: 0615445446
ISBN-13: 9780615445441
Pin Oak Bottom Press

For Anna. The measure of *my* dreams.

Warning: If profanity offends you, read no further. Shane
MacGowan is no boy scout.

ACKNOWLEDGEMENTS

Writing a fact-based book about Shane MacGowan was a far more challenging endeavor than I imagined it would be. It's difficult to separate fact from legend. Contradictions in the record abound, many of which I was not able to resolve. In the hundreds of MacGowan interviews I unearthed it is clear that Shane himself is often at the root of the confusion. In April of 1996 Spider Stacy told the *Boston Globe* "You can't completely trust him, because he says one thing one day and completely changes his story the next. I'm not calling him a liar. He says what he believes to be the truth at that particular moment." Initially I intended to footnote quotations and the like, something rock biographies seldom do. I was compelled to abandon that idea because identical quotes were often included in different articles and books. Moreover, when they were used they were frequently credited to different sources, or not credited at all. Instead, I've tried to cite sources within the text when I felt relatively certain what the original source was. I apologize for those instances where I have failed.

Shane MacGowan's life has been well documented. The best book available to learn about Shane MacGowan is Victoria Clarke's A *Drink with Shane MacGowan*. The late Carol Clerk's *Pogue Mahone, Kiss My Arse: The story of the Pogues,* and Ann Scanlon's *Lost Decade: The story of the Pogues*, while not as narrowly defined, are also good sources. I gleaned what I could from these. James Fearnley's *Tour Diary* and Joe Merrick's *London Irish Punk Life & Music...Shane MacGowan* were also helpful. In some cases I extracted interview material from these works.

I have also used interview material from the thousands of articles, letters, and emails about Shane MacGowan and his various projects I read during my research. These were found in various sources, which are cited in the bibliography. Many of the articles found in these sources were retrieved from several Internet websites. Among the most useful of these were shanemacgowan.com, shanemacgowan.de, pogueslive.com, and shane-macgowan.co.cc.

Over the years I have been fortunate to see MacGowan perform with the Pogues, with the Popes, and with Sharon Shannon's Big Band. I've also been able to obtain hundreds of live MacGowan recordings spanning his entire career. These performances and recordings informed my work.

As important as the forgoing was to this book, I am most indebted to people who provided additional source material. Many of them (like Mick Walsh, Kirk Danby, and Joe Sullivan) I know only through emails and the Friends of Shane website. Some, like Sebastian Werner who did the cover photo, I've known for years. Others, like Terry Healey and Cork-born John & Kate Shanahan, I've known most of my life. These last three I also thank for reading early drafts and providing encouragement and suggestions. I am also grateful to Kate's brother, the late Paddy Deasy of Cork, for his help early on.

I am very indebted to the people of Tiperary who helped me get to know their county: William Daly, Sally Morris, Joe Hannigan, Geraldine Reddan McKenna, and Niall Heenan were invaluable. Moreover, my wife and I will always remember the hospitality of the Henry Torpey family of Borrisokane and the Brendan Culhane family of Carney Commons who welcomed a pair of strange yanks into their homes. Nor will we forget Michael and Mary McGreeney who drove us to Thurles to experience a ceilidh.

Four people, however, require special mention. First, my editor and friend; novelist, journalist, and Shane MacGowan fanatic, Richard Massey (who once managed to get thrown out of a New Orleans MacGowan gig for being too rowdy. I didn't think that was possible.) Next, Shane MacGowan and Victoria Clarke. Shane for being Shane, and Victoria for her gracious consideration and hospitality (not to mention keeping Shane alive all these years.) Finally, Anna Friberg Mamrak, my research assistant, proofreader, concert and travel companion, reason to live, and wife.

PREFACE

"What made Ireland a nation was a common way of life, which no military force, no political change could destroy. Our strength lies in a common ideal of how people should live, bound together by mutual ties, and by devotion to Ireland, which shrank from no individual sacrifice. This consciousness of unity carried us to success in our last great struggle. Now in that spirit we fought and won. The old fighting spirit was as strong as ever, but it has gained a fresh strength in discipline in our generation. Every county sent its boys whose unrecorded deeds were done in the spirit of Cuchulainn at the ford."

Michael Collins (1922)

"I agree with that statement totally," Shane MacGowan told me the week after his 50th birthday. "And if the Brits just fuckin' accepted the fact that it was over and stuck to it. Everybody knew that they – Collins knew that they weren't going to stick to their treaty. De Valera knew they weren't going to stick to the treaty. Everybody – most people knew they weren't going to stick to the treaty because they never stuck to a treaty in their lives – ever! Anywhere."

"Like the Americans with the Indians," I suggested.

"Bloody Americans! Krssssssh," Shane laughed as only he can. (Throughout the rest of this work I've edited out Shane's trademark laugh, but you can rest assured that most of the MacGowan quotations I've used were punctuated by his laughter.) "Actually, there's always been a very strong common feeling between the American Indians and the Irish," Shane continued. "During the great famine – there were lots of them, but the big one, the really big one there was some relief in Ireland provided by the Quakers and people like that, and there was also relief sent from the Irish in America, and also from the red Indians in America."

The day before, New Years Day, I'd made arrangements with Victoria Clarke to interview Shane in their Dublin home. My wife Anna and I had been in County Tipperary researching this book when Clarke invited us to meet her and Shane in Portlaoise. He was doing his usual guest spot in a Sharon Shannon concert on New Year's Eve. The show was held in Portlaoise's best hotel, and it was outstanding. MacGowan did about a half dozen songs, including the traditional "Courtin' in the Kitchen," which we had never heard him sing before. We expected Shane to be with Victoria when we met around noon the following morning over coffee in the hotel's café. He wasn't. She explained that he had just got in from the previous night, was "a bit pissed," and was in no shape to be interviewed. She was very gracious, a lovely person all around, and invited us to come by their home in Dublin the next day.

On the way to their house we passed the Four Courts building where the Irish Civil war kicked off more than 80 years earlier. We crossed the O'Connell Street

Bridge with its elevated statue of O'Connell, the 18th and 19th century Catholic Irish Republican leader. Many of the stores still had signs up that said "Merry Christmas" in Gaelic. Our cab driver, who had once emigrated to Australia and had recently returned to Ireland to get in on its economic boom, explained that the shop owners got government grants for the signs, but not if they were in English. He dropped us off in front of a row-type house, typical of those in any large city. It was brick, not fancy, but nice, just off a main street. The cabby said it was an expensive neighborhood. MacGowan later told us that his friend Ronnie Wood, the Rolling Stone's guitarist, lived nearby.

I knocked on the door. In retrospect, I don't know why we were surprised, but we were when MacGowan himself opened the door. Shane was surprised too. He said Victoria told him we'd be by at 3:00 PM. She never told us that. She just said to come over in the afternoon. It was only about one o'clock, so I offered to come back later. Shane said, "No," and invited us in. Victoria was out. Press reports had prepared me for the possibility that he'd be semi-hostile. He was anything but. Shane was hospitable, friendly, and polite. He even kissed Anna's hand. He led us through a foyer into a small room, more of a TV room than a living room. It had a hardwood floor and shelves crammed with books and some Christmas cards. Past that room, through French doors, there was a kitchen. The room we were in had a small, black leather couch opposite a flat screen LCD television mounted on the wall. A straight back wooden chair held the top hat and long leather coat he had worn onstage with the Pogues several nights before. The chair also held a paperback of a Greek classic, Homer, if I remember correctly. He said he still reads a lot. There was a guitar in a corner, a CD player, and a large stack of CDs. Overall the house was tidy and unremarkable.

MacGowan appeared to be wearing the same clothes he had on at the Sharon Shannon concert two nights past: a black suit with white pinstripes; a black shirt with white pinstripes; and a ton of chains, amulets, and assorted jewelry around his neck. He was a bit disheveled, his clothes rumpled. It seemed a distinct possibility that he'd been in that suit for three days. I don't think he had combed his hair. I got the impression he hadn't been up long. At his feet on the floor was an array of opened beverages: a bottle of Gordon's gin, a bottle of white wine, Bulmer's cider, some beer, and God knows what else. I didn't look too closely lest he take offence. To my amazement he bent over an ordinary canvas duffel bag on the floor, reached in and pulled out an ice cold Tuborg beer, which he offered to me. All afternoon he sipped at a Bulmer's and a glass of clear liquid. I suspect it was the Gordon's gin. Shane was a little wobbly on his feet, but he was lucid and coherent.

When we arrived MacGowan was watching the Gaelic channel on the television. It was a show with people doing traditional Irish set dancing. There were subtitles in English. It struck me as a sort of Irish *Lawrence Welk Show*. When I tried to ask him some questions he stopped me, indicating that he wanted to finish watching the show first. He was really into it. When we finally got started I asked his permission to record our conversations so that I could quote him accurately in this book. He said I could and complained that nobody is ever accurate writing about him. He paid me what I took as a nice compliment by adding that my book was the most accurate he'd seen. Presumably, that was why he offered to help with the project after reading early drafts of a few chapters.

Throughout the time I spent with Shane my goal was to get him to speak about things that are important to him, and things that are important to someone trying to appreciate his work. We talked a good bit about Christianity because so much of his art is steeped in Christian imagery. Among other things, I wanted to ask him about the randy priest in "Donegal Express," but I remembered something he once said about being interviewed. "I usually know within a couple of minutes if someone's gonna be a pain in the arse," he said. "If people are gonna be stupid to me, then I'm gonna be stupid back, because at the end of the day, what I do isn't that complicated. I don't set out to confuse people. I write simple songs that people can sing along to. Like, there's no point explaining what 'Summer in Siam' is about because the bloody thing's about what it says it's about." Shane once told a critic from *New Musical Express (NME)* who was going on and on theorizing about music, "Jesus, shut up! You're boring the arse off me." So, instead of mentioning "Donegal Express," I started a conversation about celibacy in the Catholic priesthood.

"The apostle Paul said it's ok to get married if you're – basically he said if you're horny go ahead and get married," I said, paraphrasing Paul's first epistle to the Corinthians, "but if you're not it's better to be celibate. The church went and twisted that around."

"No, no, no, no. I think he was a psychopath, personally," Shane replied. "A self-obsessed psychopath. All those bloody letters! I think this, and I think that, you know? Slagging off on St. Peter who was appointed by the boss." Being an ex-Catholic Protestant, I took exception to Shane's casual reference to Peter being the first Pope, and designated as such by Jesus to boot.

"I don't know," I said. "The Bible says Jesus asked, 'Who do people say that I am?' Peter said that some think you're John the Baptist come back from the dead, and some think that you're Elijah, but I think you're the Christ. And Jesus said, 'You are Peter, the rock, and upon this rock I will build my church.' You can interpret that two ways. Some people say He was saying He would build his church on Peter, but I believe He was saying on this *truth* that you just spoke I'll build my church."

"You can interpret it loads of different ways," Shane countered, "but you're probably – that's definitely more likely than meaning let's start a worldwide organization that makes lots of money out of poor people. Because that wasn't really Christ's trip, was it? But, yes, that's the closest thing I've heard to a reasonable interpretation of something that's been doctored and translated through several languages and all the rest of it. But if He did say that, then He meant something like that, not how it turned out."

MacGowan is anything but a typical Catholic, but Catholicism is rooted deep within him. In the summer of 2006 during the *DaVinci Code* phenomenon his fiancée, Victoria Clarke, was working on a newspaper column about Kathleen MacGowan, an American woman who claimed to be a direct descendent of Jesus and Mary Magdalene. The woman had just gotten a seven-figure advance on a book based on her claim. The book contended that Magdalene was never a prostitute, but was in fact the legitimate wife of Jesus and the mother of his two children. Shane was adamant that Clarke let people know that he was no relation to Kathleen MacGowan. Stopping just short of calling the American a heretic, he told Clarke, "I think it's blasphemous, because the whole point of the Mary Magdalene story is that she was a prostitute, and not only that, a prostitute that worked on the Sabbath, which was why they were stoning her. Jesus forgave and accepted her. If she hadn't been a prostitute, there wouldn't have been any point to the story."

I was impressed with MacGowan's knowledge of Christian scripture. Most of the Catholics I know in the States don't know much Bible. I was even more impressed, but not surprised, by his knowledge of Irish history. What did surprise me was his reluctance to say anything negative about anything except the British. I asked for his thoughts on why Tipperary, Cork, and Kerry counties were so much more active than the other counties during the Irish Revolution.

"I didn't say they were so much more active," he said. "We just got it together a lot better. We were large counties. So there was a massive network going on."

When I reminded him that both Tom Barry and Ernie O'Malley had complained that those three counties did all the fighting, and that the others were content to drill, drill, and drill some more without actually shooting anybody, he relented a bit.

"Well, Tom Barry was a rabid – was a very – I mean, yes – I'm not going to start nothing with the other counties. You know, like there were various reasons. But it's true. But you'd have to put Claire in there with that. It's a massive generalization, but it is basically true. Tom Barry has got every right to – he's right, he's right, from what my family said. They did. But Ireland is Ireland, that's the main thing."

For Shane MacGowan, Ireland is indeed the main thing. He gets annoyed when people mention his English accent, asserting "I'm completely Irish!" He says his Irish accent was "kicked" out of him as a schoolboy in England. Joey Cashman, his close friend and long time manager, once cautioned an interviewer, "Don't use the phrase British Isles. It's England, Scotland, Wales and Ireland. If you say it any other way, he'll probably throw his glass at you." To understand Shane MacGowan, one must understand Ireland, and Ireland's relationship to England.

To that end we talked a good bit about Irish history. Much of our conversation was about Tipperary history, especially in regard to the Black and Tan War in the 1920s. In one regard Shane was easy to interview. I'd prepared nearly 100 questions just in case he wasn't talkative or was terse in his answers. I needn't have worried. He warmed to the subject and talked at length, often going off on tangents for ten or fifteen minutes at a time. At times I was tempted to interrupt him but thought it unwise. I did, however, have to interject periodically to guide the conversation and keep it on track. At times it was difficult to follow his line of thought as he tended to go in several directions without noticeable transitions. Frequently he would stop in mid sentence, searching for just the right word before completing a thought.

Sometimes Shane would cram so much new material into the answer to a question that I was unable to follow up on new topics he referenced. When he told me, with obvious satisfaction, that as a child he had met Dan Breen, I asked a general question about anybody he might have known who had fought in the Irish Revolution or the Irish Civil War. His answer hit on most of the themes this book explores. "My own family were very much involved... They'd all been really young from 1916. Our place was a safe house... In the country the fighting took place everywhere. Practically everybody I knew as a kid, certainly in the country, was active back in the day. The Lynches and the Deans were related somewhere along the line. They were the local – who were – who pulled off a couple of the biggest ambushes on the Black and Tans and Auxies in North Tip. People at the time were also having this huge – it followed the Land League, which was claiming back the land from the landlords, who were generally absentees. My great grandfather was one of the local leaders of the Land League. And the Land League had incited the Young IRB (Irish Republican Brotherhood), which was formerly known as the United Irishman, the Young R&D, various names – White Boys. Supposedly secret organizations, but everybody knew who they were. It was like it was happening yesterday. People were always telling me stories. They always told the right stories about other people. So then you go and check with the other people and they tell you the stories about the first people."

In one rambling response, which I've edited here for brevity, MacGowan touched on themes that permeate his art: the IRB which gave birth to the IRA; the absentee landlords who hired the Irish to farm the confiscated land they'd once owned, a confiscation that led directly to the horrendous potato famine, waves of Irish emigration, and increased hatred of the British; the old Lynch "ramblin' house" where musicians stopped by all hours of the night, playing and singing while IRA men hid from the British; and the land itself, Ireland. Moreover, he indicated that he was immersed in these themes as a young boy, soaking up the oral tradition of Irish Republicanism in the stories the adults around him told.

MacGowan heard an awful lot of Irish rebel songs in that 350 year-old stone, ramblin' safe house. For my money, nobody sings an Irish Rebel song like Shane. Most people in the know readily admit that Shane MacGowan is one of the greatest songwriters of our time. Many, however, overlook the power of his singing. Listen to his performance of "Boys of Kilmichael" in London's Brixton Academy on St. Patrick's Day, 1994. Then compare that to any other version of the song – Jimmy Crowley, Donie Carroll, or Oliver Kane. There is no comparison. The others are pretty. MacGowan makes you want to go out and kill an Englishman. Isn't that what rebel songs are supposed to do?

Every country has its share of patriotic war songs. The Irish raised the genre from that of a convenient propaganda vehicle to an art that became intrinsic to a movement, the Republican movement. The closest parallel I know is the American Civil Rights Movement, whose song catalogue pales by comparison. One thing that distinguishes Irish patriotic songs is their universality. Songs like "The Battle Hymn of the Republic" are about kicking butt for God and feeling good about it. But outside of that context, it has limited appeal. The United Methodist saw that several years ago and removed it from their hymnal. Patriotic Irish songs are not narrowly defined. Irish Republicans blame nearly all the island's problems on the English, perhaps justifiably so. That blame allows songs about emigration, songs about the famine, songs about the bastard land-lord, and of course songs about battles to fall into the box labeled rebel songs.

The tradition goes back long before the Easter Uprising of 1916. Theobald Wolfe Tone, leader of the 1798 Rebellion, often called the "Father of Irish Republicanism," wrote rebel songs. In days past the streets and markets of every Irish city were full of singers lamenting the plight of the nation. A German traveler in 1842 wrote in his journal, "In Kilkenny there were literally twice as many ballad singers as lamp posts standing in the street." In those days less than half of the island's population could read, so the songs were vital in reporting and propagating resistance against the British. The British did their best to stamp out the rebel songs. Arrests were commonplace. At the trial of a song-writer from Limerick in 1831 the judge concluded that "nothing can be more injurious than inflaming the minds of the lower orders by disseminating ballads…with an intent to create sedition against the government, and disunion among His Majesty's Protestant and Roman Catholic subjects." In many cases the seditious words weren't considered necessary to inflame those lower orders. Dinny Delaney, a blind uilleann piper born in Ballinasloe in 1819 was nicknamed the "Rebel Piper" due to his many arrests for playing "seditious tunes." In County Limerick, in 1881, a six-year-old child was arrested for whistling "Harvey Duff," a song famous for infuriating the British. The following year, in the same county, a constable struck and killed an eight-year-old girl with his baton when she whistled the tune.

Given that type of law enforcement it's not surprising that there was often a fine line between rebels and outlaws celebrated in political ballads. A case in point is "The Lamentation of the Two McCormacks Who Died Innocent in Front of Nenagh Goal." The song commemorates an infamous case that took place in Shane MacGowan's be-loved Tipperary. In October of 1857 William and Daniel McCormack, brothers in their early twenties, were arrested for the murder of a Mr. Ellis. There was little evi-dence they shot Ellis, an English landlord's agent despised in Templemore, the brothers' hometown. Suspicion fell on the McCormacks since they were thought to be holding a grudge against the English because their teenage sister was pregnant by an Englishman. They maintained their innocence to the end. In May they were hung from the top floor of the Nenagh Prison gatehouse. In the months following the execution public outrage grew, making martyrs of the McCormacks. That summer a rally outside Nenagh Prison drew nearly 15,000 protesters. Many years later, on his deathbed, an Irish immigrant living in New York confessed to the crime.

Rebel songs played a huge part in the Irish Revolution and subsequent Civil War. Padraic Pearse, the teacher-poet who was chosen to proclaim the Irish Republic from the steps of the General Post Office (GPO) during the Easter Uprising, edited an anthology called *Songs of the Irish Rebels* in 1914. He reported that in fighting lulls during the Easter Uprising, volunteers under siege in the GPO kept up their spirits by singing rebel songs like "A Nation Once Again," "The Memory of the Dead," and "God Save Ireland." New songs were written soon after the events that inspired them. When 15 of the 16 uprising leaders were executed, "Convict 95" was written about Eamon De Valera (he was spared because of his United States citizenship) while he was still incarcerated. Ernie O'Malley, an officer in both the Revolution and the Civil War, was surprised to hear songs about his own recent exploits sung at dances he attended. He wrote that people were moved by "the fierce exultance of song expressing a buried national feeling."

A basic premise of this book is that Shane MacGowan, throughout his life, has been so moved. Moreover, much of his songwriting and his impassioned vocals on the traditional songs he has covered have so moved others. While in my view this is nearly too evident to bother stating, there was a time when it was a controversial position to take. Throughout the Pogues' heyday in the 1980s the band members were at pains to play down their Irishness. Given that the IRA was setting off bombs in Belfast and England at the time, that is understandable. Jem Finer told the late Carol Clerk, "To be perceived as an IRA propaganda tool, self-appointed or otherwise, would have been a terrible thing. I mean, it would have been complete rubbish, but it would have been quite a liability to life and limb. I think we were at all pains to point that out." In 1989 Spider Stacy told the *Chicago Tribune*, "Only a fascist numbskull would think that when Shane and I played together onstage that it was some kind of political statement." It is not my contention that Shane MacGowan ever advocated blowing up anything. Nor would I call him anybody's tool. It is my belief, however, that Shane MacGowan seldom takes the stage without making a political statement. And for the record, I've been called much worse than "a fascist numbskull."

The Pogues publicity in the 1980s frequently pointed out that half of the band had no ties to Ireland, and the rest of the bands' ties were marginal. This book, however, is not about the Pogues. It's about Shane MacGowan, who is decidedly not a marginal Irishman. He is the reigning monarch in a long line of hard drinking Irish writers. He is a living legend in Ireland, a national treasure, an icon, a household name. In a poll taken to determine what people like most about Ireland he topped the list, beating out James Joyce, Jameson whiskey, and Guinness. In 1981 I was shocked to see Johnny Cash on the *Muppet Show* casually chatting with Kermit the Frog and Miss Piggy. That's it, I thought. Cash is no longer a Country and Western star. He is mainstream. He has hit the big time. He belongs to the ages. I felt the same when I saw Shane MacGowan chatting with Podge and Rodge, the plastic puppet hosts of a popular Irish TV show in late 2006. MacGowan had become far more than a gifted singer-songwriter. It was obvious that while the public perception of MacGowan had changed considerably over the years, Shane remained much the same. Also, the plastic puppets' insight surpassed Spider Stacy's in regard to what makes Shane MacGowan tick.

Rodge: Do you think he'd manage a song at all? Do ya?

Podge: No matter how bullocks he is, he can always manage an old song.

Rodge: Oh God, you know what though? It'll probably be a Brits out song. Wouldn't it?

Podge: Oh God you're right. A bash the Brits and blow them to bits song. We'd never be able to show that! A disaster.

Rodge: Not at all. Not these days. No. They wouldn't allow it. They wouldn't put that out.

From there the scene cut to Shane singing "Boys of Kilmichael," the traditional rebel song celebrating the day Tom Barry's West Cork Brigade annihilated a platoon of 18 British soldiers.

A last point I want to make is that this book is written from the perspective of an American trying to understand Shane MacGowan's work. In retrospect, it started in 1971 during the "troubles" in Northern Ireland. I was invited to my father's friend's house, John Shanahan, an Irish immigrant from Cork. The Shanahans were seeing off relatives, who after an American visit, were returning to Ireland. John's young son Tony, now Patti Smith's bass player, was there. The room where the party took place was cleared, except for a dozen or more straight-backed chairs that lined the walls. The Irish men and women there danced, sang, and told stores in the middle of the bare wooden floor. And they drank. The young parish priest, not long arrived from Ireland, probably drank the most. I'd never experienced anything like it, but I liked what I saw and heard. At one point I mentioned that one of my favorite singers, Van Morrison, was from Ireland.

"Where?" I was asked.

"Belfast," I replied.

Things got quiet very quickly.

"Belfast is not in Ireland," I was told.

I was confused. Nearly 40 years later there is still much about Ireland that confuses me. This book is an attempt to better understand Shane MacGowan's homeland, and in so doing, better understand his work.

CHAPTER 1

**"The Pogues would never have existed if I wasn't Irish.
Ireland means everything to me."**

Shane MacGowan

He'd be dead before most Dubliners had eaten their breakfasts. As he heard mass not once, but twice in his cell, hundreds gathered in the early morning light outside the walls of Mountjoy Prison. As he walked with the priest from that cell to the gallows, as he mounted the steps, as the noose was slipped over his head, they prayed their rosaries and cried their tears. There was little else they could do.

Lanky and awkward in his late adolescence, naive in his politics, Kevin Barry at 18 was hardly a threat to the British Empire. It didn't matter. In the fall of 1920 an Irish patriot, or an Irish boy who longed to be called a patriot, was an English traitor in His Majesty's courts of law. His offence has long since been forgotten by most. Few would remember even his name if not for the song.

> In Mountjoy jail one Monday morning
> High upon the gallows tree
> Kevin Barry gave his young life
> For the cause of liberty.
> Just a lad of 18 summers,
> Yet there's no one can deny,
> As he walked to death that morning
> He proudly held his head on high.
>
> Just before he faced the hangman
> In his dreary prison cell,
> British soldiers tortured Barry
> Just because he would not tell
> The names of his brave comrades
> And other things they wished to know.
> Turn informer or we'll kill you.
> Kevin Barry answered, No!
>
> Another martyr for old Ireland,
> Another murder for the Crown,
> Whose brutal laws may kill the Irish
> But can't keep their spirit down.

Lads like Barry are no cowards.
From the foe they will not fly.
Lads like Barry will free Ireland.
For her sake they live and die.

Come ye standing at attention
While he bade his last farewell
To his broken hearted mother
Whose grief no one can tell.
For the cause he proudly cherished
This sad parting had to be.
Then to death walked softly smiling
That old Ireland might be free.

Kevin Barry had joined the Volunteers, civilians determined to drive the British out of Ireland, in the fall of 1917 after attending the funeral, with 40,000 other Irishmen, of Thomas Ashe. Like Barry, Ashe had also died in Mountjoy prison. Not by hanging, but by a botched force-feeding. A key Irish Republican Brotherhood (IRB) organizer, Ashe had been on a hunger strike to press his demand that he be given POW status. Guards held him down while a doctor snaked a tube down his throat. A mixture of milk and raw eggs was poured into his stomach. Something went wrong. The procedure intended to keep Ashe alive killed him. A British newspaper wrote that his death "made 100,000 Sinn Feiners out of 100,000 constitutional nationalists." Kevin Barry was one of them.

Barry died on the first day of November during what would prove to be the beginning of the final, and surely the most savage, phase of the Anglo-Irish war. Barry was the first Irish Republican to be executed by the British since the 1916 Easter Rising, when a handful of Irish patriots took over Dublin's Post Office and declared Ireland's independence from Britain. Indeed, he was the first rebel arrested in an armed attack since 1916. He was to be made an example, a message, a warning.

A little more than a month before, on September 20, 1920, Kevin Barry was a promising medical student at National University. That morning he rendezvoused with his party of Dublin Volunteers on Bolton Street. They had planned an 11:00 a.m. ambush at Patrick Monk's bakery on nearby Church Street. Barry intended to make it to the university in time for his two o'clock class. The Volunteers were after the weapons of a rations detachment due to arrive from the Duke of Wellington's Regiment. According to army reports, as the British soldiers began to load their trucks with bread, they were ordered to surrender by a group of "armed civilians." Instead, they opened fire. Scattering, the Volunteers shot back. Barry's revolver jammed twice. Before he knew it, the battle was over. His companions had vanished. Panicked, Barry took refuge under one of the army's trucks. He was discovered, loaded gun in hand, and arrested.

He was the only Volunteer who failed to escape. Six British soldiers lay dead, the first fatalities among British regulars since 1916.

Although tortured, the young man refused to give any information concerning the other Volunteers. A sergeant threw him face first against the prison wall and pressed a bayonet to his back, threatening to run him through unless he talked. He didn't. He was then laid face down on the prison floor. The sergeant knelt in the small of Barry's back. Two other soldiers stood on his shoulders. Another pulled his head back by the hair while yet another twisted his arm until it popped lose from his elbow joint. All the while an officer badgered him for the names of his companions and any Volunteer commanders he knew. Still, Barry refused to talk.

There was no evidence presented to prove that Barry fired any of the shots that took British lives in Church Street that day. There was shock, even in England, at his death sentence. Many believed his life should be spared. Various appeals had been made on Barry's behalf during the proceeding weeks. The English Cabinet turned down a last minute petition. Even his request to be shot as a soldier was denied. That would be tantamount to admitting that Barry was an Irish soldier fighting an occupying army rather than the "armed civilian" named in the official British Army report. Some versions of the popular song were careful to point this out.

> Why not shoot me like a soldier
> Do not hang me like a dog,
> For I fought to free old Ireland,
> On that bright September morn.

In light of the political situation, the Crown was adamant that Kevin Barry would die. He would die the death of a common criminal. He would hang. He would be an example.

He became much more than an example. He became a martyr, a lightning rod that inflamed the imagination of Irish youth. Just the week before Barry's execution, Terrence MacSwiney, Lord Mayor of Cork City, had died in the 74th day of his hunger strike. The mayor had been imprisoned for possessing documents "likely to cause disaffection to His Majesty." The public outcry was deafening. Two bishops and an archbishop presided at the mayor's massive public funeral. The national sentiment over MacSwiney's death was quickly transferred to Kevin Barry. The day Barry was executed scores of students from National University enrolled in the Volunteers. In the South and West of Ireland, the "flying columns" that had begun to appear the month before multiplied quickly. The snowball had begun its decent down the hill.

Within three weeks Michael Collins, the architect of the guerilla warfare that gave birth to the Irish Free State, engineered the early morning assassination of 14 British intelligence officers. A squad of rebel Volunteers handpicked and trained by Collins shot them unawares, mostly in their Dublin homes. That afternoon a party of Royal Irish

Constabulary (RIC) Auxiliaries and Black and Tans retaliated by opening fire on thousands of Irish civilians gathered to enjoy a football match between Tipperary and Dublin in Dublin's Croke Park. By the time the shooting ended, eleven football fans and one player were dead. Another sixty were wounded. The slaughter overshadowed the morning's assassinations. That day, November 21, 1920, was thereafter known as Bloody Sunday.

The Black and Tans and Auxiliaries had begun arriving in Ireland that spring. They had been hastily recruited in England to bolster the dwindling RIC ranks. The RIC had been the British answer to policing Ireland. Initially made up strictly of Irishmen, the RIC were regarded as traitors by many of their countrymen, and especially so by the rebels. This natural resentment towards Irishmen willing to police their own as agents of the British, coupled with their vulnerability in the rural areas, made the RIC an easy and frequent rebel target. The first casualties came on January 21, 1919. Two RIC men, both Irish Catholics, were ambushed and killed in County Tipperary. During the last six months of that year, eighteen more RIC men were killed. On Easter Sunday in 1920, the Volunteers burned down more than 300 RIC stations. These actions, intended to demoralize the RIC, had the desired effect. Intimidated and ostracized in their own towns and villages, the RIC rank and file began to resign in droves.

The haste with which the Black and Tans were recruited and deployed gave rise to their name. They arrived in Ireland poorly trained and poorly outfitted. Due to a shortage of RIC uniforms, they were issued mix and match uniforms, part military, and part police. Mostly a combination of black and khaki, they looked more like stormtroopers than police. Almost immediately, the Irish began referring to the foreign police force as Black and Tans. The name stuck even after proper uniforms arrived.

They were recruited largely from unemployed soldiers back from World War I. It was a stroke of genius from the British point of view. The Crown knew it needed an army to restore order in Ireland, but sending in the army to crush the rebels would help to legitimize them as an army rather than as the criminals the Crown wanted to portray. An Irish national police force manned by British ex-soldiers seemed like the perfect solution.

To say that the Black and Tans recruits were less than the best England had to offer is an understatement. Of the original 1,500 recruits, many were uneducated, unemployable types whose baser passions had been nurtured during the war. They were given room and board and ten shillings a day. Policemen in Britain were paid the same but with little risk to life and limb. Since records show that there were many unfilled police vacancies in England in 1920, it can be surmised that these recruits were not attracted by the prospects of a career dedicated to preserving justice and upholding the law. Most, it seems, sought the excitement of military action without the baggage of discipline and boredom that normally accompanied army life.

The RIC Auxiliaries, or Auxies as they were called by the Irish, were formed in July. Intended to be an elite force of 1,500, they were recruited exclusively from ex-army officers. Their pay was twice that of the Black and Tans'. Amazingly, they were even less disciplined than the Black and Tans. With little or no authority in place and no one able or willing to check their zealousness, they became a law unto themselves.

The newly fortified RIC remained a favorite target of the Volunteers. The rebels' guerilla tactics rendered the RIC largely ineffective. Every Crown patrol travelling down a country road was a potential target. The Volunteers carefully picked the time and place of engagements. They attacked without warning. Whenever it seemed that an ambush was turning against them, they easily vanished into the rugged countryside that was their home. This invisible army frustrated the RIC. There was no way to tell an innocent civilian from a dangerous rebel. Realizing that the rebels couldn't operate without the support and co-operation of the citizenry, the difference between civilian and rebel ceased to matter to the Black and Tans and the Auxies.

Regarding the rural population as co-conspirators with the rebels, they began reprisals against civilians living on farms, in towns, and in villages. Their favorite targets were the creameries that sustained much of the rural economy. Fifty-three were burned and destroyed. They did their best to intimidate the population into abandoning the rebels. Patrols of Black and Tans and Auxies plundered the countryside. In raids on over 20,000 homes more than 400 people were arrested and shipped off to English prisons. Civilians were raped, beaten, tortured, and killed. Two hundred unarmed civilians were murdered in 1920 alone. These savage tactics backfired.

True, the RIC had the rebels on the run, but they didn't run far. Until then they had been primarily a volunteer, part-time army. With their homes rendered unsafe by the Black and Tans and Auxies, more and more Irishmen went on the run. Leaving their homes and jobs, they became full-time soldiers in a full-time army. An Irish Republican Army, the IRA. They banded into local, efficient, disciplined groups of 20 or 30 men that attacked the RIC when the opportunity arose. Compact and swift moving, they became known as flying columns. The first was probably the East Limerick Brigade. The Brigades of West Cork and North Cork were probably the most active. Flying columns were soon forming in Tipperary and other counties in the south and west of Ireland.

One week after Bloody Sunday the West Cork Brigade set an ambush on the road to Gleann, just south of the little town of Kilmichael. The target was a patrol of Auxies. The Auxies, despite having what most would regard as a higher caliber of men than did the Black and Tans, were actually far more brutal and indiscriminate in their campaign against civilians. They struck fear in the hearts of the people. Ironically, this seemed to produce in the Irish a strange kind of respect for the Auxies that was not extended to the Black and Tans. Tom Barry, the commander of the West Cork Brigade, called them "super-fighters and all but invincible."

This Barry, who had fought with the British army in World War I, had noticed that the Macroom Company of Auxies had fallen into the habit of using the same routes over and over on patrol. He positioned his column of 36 men behind rocks and boulders, the only cover available in the sparse bogland. Michael Collins' brother Sean was among them. When two truckloads of Auxies came into range, 18 Englishmen in all, Barry's men opened fire. Several Auxies were killed instantly. The survivors quickly surrendered. According to Barry, when the rebels began to come out from behind their cover, the Auxies began shooting again. The column, which had lost only one man up until that point, lost two more as a result of the ruse. One was 16 year-old Pat Deasy. Infuriated, the West Cork Brigade annihilated what was left of the Auxie patrol. It was the RIC Auxiliary's greatest single loss.

The ambush was invaluable to the IRA for the renewed pride and support it generated among a populace that had become increasingly disheartened by the brutality of the Auxies. Like most of the significant events of the Irish Revolution, the battle of Kilmichael was quickly celebrated in song.

> Much we honor in song and in story
> The memory of Pearson McBride
> Whose name's there alone in glory
> And martyrs who long since have died.
>
> Forget not the boys of Kilmichael,
> Those brave lads so gallant and true
> Who fought neath the green flag of Erin
> And conquered the red, white, and blue.
>
> On the 28th day of November
> The Tans left the town of Macroom.
> They were seated in two Crossley tenders
> Which led them right into their doom.
>
> They were on the road to Kilmichael
> And never expected to stall.
> They there met the boys from the column
> Who made a clean sweep of them all.
>
> The sun in the west it was sinking,
> Short the eve of a cold winter's day.
> When the Tans we were eagerly waiting
> Sailed into the spot where we lay.
>
> Down through all the hills went the echo
> The peal of the rifle and gun,
> And the flames of the lorries gave tiding
> That the boys of the column had won.

The lorries were out before twilight,
And high over Dunmanway town
Our banners and Tri they were waving
Just to show that the Tans had gone down.

So we gathered our rifles and bayonets
And soon left the glen so obscure.
Now we never did drink till we halted
At the faraway camp of Glandore.

Forget not the boys of Kilmichael,
Those brave lads so gallant and true
Who fought neath the green flag of Erin
And conquered the red, white and blue.

The rebel songs became a source of unity and inspiration among the Irish. On the farmsteads and in the growing network of "safehouses" where the new full-time soldiers billeted, they were written and sung and passed on from home to home and family to family and generation to generation. One such safehouse, in Carney Commons, County Tipperary, was the old homeplace of Big John Lynch. In 1901 his little farmhouse was hopelessly inadequate for his 14 children. His younger brother Tom, who had done pretty well for himself with the pub that he owned, gave Big John the money needed to build an addition. It was in this house that Shane Patrick Lysaght MacGowan spent his early childhood.

MacGowan was born on Christmas day, 1957, in Kent, England. His parents were visiting relatives at the time. Three months later he was living in Ireland on Big John's farm with his mother's family while his parents worked in England. By this time the place was owned by his uncle, another John. It was a remote property located near the villages of Kilbarron and Borrisokane. It is a rugged landscape. A terrible beauty some have said, with stone everywhere. "It's the worst land in Ireland," according to Mac-Gowan. "Very beautiful, but the soil is lye and rocky. All hills and valleys." Nonetheless, he still calls it "Me spiritual home. Some'd call it a godforsaken bog. I think it's beautiful." The closest town was probably Puckaun. The nearest town of any size was Nenagh (population 7,415 according to a 2006 census). For a family without a car it was a long and infrequent journey to the nearest city, Limerick, some 30 miles to the southwest.

It was the family of MacGowan's mother, Theresa, who lived on the farm. Intelligent, beautiful, and talented, she grew up in the rural traditions; singing the traditional Irish songs that had been passed down in sessions around the kitchen table. She spoke the native Irish tongue better than most. English rule had caused the Irish language to all but disappear in most parts of Ireland by the turn of the century. The census of 1891 revealed that less than 4% of Irish youth under the age of ten spoke it. In the 1920's, after the revolution, the Irish Free State mandated that Irish be taught in schools. Many students regarded the study of the native tongue a bother, much like mathematics or geography. Theresa, however, apparently took to the traditional language, winning awards for her fluency.

A natural beauty with a singing voice to match, Theresa left the area to make her mark in the world. Over the years her traditional Irish singing and dancing had won numerous local contests. She longed to use those talents professionally. She moved to Limerick. Her first step might be considered a relatively small one in today's world. At the time, it must have seemed a huge leap forward to a young country girl. It soon became apparent that Theresa's dream of becoming a singer or an actress was not likely to come true in Limerick. Her best chance was in Dublin.

Once she moved to the capital, Theresa did manage to find a niche on the edge of her dream. For a few years she found success as a model. She was Colleen of the Year in 1954. She made the cover of the *Independent*. That cover photograph, where she is posed with three gigantic Irish Wolfhounds, was later featured on the lyric sheet of MacGowan's 1997 album, *The Crock of Gold*. It appears next to a song about emigrating from Ireland, leaving homeland and mother behind. That song, "Mother Mo Chroi," is one of the few in which MacGowan used the Irish language (*chroi* meaning heart).

Theresa's career was put on hold soon after meeting Maurice MacGowan, a Dubliner, in a Dublin pub. An aspiring writer, he was an office worker with a charm that Theresa found irresistible. They were married, and their first child, Shane, was born within a year's time.

MacGowan invariably describes his childhood in County Tipperary as the best years of his life. At that age he was oblivious to the gripping poverty holding rural Ireland fast. Besides, the Lynch household was more comfortable than many families. "We weren't big farmers," he says, "but we were considered pretty well off. We didn't have a car, but we had two horses and a cart, a donkey and a cart, and loads of bicycles. We made our own butter and milked our own milk and I was taught to kill chickens and geese and turkeys. We shat in the fields and pissed out the front door." His Uncle John's farmhouse was home to 12-14 people during those years. There was no running water. They slept two or three to a bed. Young Shane preferred to sleep alone on the couch. Not just to have a place to himself, but to be next to the family radio. "There were songs that have been forgotten long since, like stuff by Maggie Barry, I heard on the radio. Radio Eireann was amazing in those days, a hundred times better than any pop channel I've ever listened to."

Despite a decided lack of luxuries, food on the farm wasn't a problem. They ate bacon, cabbage, and potatoes on most days. Except of course on Fridays when the Catholic Church forbid the eating of meat. Then they ate freshly caught trout, eel, or salmon. On special occasions they ate one of those chickens, turkeys, or geese MacGowan remembers slaughtering. Despite the poverty, MacGowan's memory of life in Carney Commons is positive. "It was the end of an era that I just happened to catch.

I'm glad I caught it… a hearth fire to cook on, there was no cooker. It was basic and beautiful. All I had was happy times." Day after carefree day, he played in the country-side and helped with the farm's chores.

Watching television was not an option. They didn't have one. Still, there was no lack of entertainment. Music, homemade music, homemade traditional Irish music for the most part, permeated the home. The Lynch home was what locals called a "ramblin' house," a place where people would stop by all hours of the day or night to kick back, enjoy themselves, and play music. "Our place was a safe house," MacGowan told me in 2008. "And it had a brilliant cover for being a safe house which is it was a house where there were raucous parties. A place where people were always going at all times of the day and night. All the time. You know what I mean? Going in and out. And there was loads of great music." Nearly everyone in the family played an instrument. Those who didn't sang and danced. One of the best singers and dancers, and a tremendous influence on the young MacGowan, was his mother's only brother, Sean. A flashy dresser, and a renowned ladies man, Uncle Sean sang everything: Irish ballads, Country and Western ballads, and Elvis Presley's rock and roll hits.

MacGowan's elderly Auntie Ellen played the concertina. Having been middle-aged during the revolution, her rebel song repertoire was considerable. She told stories of hiding IRA men in the bedrooms when the farm was a safehouse. The men were hidden behind the chamber pots, brimming and fouled with urine and excrement, to discourage the Black and Tans from having too close a look under the beds. MacGowan recalls her playing her concertina in the late 1950s, still rocking and shaking, banging her foot in time to the music. Theresa MacGowan recalls, "He (Shane) absorbed all that wonderful traditional Irish music and singing and dancing through his pours when he was at a very formative age."

Uncle Mick Guilfoyl, the Postmaster in nearby Cloughjordan, played accordion. Played so well, in fact, it is said that he taught the instrument to Paddy O'Brien, one of the finest accordion players ever to come out of Ireland. Uncle Mick had at one time been a local IRA commander. He probably influenced Shane as much with his stories about the Black and Tans as with his music. He told graphically of how they would line local townsmen up against a wall and play Russian roulette with Irish lives, and how they had once shot at his Uncle Willie for driving a horse-drawn cart too fast.

By all accounts Shane MacGowan was a precocious child. He remembers conversing intelligently with adults at the age of two. He was a young sponge, soaking up songs and stories. Rebel songs like the "Boys of Kilmichael." Irish Diaspora songs like "Muirshin Durkin." It wasn't long before he was contributing to the kitchen sessions. By the age of three he was up on the table singing "Kevin Barry" and "The Foggy Dew." He later recalled, "I heard a lot of traditional stuff…I'm talking about real Irish folk music. There would be a lot of unaccompanied singing of all sorts of songs like 'Kevin Barry.' You got to remember that this was the late 1950s, early 1960s. So I built up a repertoire of old famous Irish songs that were made famous later by the Dubliners and the Clancys."

MacGowan claims to have read his first book, Dan Breen's *My Fight for Irish Freedom,* when he was four. That same year he says a bad case of the measles caused him to "go mad" for a month, adding "They say I never really came back." He says that was the catalyst to begin writing stories, poems, and songs about the IRA and Irish heroes like Cuchulainn. What is certain, is that it was around that time he began to read and learn the Catechism under the tutelage of his Aunt Nora.

> Who made the world?
> *God.*
> Who is God?
> *God is the Sovereign Lord of heaven and earth and all things.*
> Why did God make the world?
> *Et cetera, et cetera, et cetera.*

There was also the Apostles' Creed, the Hail Mary, the Our Father, the Seven Sacraments, the Seven Deadly Sins, the Ten Commandments, the Act of Contrition, and the Rosary. Especially the Rosary. Aunt Nora was more than Catholic. She was a religious fanatic. Daily she led the saying of the Rosary. She, Shane, and the other participants knelt around the table on the kitchen chairs. Not for the customary 30 to 40 minutes, but for an hour on light days, often for an hour and a half. Shane absorbed her Catholicism as thoroughly as he had absorbed the rebel songs. He admits to having been a "religious maniac" until he was eleven. In rural County Tipperary such devotion to the church was not uncommon. Nearly every home proudly displayed three pictures: The Sacred Heart of Jesus, complete with crown of thorns, fire, and blood; the Virgin Mary, as often as not with her Immaculate heart exposed; and the Pope. In the 1960s most families added a photograph of John F. Kennedy to this Catholic holy trinity.

Religion was not all Shane picked up from his Aunt Nora. She was a compulsive gambler whose love of the Irish Sweepstakes and betting on the horses was soon mirrored in her young nephew. While gambling might seem an advanced habit for a preschooler, most would consider it a mild vice compared to young Shane's drinking. He came from a long line of drinkers. His Uncle John would regularly bring the boy a bottle of Guinness on his way home from Ryan's pub each night. MacGowan claims to have been downing two bottles of stout each night before bed by the time he was five years old. "We'd never even heard of alcoholism," he says. "We'd have thought it was some kind of weird religion."

All in all, it was an idyllic childhood. It came to a traumatic end in 1964, the day his parents had to drag him from the bushes he was hiding in. The time had come for the six-year-old boy to move to England. The time had come for Shane MacGowan to become part of the Irish Diaspora.

CHAPTER 2

"I started out as a healthy fucking Tipperary farm boy. I came over here, degenerated into a school truant, drunken drug user and thief."

Shane MacGowan

For the first several weeks in England, young Shane MacGowan cried himself to sleep thinking about Ireland. The family set up house in Brighton initially, but they moved around a great deal. Maurice MacGowan worked in the offices of C & A department stores, eventually becoming a department head in the London office. The family bought its first car, a used 1956 Hillman. Theresa MacGowan worked for awhile as a typist in the Catholic school in which she had enrolled six-year-old Shane. It helped a little that the school was run by Irish nuns and that most of the other kids were Irish. Still, MacGowan couldn't understand why his parents would make him unhappy, and make themselves unhappy as well, when they all clearly preferred Ireland.

Things got much worse when the MacGowans moved to London. Shane was eight. "It was complete culture shock," he says. "Black people and big city streets - the whole thing. I'd spent my childhood in a remote, country part of Ireland. Lots of hills, small farms and the River Shannon. Lots of traditional music around; hurling and horseracing and all the rest of it. I hated it, coming here." It was probably at this point that MacGowan became acutely aware that he was a "Paddy." The term probably derives from the abundant number of Irishmen named Patrick and Padraic. When used by an Englishman, *Paddy* was an unmistakable insult. Shane MacGowan's accent made sure that every English lad at his school knew he was a Paddy. Fighting became a regular part of his life. He remembers a gang of English kids getting him to sing "Kevin Barry." They jumped him when he got to the line "another murder for the Crown."

Understandably, Shane cherished any link with Ireland. His father's record collection became important to him. Maurice MacGowan, having his own considerable difficulties adapting to life in London, took increasing solace in the two mainstays of Irish culture most readily available abroad: recordings of Irish traditional music and pints of Guinness. During this time Shane MacGowan became infatuated with the Dubliners, arguably the most popular Irish folk band of the 1960's. Another important link to Ireland was his Uncle Frank's pub in Dagenham. It catered to Irish expatriates. Solid working class lads who also felt out of place in England. The jukebox was crammed with Irish music including many of the traditional rebel songs that Shane had grown up with. He loved staying behind the bar watching the frequent fights and hearing the familiar music. He spent a lot of time there when he wasn't in school.

Uncle Frank also gave MacGowan James Bond books. A precocious child, Shane had always been a reader. The isolation and alienation he felt in London, however, seems to have turned what was a pleasant pastime into a lifelong passion. He devoured Steinbeck, Hemingway, and Orwell. His Aunt Catherine loaned him books by Behan, Joyce, and Russian authors. When I visited MacGowan just after his 50th birthday, there was a paperback Greek classic, by Homer I believe, lying on his couch.

In London the MacGowans got a television. It too played a part in shaping the songwriter MacGowan would someday become. He was particularly attracted to violent shows. Shane and his mother never missed *The Untouchables* on Saturday night. They also loved the movies. The more violent the better. The brutal shower murder scene in *Psycho* was a favorite.

Still, none of these distractions could take the place of Ireland. Shane lived for summer vacations when he and his sister Siobhan, five years younger than Shane, would stay in Tipperary on Uncle John's farm. The green fields and patches of woods seemed all the more wild and wonderful now that they stood in contrast to London's streets. Like most boys, Shane and his friends played war games in the hills and fields. They pretended they were in the jungles of Vietnam. Shane took the part of the Viet Cong. When they played Black and Tans he was in the IRA.

To the people of Southwest Ireland the IRA was always more than just a game children played, or the subject of a crop of old songs harvested in the 1920s. No one denied that the IRA had seen better days, but it remained a reality. When the Irish Revolution ended in a treaty with the British in 1922, many in the Southwest's flying columns refused to accept it. A compromise that really pleased no one, the treaty partitioned Ireland into the 26 southern counties of the new Irish Free State and the six counties of the North, which remained part of Britain. When Ireland's Dail voted to ratify the agreement on January 7, 1922, it barely passed with a 64 to 57 vote. President Eamon de Valera resigned his office at once and led the dissenting delegates out in protest.

The treaty allowed that the southern Irish Free State would be a self-governing dominion in the British Empire. Much like Canada, it would enjoy constitutional status, but the members of its parliament would have to swear allegiance to the British Crown. Britain would remain responsible for defending Ireland's coastline, and therefore remained entitled to keep English Navy ships in certain Irish ports. The hated British Army, however, along with the Black and Tans and Auxies, were to be withdrawn immediately. The IRA, now recognized as the legitimate army of the new Irish Free State, began taking over the barracks, depots, and abandoned equipment of the evacuating British military.

Although excited by their new circumstances, the IRA rank and file was just as split as the Dail concerning the treaty. Those in favor of the compromise recognized it as the best deal the Irish could expect at the time. More importantly, they saw the formation of an Irish Free State as a stepping stone to their ultimate goal: an Irish Republic with no ties to England. Many of those opposing the treaty were, as de Valera claimed to be, against the Irish parliament swearing allegiance to the English Crown. The real issue for most, however, was that their job was not done; the English were still in Ireland. The IRA flying columns had left their homes, families, and jobs; they had risked their lives to drive the British off their island. And their island had 32 counties, not 26. The real issue was the same as it had been since the Norman nobleman Strongbow landed in Ireland in 1169. It was the same issue that caused an Ulster earl, Hugh O'Neill, to lead a rebellion in 1590. It was the same issue that caused Wolfe Tone to lead an army of peasants and priests in the bloody revolt of 1798. They wanted the Brits out.

Tensions between the Free State pro-treaty and the Republican anti-treaty factions within the IRA increased throughout the spring and summer of 1922. They erupted into civil war in late June. De Valera joined with the anti-treaty IRA faction in launching a new government under his presidency. They claimed to be the only legitimate government of a 32 county Irish Republic. Many Irish Republicans refused to abandon that claim even after losing to the Irish Free Staters in the brief but bloody civil war. Before it was over the following spring, the Irish had killed more Irish than the British had during the revolution.

By 1931 even de Valera saw the wisdom of using Free State status as a means to pursue a Republic. That year the Statute of Westminster gave six of Britain's self-governing dominions, including the Irish Free State, more legislative freedom. In 1932 de Valera was elected President of the Irish Free State, head of the government that he had led the revolt against a decade earlier. In 1936 he manipulated the political crisis caused by the English monarch's abdication to increase Irish sovereignty. The act allowing King Edward's abdication required the consent of Britain's Dominion governments. In Ireland, consent was withheld until the day after the other dominions consented, technically giving Ireland a different king for a day. De Valera used the time to remove all monarchical language from the Free State Constitution. Since England didn't seem eager to argue, he went further the following year, passing a new constitution naming the elected Irish President head of state and renaming the Irish Free State Éire, Gaelic for Ireland. That constitution revealed that his goal had not changed. Article 2 stated, "The national territory consists of the whole island of Ireland, its islands, and the territorial seas." Article 26 claimed jurisdiction over 26 counties, "pending reintegration of the national territory." De Valera, however, distanced himself from the idea of bringing about that reintegration militarily. He had declared the IRA illegal in 1932, allowing only a government-sanctioned army that would abide by that government's policies.

De Valera telling the IRA that they could no longer operate had little more effect than his telling Britain and the Irish Free State that he was the legitimate President of all 32 counties in 1922. In response to de Valera's 1932 declaration, IRA Chief of Staff Frank Aiken vowed never to give up the fight while the English remained on any part of the island and while what he estimated as nearly 10,000 men remained in prison. Clearly, for some the Irish Revolution was not over. In 1939 Sean Russell, a veteran of the 1916 Easter Rising with an inflexible "Brits out" stance, became IRA Chief of Staff. He promptly sent a declaration to British Foreign Secretary Lord Halifax demanding full withdrawal of British forces from Ireland. Two days after the demand was ignored there were seven sizable explosions in English power plants in London, Manchester, Birmingham, and elsewhere. During the 1940s the IRA's war against the British was primarily limited to skirmishes along the northern border. Ireland was neutral in World War II and refused to co-operate with England in establishing much needed additional North Atlantic ports. Various official reasons were given for Ireland's stance. But for many Irishmen, and certainly for most of the IRA, the real issue went back to 1922. There was a general feeling that anyone fighting a war against England could not be all bad. Besides, what had Hitler ever done to them? Once, when asked if Frank Ryan (introduced to the non-Irish world in MacGowan's "Sickbed of Cuchulainn") collaborated with the Nazis, an incredulous MacGowan replied, "Of course he collaborated! England's misfortune is Ireland's opportunity, you know."

By the end of the war the government of the island's southern 26 counties had ceased participating in British government. In 1949 it renounced its Dominion status entirely and declared itself a Republic, cutting all ties to London. No doubt the IRA was pleased, but not entirely satisfied. There were still six counties to go. The border raids continued throughout the 1950s. Using the guerilla tactics of the 1920s, the IRA launched weapons raids and operations to blow up bridges. Once, a BBC relay station was destroyed.

Coincidentally, the IRA increased its activities when Shane MacGowan was born. In January of 1958 there were 25 reported incidents. In July there were 13 explosions. De Valera issued a number of statements denouncing the violence as a means to force an end to the partition of Ireland into separate states. The old rebel's views had clearly changed since 1921, as had the views of most of the citizens in the 26 counties. No doubt many in southern Ireland would have liked to see the British leave the north, but fewer and fewer were dissatisfied enough with the status quo to fight a war to establish a 32-county republic. As the decade came to an end the IRA was in danger of becoming irrelevant. In 1962 Cathal Goulding, fresh out of an English prison, became IRA Chief of Staff. He introduced policies geared more towards achieving their goal politically. What little IRA military action remained was unauthorized and sporadic. In 1963 on St. Patrick's day in Cork, a freelance mission gave a good indication of the state of the IRA's military capacity. Two IRA men tried to blow up, of all things, a Republican monument de Valera was scheduled to dedicate. The explosion killed one of them and injured the other. It was evident that the glory days were over. The Black and Tans ambushes that Shane laid on his friends during summer vacations on his uncle's farm were probably better planned and executed.

Except for those vacations, MacGowan's life got even more difficult as he moved into adolescence. The MacGowan family had become what today might be glibly labeled dysfunctional. His mother had become depressed and started drinking much more. A doctor had told her it would be dangerous to have more children. She began taking birth control pills despite the Catholic Church's adamant stand against any birth control method save rhythm or abstinence. A priest, an English priest as MacGowan is quick to point out, told her that she would have to stand in the back of the church during mass, and that she would be denied the communion sacrament. In addition to throwing his mother into depression, the priest's obtuseness severely scarred what was once Shane's fanatic Catholic devotion. Maurice MacGowan did little to help the situation. Shane remembers waiting outside pubs and bookie joints when he was left in his father's care. More often than not he looked after himself and his younger sister Siobhan. Most of his friends were other Irish kids who felt exiled in London as well. One exception was a boy he describes as "half-cast." This non-Irish friend, who disliked the English at least as much as Shane did, introduced him to reggae.

Things began to look up when Shane's blossoming writing talent, in this case manifested in an essay on the works of Blake, won him a scholarship to the very prestigious, very ancient, very expensive Westminster School. Founded by the Benedictine monks of Westminster Abbey in 1179, it received royal patronage from Henry VIII after the dissolution of the monasteries in 1540. Considered the fast track to Oxford and Cambridge, its alumni include Ben Johnson, Christopher Wren, John Locke, Sir John Gielgud, Lord Havers, Peter Ustinov, Andrew Lloyd Weber and Lord Lawson of Blaby. It was pretty posh compared to County Tipperary. "My accent changed," MacGowan asserts. "There were a few others like me at Westminster. They let in a bit of a rough now and then. I'd already had one huge culture shock coming over here, so I was getting used to culture shock. There were huge anti-Irish feelings at the time."

Even when cutting-up Shane's intellect was evident. One classmate recalls the time he and Shane were talking in the back of an English literature class. The teacher became annoyed and asked Shane's friend, "What figure of speech is indubitably?" Shane whispered under his breath, "It's an onanism." His friend blurted out, "It's an onanism, Sir!" The teacher made the student come up to the front of the class and read the definition of onanism out of the dictionary: "withdrawal of the penis in sexual intercourse so that ejaculation takes place outside the vagina; coitus interruptus."

The school's location gave MacGowan a different view of London life. It sits on its original site in London's center, next to Westminster Abbey and the Houses of Parliament. The cultural life of the South Bank and West End help create a heady atmosphere. Shane began to split his time between affluent schoolmates in Hampstead and a rougher crowd in Islington and King's Cross. While all this may have proved stimulating to MacGowan, the rigorous academics and regimented daily routine weren't to his liking. Rather than attend chapel three times a week he preferred to turn his attention to extra curricular matters: drugs and alcohol. He wore black trousers, black T-shirts, a black leather jacket, and his hair all up in a quiff. It was a sort of James Dean/Elvis Presley look. Shane told the BBC's Jack Doherty, "I didn't fit in there… I got kicked out at 14. I was basically running, selling drugs to other kids and drinking in the local pubs when I should have been in classes… I didn't know what the hell I was doing there. Priests and teachers at other schools convinced my parents that I should try for a scholarship in this place… I wrote. It was because of my English compositions that I got in." It wasn't long before he was expelled for getting caught smoking pot in public. Apart from a later brief stint at Hammersmith College, it was MacGowan's last brush with formal education.

It was 1971. He was a young Irish teenager in London. He had just squandered what seemed to have been the opportunity of a lifetime. He had little or no adult super-vision. But he had a plan. He planned to wring whatever pleasure he could out of the city he hated. London, he had discovered, did offer certain opportunities not as readily available to a Tipperary teenager. There were drugs, discos, rock and roll, and a great many more girls. Shane MacGowan availed himself of the lot.

Like most teenagers, his musical tastes began to broaden. As a 14 year-old he saw his first rock concert: Mott the Hoople. Several American rock and rollers became favorites: MC5, the Stooges, the Velvet Underground, the New York Dolls, Jimi Hendrix, and Bo Diddley. He still loved Irish music, but Ireland's contemporary song-writers like Van Morrison had an increasing appeal. A special favorite was the Irish rock band Thin Lizzy. MacGowan admired singer Phil Lynott's songwriting and the band's rock version of the traditional Irish song "Whiskey in the Jar."

MacGowan had grown into a strapping youth by this point. He worked a series of menial jobs where his brawn was far more useful than his brain. For a time he stocked shelves and unloaded trucks for a supermarket. He worked in a warehouse. For a time he was a porter at the Indian Embassy. The money he earned allowed him to pursue his increasingly hedonistic lifestyle. His nights became a dizzying whirl of uppers, down-ers, acid, pot, and alcohol. He still went to Ireland every chance he got. He generally kept a job just long enough to save the money he needed for trips back home.

At seventeen Shane MacGowan started his first band. Called Hotdogs with Eve-rything, they played loud rock and roll. Included in their repertoire was MacGowan's first rock composition, "Instrument of Death." Much of the rest consisted of songs by Van Morrison's sixties Irish rock band, Them. Shane had come to regard Morrison as Ireland's greatest living poet. At the time he considered Morrison's old band the great-est in the world. Hotdogs with Everything might have been an important formative step in what would become Shane MacGowan's musical career, but it still wasn't time to quit the day job. The band rehearsed a lot but never actually played a gig.

That same year Shane's lifestyle caught up with him. He was committed to what he usually refers to as "the loony bin." Located in Central London, St. Mary of Bethlehem Hospital was basically a detox center. He was treated there for anxiety, depression, and hallucinations. The official diagnosis was "Acute Situational Anxiety," which he says meant that, he didn't like living in London. The treatment, such as it was, included painting. Shane recalls his paintings being so horrific that they scared the other patients. He was also encouraged to play guitar during his six-month stay. He celebrated his 18th birthday as a "loony."

Shortly after his release, MacGowan landed the job he seemed best cut out for. He became a barman at Griffin Tavern, right next to Charing Cross station. It was a big, busy place with three bars. He hauled beer barrels around, collected cases of empty bottles, and sometimes got to tend the seediest of the three bars, which was located in the basement. He worked a 12-hour shift with an extended break from 4:00 to 5:30 in the evening. During that time he went home to check on Siobhan and see to it that she had something to eat. He also took the opportunity to fortify himself for the night shift by drinking several shots of vodka. Siobhan, just entering her teenage years, had yet to find the means to cope with living in London. She recently said, "I always felt in a constant state of trauma, to tell you the truth. I always felt when I came back (to Ireland) I let my breath out, and over there (in England) was... I felt lonely, you know? You really feel that a part of yourself is missing and you must be reunited with it."

The new job seemed to give MacGowan a new lease on life. "Being a barman, for me, meant cleaning myself up... I had a whole new attitude. I wasn't a druggie zombie, and I wasn't constantly having rows with my parents, and generally being in a state, like I used to be... I felt sharp, alive. I had money in my pocket, y' know. I was looking good."

"Looking good," meant that the longhaired, bearded look that had become part of his Hot Dogs with Everything persona was out. MacGowan became what was called a "soul boy." Soul boys looked sharp. They wore suits and had good, short haircuts. For the most part they listened to black rhythm and blues music and slick English dance bands like Roxy Music. They went to discos to dance, dance, and dance some more. It wasn't for exercise; it was the practice of a mating ritual perfected in antiquity. Discos were where the girls were.

The ritual was largely fueled by booze. Most soul boys drank quite a bit, but they were not into the wide open drug scene that had landed Shane in St. Mary's. Soul boys generally stuck with just one illegal drug: amphetamine. They took it so that they could dance faster and longer, and it helped loosen the tongue when it came to talking up the women. MacGowan viewed limiting himself to various forms of speed and prodigious quantities of booze as a positive step in his life.

Perhaps Shane's soul boy fling was, as he claims, an improvement in the area of substance abuse. He even made some inroads towards repairing his strained relationship with his father. They sometimes spent evenings together drinking in pubs. One area of Shane's life, however, worsened during his disco-hopping phase: violence. That's understandable. A disco full of drunken teenage boys hopped up on amphetamines, testosterone raging as they competed for the attention of the opposite sex, was a place where fights broke out. The fights were even more likely to occur when there was a mix of English and Irish lads. More likely still, when Shane MacGowan was one of the Irish lads. One night he was jumped by six Brits. They kicked him senseless, breaking his nose in the process. "I think my hatred of them came from the old folks at home, originally," he says, "but it was reinforced by the fact that they turned out to be as big a bunch of bastards as I'd been told they were."

MacGowan's anti-British feelings had no doubt been stoked by events in Northern Ireland during his teenage years. From 1969 on, he didn't have to rely on old-timers' tales to hear of daring IRA exploits. All he had to do was pick up a newspaper, or turn on the radio or television to hear about the renewed "troubles." They had intensified in 1967 with the formation of the North Ireland Civil Rights Association (NICRA). Northern Catholics had become increasingly marginalized by the growth of extreme Protestant loyalism. Formed by Catholics, NICRA had taken notice of the advances made in America by blacks following Martin Luther King's non-violent strategies. The group held no pretensions about running the British out of Northern Ireland's six counties. They sought, like American blacks, equal rights under the laws of the land they lived in. They demanded good housing for Catholics and fair employment practices. Most of all, they rallied behind the call for "one man, one vote." Elections in Northern Ireland had long been gerrymandered to all but remove any Irish Catholic influence. The most effective method was to allow only those who paid local taxes the right to vote. Since Catholics in the North tended to be poorer, and more likely to be unemployed, they were less likely to pay those taxes. Elections in Derry were a good example of the system's effectiveness. The Catholic laborers in Derry lived under horrible conditions. Unemployment was high. Most were crowded into a ghetto called Bogside. What frustrated them the most was that the Catholics of Derry were the majority in the city. Yet the election laws used their poverty to prevent Derry's Catholic majority from electing officials willing to address their problems.

In August of 1968 NICRA organized a public march to protest the removal of a Catholic family in Dungannon from council housing. The family had been evicted to make room for a single Protestant woman. She worked for a Protestant Unionist Councilor. Unionists, though Irish, supported British rule in Northern Ireland. When a second larger march was planned, the government banned it and rioting broke out. It began to become clear that non-violent means were not going to take hold with the Irish. It was not natural for the typical Irishman to go out into the streets and allow himself to be battered. It was just not in his nature. Thirty years later, reflecting on "the troubles," MacGowan alluded to his countrymen's unwillingness to always play by the rules. "We inherited a British set of laws unsuited to the Irish temperament, which is essentially inclined towards lawlessness. The Irish are pragmatic, not dogmatic. We're not averse to lying or cheating to get what we want. It goes back to the Famine and before it; when your first instinct is survival, it doesn't leave much room for questions of morality. I shouldn't say it, but I'm not too worried that we're not a bunch of fucking wimps like the English." "The Orange and the Green," a popular song about a young Irishman with one Catholic and one Protestant parent, references the fighting Irish temperament.

One day me mum's relations
They came to visit me.
By chance me father's kinfolk
Were just sitting down to tea.
Well, we tried to smooth things over,
But they all began to fight,
And being strictly neutral
I bashed everyone in sight.

The violence spread. Riots in Derry, Newry, Dungannon, Armagh and Belfast alarmed British loyalists. They responded with attacks on Catholic homes. In the Battle of Bogside in August of 1969, Catholics barricaded themselves in their community in order to keep out British forces that had resorted to using huge quantities of CS gas; a tactic that had never before been used in peacetime. That same month saw what became known as the Belfast Burnings. The skirmishes and riots that raged throughout the Northern capitol were even more intense. In Belfast the individual Catholic and Protestant communities were smaller and more interspersed among each other than in Derry. Small communities barricaded themselves in, creating "no go areas." A siege mentality took over.

In 1970 Edward Heath's conservative government took office in England. Heath, who had close ties to Northern Ireland's Unionist leaders, decided that the reforms the Catholics were after were not the answer. Instead, he repeated the mistakes the Crown made a half century before. He opted to crush all signs of rebellion using Britain's superior military strength. The war was on.

An army is needed to fight a war. The only army Northern Catholics could turn to was the IRA. By this time there had been a split in the organization. The scope of this book does not allow a close look at the reasons. It must suffice to say that the IRA's more militant faction felt that the leadership's preference for diplomacy over violent confrontation was misguided. They cited the IRA's inability to protect Northern Irish Catholic communities during the renewed troubles as validation of their position. Some said that IRA had come to stand for "I ran away." On December 28, 1969, the militant faction formerly announced the new "Provisional IRA." The Provos, as they were soon called, chose their name to historically align themselves with the "Provisional Government" declared by Padraic Pearse from the steps of the Dublin Post Office during the Easter Rising of 1916. In a public statement they asserted that they were the army of the 32 counties of Ireland. The civil rights movement had escalated into that same old issue. The Provos wanted the British off their island.

The Provos' cause got an unexpected and unwanted boost a month after Shane MacGowan's 14th birthday — a massacre that made headlines around the world. Since August of 1971, the British had pressed a policy of internment without trial in Northern

Ireland. The idea was to get as many Provos in jail as possible without the bother of proving they had actually done anything illegal. In a single day over 350 key Republicans were arrested in one swoop. Several thousands went to the streets of Derry that cold Sunday morning to protest the policy. A special, and extremely tough, battalion of British troops were sent to the Catholic ghetto of Bogside. The community had been a barricaded "no go area" for nearly two years. When the demonstrators began throwing rocks at the soldiers, the British opened fire. Thirteen protesters were killed immediately. Some had been shot more than once while lying on the ground. A fourteenth later died of his wounds. Thirteen more were wounded but survived.

People who were not even quite sure where Ireland was were horrified by the news. One can easily imagine the effect it had on a young Irish teenager weaned on rebel songs and stories about Tom Barry, Dan Breen, and the flying columns of 1920 and 1921. The world press dubbed January 30, 1972 "Bloody Sunday." To the IRA it was the second Bloody Sunday in a very long war.

The official British inquiry maintained that the murdered civilians were gunmen and bombers. The residents of Bogside knew that to be untrue. The British soldiers were exonerated. It would take 26 years before the British government would acknowledge possible wrongdoing when Prime Minister Tony Blair announced a new judicial inquiry into the incident. In the meantime, the Provos' ranks swelled. They began to be generally regarded as the legitimate IRA.

England's immediate reaction to Bloody Sunday was to dissolve Northern Ireland's parliament and impose direct rule by the Crown. The IRA's response came in July on Bloody Friday. They set off 26 bombs in Belfast. Nine people were killed. One hundred and thirty were injured.

The IRA was in the middle of a cease-fire when Shane MacGowan went back to Ireland at age 18. He made the trip with a friend, Peter Gates. They took the boat train from Liverpool to Dublin. The Republican hero de Valera had just died and was lying in state in the capital. When they finally made it to County Tipperary, they took their guitars each night to Reddan's, a pub in Borrisokane. Known by locals as "the Yank's," the pub has a good-sized hall in the back of the building. The nightly sessions there were large and wonderful. MacGowan and Gates, for their part, threw a good bit of rock and roll into the usual mix of traditional Irish songs of rebellion, emigration, and lost love. Even he did not yet know it, but MacGowan was beginning to feel around the edges of the formula that he would use to lead the Pogues to international acclaim. When he returned to London, it was back to the soul boy scene. It must have seemed pretty vacant in comparison to the sessions in the Yank's pub.

Still, it would have to do. Shane MacGowan had found ways to cope, to enjoy himself in London, but he still hated England. He was full of fury. He was full of anger. He was full of rage. Most of it was directed at the English. He was about to find an outlet for it.

CHAPTER 3

**"There's one punk band. The Sex Pistols. The rest of them were rubbish...
I probably wouldn't have been that interested in them if Johnny Rotten
hadn't been so bloody obviously Irish."**

Shane MacGowan

"I went along to see the 101ers and supporting them was the Pistols. And that's when I saw God. I saw this little-red haired Paddy up there pouring beer over his head and sneering at the audience shouting insults at him. And then he'd launch into this loud, raucous rock 'n' rollin' number with foul lyrics, I thought this was the pop band I'd been waiting for all my life." It's not surprising that Shane MacGowan's recollection of seeing the Sex Pistol's for the first time focuses on lead singer Johnny Rotten. The Irish singer, born in England as well, stalked the stage with an energy and anger that mirrored MacGowan's own.

It was June 15, 1976. The early days of punk rock. The Sex Pistols were the vanguard of a young army of bands whose influence on popular music remains vital to this day. They, more than any other band, put punk rock on a global stage. They did it not with musical prowess, but by taping into an enormous energy born of the bottled up frustrations and anger in Britain's youth. "It was a very, very squalid period. Massive unemployment," Rotten remembers. "Class warfare rampant. Quite literally, no future."

The Pistols anti-establishment, indeed, anti-everything attitude surely hit a nerve with MacGowan. In *A Drink with Shane MacGowan*, he told Victoria Clarke, "The Pistols were the only pure punk band, with the real attitude. Any real punk will tell you that. They just didn't give a shit, they were nihilists. Which is a comical way of saying... it's an easy way of saying you don't give a shit. You don't give a shit about starving people in some country, you don't give a shit about starving people in your own country. You don't give a shit about class, color, creed, sex... you don't give shit about yourself, know what I mean? You don't allow yourself the arrogance of self respect."

No small part of the Pistols' disdain was aimed at the hand they hoped would feed them: the music establishment. By the mid-seventies rock and roll had become a major industry. Unemployed British working class teenagers and an ever-growing number of middle class teenagers trapped by England's recession found it hard to relate to millionaire rock stars. Mick Jagger, the bad boy of the sixties, hobnobbed with royalty. Given the Pistols' anti-business posture, it is ironic that the band was formed as a business venture by Malcolm MacLaren, a self-proclaimed haberdasher.

Rock historians cannot seem to agree if it was Ike Turner, Little Richard, Bill Haley, Elvis Presley, or Chuck Berry who contributed most to the birth of rock and roll. There is little more agreement over the origins of punk. Malcolm MacLaren, Johnny

Rotten, Patti Smith, Richard Hell and the Ramones all have their champions; but to get back to the very beginning, one must look to the Velvet Underground.

Roxy Music's Eno once quipped that everyone who ever bought a Velvet Underground album started a band. That may not be far from the truth. Surely, if every musician who claims to have been influenced by the band had actually bought their records; Lou Reed, the Velvet Underground's singer, songwriter, and leader, would not have walked out in 1970, discouraged and broke.

A major contributor to the band's lack of commercial success was one of the very things that so appealed to punk's pioneers: attitude. Reed once referred to a feeling of "despondency" in the Velvet's music. "In those days, I thought there was a certain kind of aloneness going on and I felt I wasn't the only one feeling that." Perhaps he was not the only one. The average American, however, preferred the melodic angst of Paul McCartney's "Yesterday" to Reed's brutal narratives of heroine addiction and gritty New York street life when the Velvet Underground's first album was released in 1967. When the band was recording the album in April of 1966, the top hit in America was Sgt. Barry Sadler's "The Ballad of the Green Berets." While most of the nation marched patriotically in time to their nearest record shops, Reed was in the studio singing about nervously waiting to meet his black drug dealer on the streets of Harlem.

James Osterberg was one record buyer who opted for the Velvet Underground in 1967. That year, under the stage name Iggy Pop, he formed The Stooges. Their 1969 debut album, produced by the Velvet Underground's John Cale, was cited as a major influence by nearly every punk rocker of the 1970s. It was more than attitude that caught Iggy Pop's ear. The Velvet Underground had an unsophisticated, unpolished, unprofessional sound. Years later he alluded to it when discussing the birth of the Stooges. "The American bands that were influencing me were the MC5," he said. "That was just a very heavy, brutal, Detroit, industrial, rock ethic. You were supposed to go out and just kick the audience's ass and everybody gets sweaty and gloriously beat up. When I first heard the Velvet Underground, it gave me hope. Here's a band playing super simple songs, and the singer can't sing. And I couldn't sing either. And I thought, this is great! He can't sing, I can't sing, let's sing!"

The lack of polish that characterized the band's music is evident in punk's Do It Yourself (DIY) ethic. Richard Hell remembers what the Velvet Underground's harmonic drones and precedent setting electronic feedback meant to him. "It seemed as if you didn't have to know how to play with the Velvets. Obviously, it's not as easy as they made it sound, but it was inspiring." The seeds of inspiration the Velvet Underground sowed began to sprout in New York soon after the band split up.

One of the first to pop up was the New York Dolls, a prototype punk band led by David Johansen and Johnny Thunders. The cynicism of the Doll's songs and their basic, simple sound formed a direct link to the Velvets. The Dolls began performing in Greenwich Village in late 1971. They soon settled in as the house band at a club called the Oscar Wilde in the Mercer Arts Center. Earlier that year, on the other side of the Village, Patti Smith had begun reading her poetry in small clubs. Smith, who had published three volumes of poetry by then, found a manager who secured her a regular ten minute spot opening for the Dolls at the Oscar Wilde.

In 1973, in true DIY fashion, Patti Smith's poetry readings evolved into a rock and roll performance. First, she added part-time music critic and record shop clerk Lenny Kaye on guitar. Chris Stein, later a guitarist in Blondi, remembers Kaye's playing as "really lousy, just bashing these chords out..." Soon they added Richard Sohl on keyboards. Classically trained, Sohl could play anything from Mozart to blues. The poetry, the power chords, and the accomplished keyboards came together in a way that produced something unique. Something was happening, but no one knew quite what it was.

By the spring of 1974 the scene had shifted from the Mercer Arts Center to the Lower East Side of Manhattan. CBGB's, short for Country, Bluegrass & Blues, was a rundown club in the Bowery with a clientele made up primarily of bikers and alcoholics. That March the owner, in a "What have I got to lose?" gesture, allowed Richard Hell and Tom Verlaine's band, Television, to play in the club. Patti Smith had become friendly with Hell when he was concentrating on writing poetry rather than on playing bass. She went to see Television at CBGB's and was ecstatic. Soon, she too was performing in the club. In August they were joined by the Ramones, a DIY three-chord band formed by four high school friends from Forrest Hills, New York.

CBGB's quickly became the place where new bands, no matter how crude and sloppy, could get a chance to play before an ever-growing, appreciative audience. It became a place not only for the bands to play, but to hang out and see what the competition was up to. On any given night Television, Patti Smith, the Ramones, Talking Heads or Blondi would be onstage or at the bar. The New York Dolls' David Johansen and Johnny Thunders were regulars. Even Lou Reed showed up. Roy Traykin of the *SohoWeekly News* recalled: "The feeling of CBGB's was that it was like a basement or recreation room that you took over. Every night you would meet someone else who was involved, a lot of artists and students in a melting pot. There was a real feeling that here were new ideas, something happening, like Paris in the twenties or London in the early sixties. It was a scene you could really call your own."

Other than *their own*, nobody, not even the musicians, knew exactly what to call it. It is only in retrospect that we can see the birth of punk rock at CBGB's. One of the Ramones later said, "We thought we were playing bubblegum music. Sort of like a sick bubblegum music, which later became punk." Their debut recording in 1976 was the first pure punk rock album ever recorded. Countless English punks learned their instruments by playing along with it. Within a few years the Ramones' two and three chord, full speed ahead, power charged style came to define punk rock for many. But that is a terribly shortsighted view which minimizes what actually happened. What occurred was a rock and roll Renaissance. Cynical street poets had put the rebellious sneer back on the face of rock music. More importantly, for the first time in years, the idea that anybody could do it was again viable. David Byrne, singer, songwriter, and guitarist for the Talking Heads (a band many later punks dismissed as unauthentic) summed it up well. "Punk wasn't a musical style. At least it shouldn't have been. To many people it turned into a particular musical style. But, it was more of a kind of do it yourself, anyone can do it, kind of attitude. If you could only play two notes on a guitar, you could figure out a way to make a song out of that. And that's what it was about."

Another regular at CBGB's was Malcolm MacLaren, the owner of a series of clothing shops in England. He had just concluded a remarkably unsuccessful stint as manager of the New York Dolls. After presiding over the Dolls' demise, he headed back to Britain in 1975 with a vision. He would reproduce the CBGBs scene in London. But to MacLaren the scene was more important than the music. He was more interested in reproducing Richard Hell's trademark ripped and safety-pinned T-shirts for sale in his clothing shop than in starting a musical revolution. He once told a journalist about his initial reaction to the New York Dolls' music. "It was so bad. When they attempted to play rock and roll, I thought it was such a cacophonous racket, it made me laugh. Their sheer audacity I thought was phenomenal."

MacLaren's timing was perfect. England's high unemployment and the strangling effect of class-consciousness had stolen the hope of a better future from many British teenagers. What Lou Reed called the "despondency" of the new music would find a ready audience with them. Also, the slick dance music that had attracted soulboy Shane MacGowan was growing increasingly vapid. A new trend had surfaced. Generically dubbed "pub rock," it was a more basic, stripped down form of rhythm and blues, owing more to Chuck Berry and Bo Diddley than to Motown. Bands like Dr. Feelgood, the Hot Rods, and the 101ers were bringing simple, exciting rock and roll back to London's pubs. Just as importantly, they were doing it without synthesizers, drum machines, and several thousand dollars worth of equipment. It was this back-to-the-roots movement which set the stage for punk in England. It was a short step for a musician like the 101ers' John Mellors to change his name to Joe Strummer and form the Clash once he had seen the light in a Sex Pistols' performance. MacGowan's experience was typical of the route many soulboys took from the disco to the punk club. "I got this impulse to cut off all my hair and started wearing it like a fifties greaser," he recalls. "Then I got into the tail end of the pub rock scene: Eddie and the Hotrods, the 101ers. It was at a 101ers' gig at the Nashville when I first saw the Pistols. I just couldn't believe it. There it was. The band I'd always been waiting for, playing stuff by the Stooges and Dolls. I just thought, this is what I'm about, and I started following them."

Malcolm MacLaren manufactured the Sex Pistols in the grand tradition of Fabian, the Monkees, and the New Kids on the Block. He assembled the band in a clothing shop on Kings Road. In different incarnations he called the shop Let It Rock and Too Fast to Live, Too Young to Die. In 1975 it was called Sex; a sort of pseudo S&M boutique that, according to Johnny Rotten, appealed to "perverts, freaks, oddballs, and people with disturbed personalities." Guitarist Steve Jones and drummer Paul Cook were the first recruited. Glen Matlock, a part-time clerk in the shop, was added on bass. In MacLaren's concept of the band, the all-important frontman needed a riveting, outrageous stage presence. Ability to project far outweighed the ability to sing. In this, Johnny Rotten was very fortunate. His audition took place after hours in MacLaren's shop. Rotten remembers it like this. "I could mime fine, but of course I couldn't sing a note. I knew all the words to Alice Cooper's songs, whereas I knew practically none of the records inside Malcolm's jukebox because it was all that awful sixties mod music that I couldn't stand. The only song I could cope with was Alice Cooper's 'Eighteen.' I just gyrated like a belly dancer. Malcolm thought, 'Yes, he's the one.' Paul thought it was a joke and couldn't have cared less. Steve was really annoyed because he instantly hated me."

With the Sex Pistols' lineup in place they faced one major obstacle. Matlock was the only member who could play even moderately well. Jones recalls, "I couldn't play and Johnny Rotten couldn't sing, and it created this horrible noise." They went to work over the next few months. Jones began practicing early each morning in the studio MacLaren had procured on Denmark Street. Propelled by amphetamines, he played along with Stooges' and New York Dolls' records all day long. He picked up a few basic Chuck Berry riffs. Rotten wrote lyrics and developed a stage persona based on Laurence Olivier's hunch-backed portrayal of Richard III. Each night they all came together to rehearse. They put together a set covering songs by the Who, Small Faces, the Stooges, and the Monkees. Matlock's musicianship and Rotten's lyrics eventually produced original material. By November they were ready. The Pistols played their first show at St. Martin's Art College. A school official pulled the power plug after the fifth song. It was too late. The holocaust was out of the bag.

The Sex Pistols were an immediate, if small, sensation. Initially, a fanatical fan base of about 100 "punks" followed them to whatever tiny, out of the way club allowed them to play. An infectious energy permeated every performance. Imitators began to spring up almost immediately. Pub rock bands like the 101ers and the Stranglers retooled themselves into punk rock units. Musically inclined fans, some more adventurous than musically inclined, started their own bands. The scene that Malcolm MacLaren had envisioned for London quickly became a reality. But it was bigger than its prototype on Manhattan's Lower East Side. Punk clubs multiplied. Louise's, a lesbian bar, became a punk hangout. The 100 Club became a regular Sex Pistols' venue. The Nashville, the Marquee, Dingwells, and Screen on the Green all booked punk bands. But if there was a London counterpart to CBGB's, it would have to have been the Roxy.

In December of 1976 the Roxy wasn't doing very well. That month the owner was persuaded to try a punk rock band for one night. By January the Roxy was a punk rock club. By April it was *the* punk rock club in London. Able to hold about 2,000 people, it became a place for people to hang out, exchange ideas, and form bands. The Roxy didn't do much advertising. The crowds came by word of mouth. Knowing where the action was, knowing what bands were playing where, was an important part of the early punk scene. There was the feeling among the punk crowd that the scene, the music itself, was for them, not the general public. There developed a nucleus of a few hundred or so hard core fans that made it their business to be in the right place at the right time. Wherever that place was on a given night, Shane MacGowan was there.

Decked out in a Union Jack jacket, MacGowan became a front and center fixture at every important show. By 1977 he had become one of the most recognizable faces on the punk scene. He got more press than some of the bands themselves. His picture appeared frequently in the media, and he was often interviewed as to the meaning and philosophy of the punk movement. The *Evening Standard* did a two-page spread on him. At one point he made the cover of *Sounds* magazine. Undoubtedly the most widely seen photograph of MacGowan was one in which he was covered in blood. It stemmed from something that happened at a Clash gig. To a press all too anxious to exploit the violent side of punk, the photo was a godsend. They claimed his earlobe had been bitten off. Some actually referred to the incident as an act of cannibalism. In Ann Scanlon's *Lost Decade*, MacGowan provided the real story. "Me and this girl were having a bit of a laugh which involved biting each other's arms till they were completely covered in blood and then smashing up a couple of bottles and cutting each other up a bit. That, in those days, was the sort of thing people used to do. I haven't got a clue now why I did it or why anyone would want to do it, but that was how teenagers got their kicks in London if they were hip. Anyway, in the end she went a bit over the top and bottled me in the side of the head. Gallons of blood came out and someone took a photograph. I never got it bitten off, although we had bitten each other to bits, it was just a heavy cut. It's like the old story about the bloke who catches the fish. He says that it weighs this much and it's that big, and within a couple of days it's a whale."

By this time Shane MacGowan had followed the lead of Iggy Pop, Johnny Thunders, Joey Ramone, Johnny Rotten, Rat Scabies and countless others. He adopted an alias. He opted for the punkish, yet very Irish, Shane O'Hooligan. As O'Hooligan he took a step that added to his notoriety. The punk scene had developed its own print media. In true DIY fashion, several fans began to publish fanzines that were printed on copy machines. *Sniffing Glue* was probably the first. Small, cheap, handmade, and stapled; it set a precedent by focusing on only one band per issue. *Sniffing Glue's* premiere issue was dedicated to the Ramones. Shane published a fanzine called *Bondage*. The first and only issue featured the Sex Pistols on the cover and MacGowan raving about his favorite band inside. He also wrote an article predicting that the Jam would be the next big punk group. *Bondage* had a different look that separated it from the others. MacGowan has called it the first "graphic" fanzine. Rather than type it, he wrote it out by hand. He also attached chains and safety pins to the master copy before having it printed. He sold *Bondage* for at least three times the cost of the other fanzines and made a tidy profit. The Sex Pistols issue included a table of contents for a second issue that never materialized. Shane O'Hooligan was having too much fun being a punk to be bothered with it.

Apparently, part of that fun was getting into fights. London's youth seemed to have it in for just about anyone that was different from themselves. Different classes, different races, even different musical subcultures fought at the drop of a slur. If there was one thing that blacks and whites, working class and middle class, and teds and rockers could all agree upon, it was that they did not like punks. And punks were easy to find. Malcolm MacLaren's clothing shop had done its part to make punk a fashion statement as much as an attitude or a guitar churning out three chords. Adorned with colored and spiked hair, torn and safety pinned clothing, chains, plastic garbage bags, and swastikas; the average punk stuck out more than young Shane MacGowan's Irish accent did when he began public school in London. The letters *IRA* written on Shane O'Hooligan's forehead no doubt prompted a few fights on London's streets as well.

As much as anything, it was the punk scene's reputation for violence that attracted anyone looking for a fight. Ex-punks looking back on the good old days are quick to point out that the media exaggerated the violence because it made good copy. Surely that was the case. That truth, however, does not change the fact that violence was part of the punk package. Howard Thompson, an A&R man for Island Records remembers what it was like at a Sex Pistols' gig. "The Pistols' fans wanted to bring down the walls and change the face of music. So here I was, watching all this stuff going down. There were constant fights. I'd never seen any band jump off a stage and join in on fights before. That was novel. On the stage, the Sex Pistols were pretty damn good! John was fairly nasty - ranting, spitting up phlegm between songs and being cynical. He would try to cajole the audience into reacting to him. He was like a red rag to a bull."

Some have contended that with the Sex Pistols Johnny Rotten was creating a "Theater of Rage." An orchestrated event designed to vent one's frustrations. This may have been Rotten's intent, but many with a lesser intellect and artistic temperament were just plain violent. Sid Vicious, who replaced Glen Matlock as the Pistol's bass player, is a case in point. Most of the other band members blame Vicious for the fistfight that broke out in the limo they took to sign a contact with A&M Records. At one gig he bashed a female fan over the head with his bass. Then there was the time he beat a journalist with a chain. Once, while in the audience at the 100 Club, he threw a glass at the band. It ricocheted off a post and cut a girl's eye. Given his appetite for mindless violence, few were surprised when he was accused of murdering his girlfriend a few months before he himself died of a drug overdose. Johnny Rotten's father once gave this insight. "Sid was a suffering idiot. He was like a gimmick. If he was sitting here and nobody was taking any notice of him, he'd cut his hand or something to attract attention. You'd have to take your mind off everything else and look at him. That was all Sid ever did. He could never sing or play anything. He used to come here to the house with Johnny when they went to school together. Stupid, he was. Really stupid."

The punk revolution that so inspired Shane MacGowan did not last long. "The punk scene was great while it was small," he has said. "To be quite honest, punk was over for me by the end of 1977." Ironically, it was not punk's excesses that did it in.

The excesses made punk rock more and more successful, and that success guaranteed its demise.

The first big boost came in December of 1976. The Sex Pistols, drunk on daytime TV, let fly with a flurry of expletives when goaded by talk show host Bill Grundy. It seemed the entire nation became enraged. In Essex a 47 year-old truckdriver kicked in his TV screen. The BBC's phones rang continuously. Nearly every paper covered the Grundy affair. The *Daily Mirror* gave the story the entire front page. By the next morning everyone in Great Britain had heard of the Sex Pistols. Their first single, "Anarchy in the UK," was promptly banned. This of course, resulted in more free publicity. The record, which had not sold all that well in the two months it had been out, suddenly entered the top 40.

In May of 1977 the Pistol's release of their second single, "God Save the Queen," coincided with the Queen's Jubilee, a national holiday to celebrate the 25th anniversary of Queen Elizabeth's coronation. Because of lyrics like "God save the Queen, the fascist regime," it too was banned. Malcolm MacLaren responded by filling a rented boat with journalists, punks, and the Sex Pistols. They floated down the Thames just behind the Queen's flotilla on Jubilee Night, the band blasting out "God Save the Queen" live. Police boarded the boat and several people, including MacLaren, were arrested. Money could not buy the resulting media coverage. "God Save the Queen" rocketed to the top of the charts. "We were a bunch of spotty kids being naughty. But somehow it worked," Rotten said years later. "We hit on something there, not deliberately so. Instinctively."

In the space of about two years punk had evolved from an anti-establishment movement against the fat of the rock music industry into that industry's latest fad. By 1978 punk bands were everywhere. A&R men from major record labels stalked the clubs looking for the band that would help their company cut a piece of the pie. Many new bands were being formed not by disenfranchised youth but, heaven forbid, professional musicians. The outlandish clothing that trend setting punks had created as personal expressions were being mass produced and sold in MacLaren's shop (and a growing number of others) to suburban kids who came into London to be part of the scene. Punk had become acceptable. It had to die. As surely as rockabilly had to die when Eddie Arnold cut "Hepcat Baby," as surely as the British Invasion had to die when Freddie & the Dreamers introduced "The Freddie," as surely as folk rock had to die when Sonny and Cher topped the charts with "I Got You Babe," punk rock was doomed when Generation X recorded "100 Punks." Shane MacGowan knew it. The rest of the world would catch on in a few years.

Generation X was one of several bands started by Sex Pistols fans. Instigated by William Broad, a Pistol fanatic who called himself Billy Idol, the band had a quick top 40 hit with "Your Generation." Susan Dallion (AKA Siouxsie Sioux), one of the first Pistols' fans, fronted Siouxsie and the Banshees for two decades until they split up in 1996. Of all the DIY bands to emerge from the Sex Pistols' audience, Billy Idol's Generation

X was probably the most successful, Siouxsie Sioux's Banshees was the longest lasting, but Shane O'Hooligan's Nipple Erectors was certainly the best.

MacGowan started the band with his friend Shanne Bradley, a female bass player. The Nipple Erectors did more than give MacGowan the opportunity to put his budding creativity on vinyl; the band gave him a focus that would change his life. He summed it up well from the stage during their last performance. Using Winston Churchill's line, he said it was "only the end of the beginning." By then MacGowan had left his job at Griffin Tavern, moved out of his parent's flat, and moved in with some old school friends. A good resume writer would say he spent much of this period doing research for one of the most compelling of his early songs, "The Old Main Drag." MacGowan was on the dole. He claims to have lived on porridge and water all week until his check came in. Then it was a fried egg sandwich banquet. He used to break into restaurants to steal commercial size cans of peas and baked beans that could be turned into cash on Petti Coat Lane. He tells stories of being beaten in police cells after drunken revelries.

Things began to turn around when he found the perfect job. The only other job he was as well suited for as he was for barman. He was hired as an assistant in Stan Brennan's Rocks Off, a record shop in Soho Market. All the pieces were in place for the launching of a recording career that has thus far lasted more than three decades. During the day MacGowan was immersed in what was for him an immense record library, and he was getting paid for it. Most evenings afforded the inspiration of a live band in a club that was part of the still vital punk scene. Most of all, once Shane and Shanne recruited guitarist Roger Towndrow and drummer Gerry Mcllduff, he had a band.

The band had been performing in the clubs for about a year when they made their first studio recordings in the spring of 1978. Stan Brennan, Shane's employer, produced the session. At their formation, the Nipple Erectors were a dedicated part of the punk scene. By the time they entered the studio, real punk was, by Shane's own reckoning, a thing of the past. That circumstance probably influenced the choice of "King of the Bop" as their debut single. The other three tracks recorded at that first session were "Nervous Wreck," "So Pissed Off," and "Stavordale Road, N5." "King of the Bop" was the least punkish of the four. It was far more rockabilly than punk. Rockabilly had influenced punk from as far back as the early days at CBGB's. Robert Gordon, who fronted CBGB regulars Tuff Darts, did his best to start an American rockabilly revival when he left the group in 1976. In England, what few solos early punk guitarists could manage were invariably of Chuck Berry and Scotty Moore lineage. "King of the Bop" was released on Soho Records in June of 1978. It was fast. It was basic. It was powerful. It is the only Nipple Erector song MacGowan still performed 15 years later when he formed the Popes. Despite its obvious rockabilly roots, Shane's vocal was punk. Exercising its God-given right to label and pigeonhole bands, the press dubbed the Nipple Erectors "punkabilly." The flipside, "Nervous Wreck," was closer to, but not quite punk rock. When the band echoed Shane's lines, "I'm a nervous wreck. I think I'm going balmy," the song approached novelty number territory. It also included the self-censored line,

"Kicking me in my you know what," words it is hard to imagine MacGowan singing later in his career. The single went nowhere.

The band's name was perceived as part of the problem. MacGowan later explained, "Well in those days, people thought the name was sexist, which was pretty stupid because it was thought up by our girl bass player. We couldn't even get gigs as the Nipple Erectors and our records just weren't played then." Later that year, they shortened the name to the Nips. As the Nips, they began to build a small following in London. Shane's punk notoriety helped. Many came secure in the knowledge that any band fronted by Shane O'Hooligan was going to be fun. They came back when they discovered that the Nips were also very good.

By the end of the year the Nips had a second single on Soho. "All the Time in the World," while certainly not a rockabilly number, was not punk either. It was pretty much a rave up rhythm and blues. Shane's vocal and the bluesy harmonica owed far more to the Rolling Stones and the Pretty Things than to the Sex Pistols and the Clash. The B-side, "Private Eye," was probably the Nips' most successful merging of punk and rockabilly. It opens with a full speed punk rip before reaching a classic rockabilly break born of Little Richard's "Long Tall Sally." Despite having a more radio friendly band name, despite having a solid recording on both sides, the second single also disappeared without a trace.

Throughout 1979 the Nips continued to play to appreciative audiences, all the while surviving frequent personnel changes. They went through four guitarists including future Pogue James Fearnley. Even more drummers came and went. Only the founders, Shane and Shanne, remained for the duration. Switching to the Chiswick label, the Nips recorded what they felt sure would be their first hit. Released in February of 1980, "Gabrielle" gave the first real hint of the songwriter Shane MacGowan would become. Musically reminiscent of the Velvet Underground at their most melodic, it is a love ballad with a timeless quality. Replete with hooks and "Gab, Gab, Gab, Gabrielle" harmonies, the record inexplicably went nowhere. The flipside, "Vengeance," was nearly as good. Steeped in a punk mood, Shane's lyrics threatened to beat and kill his lover's "fancy man, a skinny little runt from Birmingham." The mood was punk, but MacGowan had obviously moved beyond the Sex Pistols and their legion of imitators. "Gabrielle's" failure frustrated Shane. *NME's* Gavin Martin remembers running into him at the publication's offices. "He'd arrived in the lobby to demand a meeting with the writer who'd given 'Gabrielle,' his then current single with the Nips, a curt, dismissive review," Gavin remembers. "Wild-eyed, drunk, obviously speeding, a London Irish public school dropout turned minor punk celeb famed for having his ear bitten off at a Clash gig months previously, he seemed like a guy with chips on the chips on both of his shoulders. I gave him a wide berth."

By the time their fourth and last single, "Happy Song," was released, the Nips were history. Backed with "I Don't Want Nobody to Love," the record was produced by

Paul Weller on Test Pressing Records. Weller was the singer for one of the most successful early punk era bands, the Jam. He owed MacGowan a favor. It was Shane who introduced the Jam to Chris Parry, the A&R man who signed them to Polydor Records. Parry had narrowly missed signing the Sex Pistols and the Clash after pursuing both bands for half a year. MacGowan convinced Parry there was a third band worth his trouble, and took him to a Jam gig at the Marquee. Despite Weller's input, "Happy Song" was the Nips' fourth and final failure. All four singles, along with the two unreleased tracks from the Nipple Erectors' first recording session, were eventually re-released on *Bops, Babes, Booze and Bovver* (Big Beat Records) in 1987.

MacGowan has modestly called the Nips "nothing to write home about," before adding, "we were a good live band." Anyone lucky enough to have seen them perform readily attests to that. Many recall his sneering, over-the-top Teddy boy persona. But it would be a mistake to assume that MacGowan's arresting stage presence was all schtick. MacGowan was a genuinely angry young man, and his audience responded to him. "We were a no bullshit group," he says matter of factly. "We just used to get up, whatever state we were in, and without all the posing that a lot of other people did. We never gave all this 'I'm an artist' shit; we were always in touch with the audience. It sounds corny but it's true."

In the spring of 1980 the Nips took the stage of London's Rock Garden for what would be their final performance. Fortunately, and remarkably considering the band's dismal record sales, the show was recorded and released as a live album on Soho Records. *Only the End of the Beginning* is more than documentation of that night's 45-minute set. It is more than documentation of Shane MacGowan's art in an early stage of development. *Only the End of the Beginning* is a damn fine record.

When the Nips came on stage, MacGowan took the microphone and said, "Alright. Lets go!" And go they did. They started in overdrive with the punkish "Love to Make You Cry." Rather than save the best for last, they followed with "Vengeance," "Gabrielle," and "King of the Bop," arguably their best material. Shane introduced "Gabrielle" as "a bit of a smoocher." It was simply terrific. By the time "King of the Bop," which Shane called a "Teddy boy number," screeched to a halt, MacGowan had shown that he was the most significant artist on the punk scene. Consciously or not, he used the rest of the gig to show he was through with that scene.

"Ghost Town," a song about wanting to leave a dead, boring town, came next. The theme of boredom had been a staple of punk songwriters from day one. This night, however, the charge of being boring and dead seemed directed at punk itself. "Stupid Cow," perhaps the most straightforward punk rocker of the set, Shane called "a bit of a punky one, for the Clapham yobs." They closed with two songs that were anything but punk. "Infatuation," a song with hooks and breaks aimed at a pop audience, was ambitious, if not terribly successful. The last number, "Maida Ada," opened with a guitar riff dating back to the Champs' "Tequila."

If any of the "Clapham yobs" had missed the change of direction in the perform-ance, the encores should have corrected that. First up was "Hit Parade," a song about the hypocrisy of bands taking anti-establishment stances while being consumed by a quest for commercial success. MacGowan told the crowd that the song was "for the Sex Pistols and the Clash, and all the other old wankers." The final number was very different from anything else they had done that night. To introduce "Can't Say No," Shane said, "This is our last number. It's a progressive, psychedelic type rocker, see? Takes a bit of getting into, ya' know?" One gets the feeling that MacGowan suspected that few in the crowd did know, and for that reason the song would indeed be the Nips' last number.

The song "Hit Parade" gets to the heart of Shane's disillusionment with punk. Rebellion was gone. Anger was gone. He still had plenty of anger to exorcise, but punk rock no longer seemed a suitable vehicle. With the Nips he had incorporated nearly every musical style he loved, but could not interest anyone beyond a small remnant of ex and neo-punks. And even they did not have that spirit of rebellion. The scene did not seem important anymore. MacGowan needed a new focus. Perhaps he came to realize that there was one type of music he had not injected into the Nips' mix. Perhaps he realized that a rebellious spirit was an intrinsic part of that music. Or perhaps, in his time of transition, like many of us he just instinctively returned to what he knew best, what he had grown up with. For whatever reason, Shane MacGowan began to focus on Irish Republican rebel songs.

CHAPTER 4

**"The best compliment we ever got was that
the Pogues were 'like The Dubliners on-speed.'"**

Shane MacGowan

While Johnny Rotten was still perfecting his "Theater of Rage" with the Sex Pistols, real rage was erupting in Northern Ireland. Since the carnage of Bloody Sunday in January of 1972, the IRA Provos had been taking the offensive. They had retaliated in July by setting off 26 bombs in Belfast on what became known as Bloody Friday. Before the month was out there had been 2,000 explosions, 95 dead, and 2,800 shooting incidents. In late November of 1974, bombs exploded in two Birmingham pubs. Twenty-one people died, bringing the year's fatalities up to 140. The attack shocked and outraged people on both islands and around the world. A half dozen suspected IRA Provos, the Birmingham Six, were charged with the crime. Soon negotiations began for a cease-fire that went into effect in February of 1975. It did not last.

The cease-fire had fizzled out by March of 1976 when the British instituted a policy of criminalization. In short, it meant that Irish political prisoners would no longer be given special category status. In future, any rebels arrested would be treated as common criminals. They would be housed with the general prison population and be made to wear the standard prison uniform. These men were not members of an uneducated underclass. They viewed themselves as patriots involved in an idealistic struggle on behalf of their communities. Kieran Nugent became the first convicted IRA man to be criminalized. When his own clothing was taken from him he refused to put on a prison uniform. Opting to wrap himself in a blanket, he set the precedent that mushroomed into the Blanket Protest. By August, 300 arrested Irish Republican rebels had become Blanket Men. Most did not shave or cut their hair. Seeking means to intensify their protest, they began smearing their own excrement on the prison walls. The media called it "the dirty protest." The Catholic Church's Cardinal O'Fiaich was horrified at the condition of the Blanket Men when he visited Maze prison that month. Most of the world was horrified as well when O'Fiaich made a public statement concerning the protester's conditions. The image of bearded, long-haired, blanketed men, powerless against their oppressors, resonated with Irish Catholics. The prisoners came across more like Christ on Calvary than the jailed thugs the British had intended. Many of the demonstrators who marched in their support wore blankets and crowns of thorns. Britain's Prime Minister, Margaret Thatcher, intractable in her resolve to keep up the pressure on the IRA, was unmoved.

The violence rolled on. There were new bombs and more killings at every turn. British soldiers, Catholic and Protestant civilians, police officers, and priests were shot and blown up individually and in gatherings. Three members of an Irish showband were shot and killed after a concert in County Down. A car bomb claimed the British Ambassador to Ireland and his secretary. The British Royal Air Force base in County Londonderry was bombed destroying a terminal, two hangers, and four planes. Between 1977 and 1983 the IRA killed 425 people. An alphabet soup of new paramilitary groups began appearing. The Republican Action Force (RAF), the South Armagh Republican Action Force (SARAF), the Red Hand Commandos (RHC), the Irish National Liberation Army (INLA) were among those claiming responsibility for terrorist attacks. Inevitably, they began fighting among themselves and killing each other. The Official Irish Republican Army and the Irish National Liberation Army feuded and began assassinating each other's members. The Unionists loyal to the British government in North Ireland did the same. For awhile the Ulster Volunteer Force and the Ulster Defense Association killed more of each other than they did Catholics.

In 1979 the IRA made two dramatic strikes on the same day. In Warrenpoint, County Down, explosions claimed the lives of 18 British soldiers. About 100 miles away in Mullaghmore, County Sligo, a smaller explosion had even bigger repercussions. A radio-controlled bomb had been placed on a boat carrying Queen Elizabeth's uncle. It blew the craft to pieces, instantly killing Lord Mountbatten, his fourteen year-old grandson, and two others. Margaret Thatcher tightened down security.

In the spring of 1981, when a bandless Shane MacGowan was looking for a new direction, Bobby Sands began a hunger strike in Maze prison. Joined by other imprisoned IRA men, he refused to eat until the British relented on the policy of criminalization and reinstated their special category status. Unwilling to make any concession, or for that matter to even enter into a discussion with "terrorists," the Thatcher government sat back and watched ten rebels starve to death one by one. Sands was the first to die.

He had joined the IRA in 1972 while the death toll produced by the "troubles" was peaking. Late that year he was arrested for gun possession and sentenced to five years imprisonment. Released in 1976, he returned to his Belfast neighborhood and the IRA. In October Sands was arrested with three other young IRA men when police found a handgun in their car. They were in Dunmurry, close to the Balmoral Furniture Company, where a shootout and bombing had taken place. At their trial the judge admitted there was no evidence connecting them to the bombing, so he sentenced each of the four to 14 years for possession of the single revolver.

Bobby Sands' fame began to spread even before his hunger strike began. His fellow IRA prisoners chose him as their commanding officer. He began writing in prison, publishing stories and poems in *An Phoblacht*, an Irish Republican newspaper. A beautiful song he wrote about an Irish rebel exiled to Australia in 1803, "I Wish I Was Back Home in Derry," became popular. On April 9th, 40 days into his strike, Sands was elected Member of the British Parliament for Fermanagh-South Tyrone with 30,493 votes. He died 26 days later. Thatcher told the English Parliament, "Mr. Sands was a convicted criminal. He chose to take his own life." Much of the world seemed to disagree. Thousands marched in the streets of Paris. In Milan 5,000 students marched and burnt the British flag. The International Longshoremen's Association in New York announced a twenty-four-hour boycott of British ships. New York's Irish bars closed for two hours of mourning. New Jersey's legislature passed a resolution honoring his "courage and commitment."

Twenty-seven year-old Bobby Sands' death had an enormous impact on the Irish Republican cause. An estimated 100,000 marched the day of his funeral. The inevitable rioting shook Northern Ireland. IRA recruits and donations rose dramatically. Another murder for the crown.

That same spring Shane MacGowan took the stage of the Cabaret Futura as frontman of a haphazard group singing Irish rebel songs like "Bold Fenian Men" and "The Patriot Game." Billed as the New Republicans, it would be the band's first and last gig. Still, it moved MacGowan a good bit further down the road that lead to the Pogues. He later told Victoria Clarke, "The Pogues would never have existed if I wasn't Irish. Ireland means everything to me. I always felt guilty because I didn't lay down my life for Ireland. I didn't join up. Not that I would have helped the situation, probably. But I felt ashamed that I didn't have the guts to join the IRA. And the Pogues was my way of overcoming that guilt. And looking back on it, I think maybe I made the right choice."

The New Republicans consisted of MacGowan and a few members of the Millwall Chainsaws, a band he played guitar with occasionally. They all lived on Burton Street in King's Cross, London. The Cabaret Futura performance was not too well received. MacGowan recalls the sparse crowd throwing French fries at the band. "There was a bunch of squatties in the audience," he said. "It was a perfect ending. Squatties started pelting us with fish and chips." Still, the experience exhilarated Shane. Something felt quite right on that stage. He remained very enthusiastic about the band despite managing only a few New Republican rehearsals over the next six months.

Near the end of the year Shane invited Jem Finer to play guitar with the band that existed more in MacGowan's mind than anywhere else. Finer, like Shane and the Chainsaws, lived on Burton Street. Today the row houses once occupied by the future Pogues are neat and tidy in a quiet residential street. Burton Street at that time was a less than desirable neighborhood. In the early 1980s there were an estimated 30,000 squatters living in London's abandoned buildings, and Burton Street had its share of them. Gavin Martin has described what the area was like then. "Kings Cross in the early '80s was a kind of inland urban port in the island state of the metropolis," he wrote. "In short the dumping ground- in rightest sociologist terms- for the dregs of Thatcher's Great Unwashed. Nailed to the cross of Kings. The place where liars, scumbags, junkies, backbiters, syndicators' dreamers, lost souls and alcaholics- and some REALLY nasty sorts- hung out."

Like most Londoners his age, Finer liked rock and roll, particularly the Small Faces. Unlike most young London rock guitarists, he also loved country music. That love of country complimented the musical direction MacGowan was taking. In addition to performing traditional Irish material, Shane was beginning to write his own songs. Songs that were decidedly not rock and roll. The first was "Streams of Whiskey." They rehearsed their set in private, and in the grand old London busking tradition, tried them out on commuters at the Finsbury Park subway station. It was not exactly the Beatles honing their act with seven or eight hours on stage each night in Hamburg, but a band was coming together. MacGowan and Finer decided to take it up a notch and tried to get a license to busk in Covent Garden. The morning of their audition the only one on the piazza was an old Irishman who kept asking them to play "Carrick Fergus." After a poll of the piazza's shopkeepers the official in charge of granting licenses told them, "I'm afraid to say you just haven't got what it takes."

By the next summer's end something new and infinitely superior was rising from the New Republicans' ruins. MacGowan and Finer had recruited James Fearnly, the Nips' last guitarist. Since the Nips' breakup, Fearnly had been trying his hand at writing professionally. Although he had completed a play and a few short stories, he decided to turn back to music. He loved the blues, and played decent blues guitar, but Shane and Jem wanted an accordion player. They reckoned that since Fearnly played piano, which also had keys, he could learn the accordion. "I had seen neither Jem nor Shane for 18 months," Fearnly remembers, "and Jem came around with a laundry bag with an accordion in the bottom of it and said, 'We want you to learn how to play this.'" They had also recruited John Hasler as the band's drummer. Peter "Spider" Stacy, an original New Republican and Millwall Chainsaw, shared vocals with MacGowan.

They played their first gig at the Pindar of Wakefield, King's Cross on October 4, 1982. The night before the show they still had not renamed the band. The New Republicans had for all intents and purposes expired. The name was nearly perfect for a band with a rebellious spirit playing Irish rebel songs. It was, however, limiting for a band with a broader repertoire. It was Spider Stacy who came up with Pogue Mahone, Gaelic for "kiss my ass." It seemed a good fit.

That first show held out real promise. The sound was unmistakably Irish, but nothing like the purist Irish folk music of the past. They seemed simultaneously to celebrate and defy tradition. Undeniably, there was something there, but there were problems. The drumming was not right, and coupled with a lack of bass guitar, the sound lacked a proper bottom. Then there was Spider. With a vocalist like Shane MacGowan onstage, Stacy's singing was, to be polite, superfluous. Rather than hang around like a paralyzed arm, Spider compensated by jumping, shrieking, whirling, shouting, and generally acting the fool. Finer and Fearnly were not amused. Unsure that he was acting, they would just as soon have made the show Spider's last performance, but Shane would not hear of it. "Shane and I shared vocals, and I didn't know what the fuck I was doing," Stacy remembers, "I managed to annoy everyone by bellowing inanities out during every song. And after the gig I nearly got kicked out of the band, but Shane stepped in and said, 'He'll be a natural tin whistle player...'" MacGowan and Stacy went way back. They had met at a Ramones' show when the New York punks played London's Roundhouse on their first English tour. Stacy had invited Shane to sit in with the Millwall Chainsaws after the Nips' demise. It was Stacy who had sat around Shane's flat listening to old Dubliners' records while the idea for the original New Republicans was germinating. As for his bizarre performance at the Pindar, it was probably that kind of behavior that attracted Shane to Spider in the first place. It was decided that the very English Spider Stacy would learn to play that most Irish of all cheap instruments, the tin whistle.

Almost as quickly, a bit more bottom was found. The day after the Pindar gig MacGowan ran into Caitlin O'Riordan. She knew Shane from her days as a Nips' fan. She had met him on a trip to the Rocks Off record shop to buy "Gabrielle" and was surprised to be served by the lead Nip himself. Born of a Scottish mother and an Irish father, who had long since introduced Cait to the Dubliners, O'Riordan had a natural interest in what Pogue Mahone was doing. Although she did not really play bass guitar, she did own one. That was good enough for MacGowan. A few weeks later Cait debuted at Clapham's 100 Club, the band's second gig. There were less than two dozen in the audience. Stacey, who had yet to master the tin whistle, played a metal beer tray with his head.

Pogue Mahone continued to play when and where they could, usually to tiny audiences. As often as not it would be the Pindar of Wakefield. For awhile they billed themselves as the Black Velvet Underground. In December drummer John Hasler quit the band. MacGowan and Finer had never been satisfied with the drums. With Hasler's departure they began to think in terms not just of who would play them, but how the drums would be played. The traditional rock and roll drum setup was not conducive to their traditional Irish sound. They decided to use a stripped down two-piece drum kit: tom-tom and snare. By the time they played the Hope & Anchor in Islington the following March, they had found the drummer they wanted to man the sparse drum kit. Actually, they had found Andrew Rankin, another King's Cross neighbor, about nine months earlier. At that time he had other commitments and declined to come on board. One of them was to a rhythm and blues band called The Operation. In addition to rhythm and blues styles, Rankin had a real liking of jazz drumming, especially Elvin Jones. Rankin was born in England, but he had been introduced to Irish music by his grandfather when he visited him at his rural home in Ballyneety, about 25 miles from MacGowan's boyhood home in Tipperary.

For the remainder of 1983 Pogue Mahone played as often as they could, earning just enough to make their day jobs essential. Shane was still working for Stan Brennan's Rocks Off. The shop had moved to Hanway Street, a better location on the corner of Tottenham Court Road. Little by little the band began to build a fan base. MacGowan and Finer had evolved into dual managers. Jem looked after most of the business side of things. Recognizing that Shane knew more about the Irish music the band was playing, the others left him in charge of most creative decisions. This is not to suggest that Pogue Mahone was well organized. They were by all accounts a shambolic affair. Professional they were not. They lugged their equipment, such as it was, from gig to gig in a van. A far cry from a tour bus, their transportation offered little comfort beyond a cassette deck and tapes of the Dubliners and Clancy Brothers. The band established a reputation for excessive drinking and rowdiness during this time. Drunken Paddies. As is always the case, their exploits were exaggerated by the press. Still, MacGowan himself acknowledged that Pogue Mahone gave journalists plenty of raw material to work with. "Basically, the way we perform depends entirely on how pissed we all are," he admitted. "We are trying now to reach that perfect state where we are pissed enough to play well and enjoy ourselves, but not so out of it that we don't know what we're doing. We're getting close to it, and when we get there, we'll really be going full steam."

The Sex Pistols were known for fighting with the audience. Pogue Mahone fought each other. Usually it was over what song they would play. Rather than work from a list, they generally made up a set as they went along. Finer recalls MacGowan as the catalyst for most fights. Halfway into a song's introduction Shane would bring the show to a halt, shaking his head and saying, "Nah, nah, nah." Inevitably, an argument would ensue. On many occasions they actually came to blows. One night at the Wag Club, Shane hit Cait in the head with a full can of beer, knocking her off the stage.

To many in the audience the chaos of early Pogue Mahone shows was part of the appeal. Surely to some, it was a distraction. But no matter where fans stood on the band's demeanor, it was the music that mattered most. Early on, by their own admission, Pogue Mahone could not play traditional Irish music all that well. Nonetheless, they were doing it, and doing it with an attitude and spirit that was infectious. They were not great, but they were playing great music. They were exciting. They were different. Pogue Mahone was an oasis in a pop music desert whose sheiks were Duran Duran, Spandau Ballet, and Culture Club with Boy George. "It was a time where everything was very boring again," MacGowan recalls. "The time of New Romantics and all that…it was the era of the one faggot and a guy on a synthesizer bands."

Pogue Mahone had no synthesizer. The only electric instrument was Cait's bass. In the beginning less than a third of their set was original material. They covered a few American tunes like the Velvet Underground's "All Tomorrow's Parties" and Kris Kristofferson's "Me and Bobby McGee." The only Nips' number to make the transition with Shane was "King of the Bop." Most shows kicked off with about half a dozen full speed dance numbers: traditional tunes like "Muirshin Durkin," "Greenland Whale Fisheries," "Rocky Road to Dublin," and MacGowan's up tempo composition "Dark Streets of London." "The Repeal of the Licensing Laws," a tin whistle showpiece written by a rapidly improving Spider Stacy, was usually a part of the furious opening. The frenzied pace defied anyone in the audience not to dance, or at least to jump up and down in a sort of post-punk pogo. MacGowan's snarling vocals still dripped punk attitude. When not playing whistle, Stacy screamed and repeatedly smashed his head with a beer tray. "Me and Spider are both ex-punks from 1976," Shane said at the time, "and I suppose we still retain that spirit to a large extent in what we are doing now. Only today, that spirit has been tempered by realism, or to be more accurate, by drink." Pogue Mahone's shows were soon dubbed Irish punk, a cross between the Sex Pistols and the Chieftains. MacGowan was always uncomfortable at the thought of being an Irish punk band. He saw the band's sound as an attempt to give Irish folk music "a shot up the arse!" The idea was to use a new context to introduce the music he had grown up with to a new audience. "During the seventies Irish music got hippified and intellectualized by various people," he explains. "They started off with good intentions, but they softened it up, and a lot of purists got involved and they took it away from the people. And what the Pogues played was just Irish music the way it's played by bands in the country, by normal pub bands in Ireland. So we just took it back to the roots. The Dubliners had done it, but then it got softened. All the fusion stuff really fucked it up. It was nothing to do with punk. We didn't use any electric instruments. The lyrics certainly aren't punk-style lyrics. They weren't just 'Oi! Oi! Fuck you, fuck you!' If you mean punk in the sense that the Pistols took rock back to the roots, we did the same with Irish music. Then you've got a point, but it's wrong to say that we were an Irish punk group."

Lest any ex or neo-punk in the crowd be mislead, Pogue Mahone always downshifted to a near waltz tempo after their blitzkrieg opening. More often than not they did it with Eric Bogel's anti-war gem, "And the Band Played Waltzing Matilda." While dancers were still gasping for breath, Jem Finer's solo banjo notes announced the gearshift. Juxtaposed against the dance numbers, the delicate sound of his individually plucked strings was mesmerizing. The drama built slowly as MacGowan's heartbreaking vocal began to tell the story of an aged Australian World War I veteran, an amputee maimed in the Battle of Gallipoli. When Shane reached the chorus Fearnly added a frail accordion line to the banjo. By the time the rhythm section took up the cadence at the start of the second verse, most crowds had been transformed. "The slower tunes were amazing, emotional, and heart wrenching," MacGowan remembers. "And we had drunken yobs in the audience, swinging from side to side, and putting their hands up with peace signs and stuff. These were guys who normally beat each other shitless at gigs. Skinheads, psychobillys, punks..."

After the ballad Pogue Mahone would reel off several more dance numbers: traditional tunes like "Dingle Regatta" and "Waxies Dargle" mixed with new MacGowan songs like "Streams of Whiskey" and "Boys from the County Hell." The pace was relentless. Once again, when the crowd reached critical mass, a slow number brought relief. Sometimes it was Brendan Behan's "The Auld Triangle." Sometimes it was "Kitty," an obscure Republican folk song that Shane called "a Fenian song about the Fenian uprising." He had learned it in his Uncle John's kitchen. Few outside of West Tipperary had ever heard it. Sometimes Cait slowed things down with a cover of Crystal Gale's country and western hit, "Don't It Make My Brown Eyes Blue?" O'Riordan had been singing the song with Pride of the Cross, a band with which she sometimes moonlighted. If the truth were told, O'Riordan often murdered the song. Nonetheless, the juxtaposition of several dance numbers with a ballad was so effective that even Cait's clunker became a favorite. At times it served as an encore.

By the summer of 1983 Pogue Mahone felt ready to make a demo recording in order to shop the band around. Justin and Vickie Ward, owners of the Pindar, produced that initial recording in their apartment. By August the band's following had grown sufficiently to interest the music press. A going concern for just under a year, they were beginning to attract attention. By the end of the year, record company A&R men were showing up at gigs. Several labels were interested. They were drawn by the band's increasing crowds. Crowds who were growing increasingly fanatical. It was obvious that Pogue Mahone was on to something, but the record industry was not quite sure what. It was unusual and exhilarating, but it was chaotic and unpredictable; too chaotic and too unpredictable for a label to take a chance on the band. The industry took a wait and see stance. *MusicWeek's* year-end poll of industry insiders named Pogue Mahone the band to watch in 1984.

Pogue Mahone wanted to capitalize on their momentum as the new year began. In January they decided to make a video to promote one of the five songs recorded in the Ward's apartment. They chose "Streams of Whiskey." Lacking a recording contract and the deep record company pockets that a contract would give access to, the video was of necessity a cheap, homemade affair. Made for about $100.00, it opened in the Hillview tenements with MacGowan popping up from behind the middle of what appeared to be three large garbage cans. The rest of the band popped up to join him on the first chorus. The scene cut to the Camden Canal for the second verse. In this sequence, despite it having been a cold winter day, MacGowan and Finer were filmed in their underwear. They sat, as if on a seaside vacation, sipping drinks in lounge chairs amid the rocks on the canal's dirty edge. Another scene taken at the canal had MacGowan staggering around, beer bottle in hand. The last half of the video was shot in the Pindar of Wakefield. Near the end, MacGowan turned over a table full of pints of beer.

The video was crude, but that was to be expected going in. Pogue Mahone was launched in defiance of the music industry trend towards bands like Duran Duran. Bands that looked better on video than they sounded on record. Considering it cost less than the catering budget for most rock video shoots, the results were not without merit. The video managed to capture the raucous, party spirit that was central to the band's live performances. Without a record to promote, the "Streams of Whiskey" video had no chance of launching Pogue Mahone's recording career. So in late January the band entered London's Elephant Studios to cut their first record. They passed on "Streams of Whiskey," MacGowan's choice for their debut single, after Stan Brennan, Shane's employer at the Rocks Off record shop, suggested that the song's adulation of drink and Irish Republican icon Brendan Behan would hinder radio airplay. They opted instead for a newer MacGowan composition, "Dark Streets of London." It was backed with "And the Band Played Waltzing Matilda." Brennan paid for the sessions, earning himself the producer's credit for his faith in the band. It was independently released on the Pogue Mahone label.

The single didn't sell very well, but things were still happening rapidly for the band. In February they did their first recording session for the influential John Peel radio show. In March Shane asked old friend Joe Strummer for a favor and Pogue Mahone was subsequently booked to open for the Clash at Brixton Academy. It was their largest audience to date. They landed a small bit on a BBC television show at Easter time. Around this time they began getting their first bookings out of London. Given their widening audience, the inevitable happened. A Gaelic speaker whose influence was greater than his sense of humor blew the whistle on exactly what Pogue Mahone meant. He worked for the BBC in Scotland. In short order "Dark Streets of London" was removed from playlists throughout Britain. Only John Peel continued to play the single.

The lack of airplay did not help Stan Brennan's efforts to sell the record to a major label. There were no takers. He finally convinced a relatively new company, Stiff Records, to re-release "Dark Streets of London." Stiff Records founder Dave Robinson remembers a certain amount of anxiety on signing Pogue Mahone. "The buzz around the business was, 'How could anybody sign this group?' They were so out of it," Robinson says. "They couldn't even perform a gig from beginning to end. They were the opposite of safe. But that was part of their appeal. They were fantastically exciting; they could whip up that football crowd sort of fervor in an audience. I remember watching them play in a pub and after three numbers they fell into the audience and never reappeared. I thought if this could be bottled, if the band could be coerced into performing at full length, people would love it."

Accordingly, Stiff did have a few conditions before they were willing to get involved with Pogue Mahone. First, the band's name would have to be changed in order to facilitate airplay. That presented no real problem to any of the members. Shane had been through the same circumstance with the Nipple Erectors. Just as the Nipple Erectors' name had been shortened to the Nips, Pogue Mahone became the Pogues. The second condition found less favor with the band. Stiff wanted the Pogues to cut back on their rowdy ways, particularly their drinking, and to get down to the serious business of selling records. MacGowan recalls, "When we signed to Stiff, we had to pretend to stop drinking. So in the photo sessions we had to hide our drinks. And in the pictures we look really miserable and uncomfortable because we're sitting on our beer cans."

Things continued to look up for the Pogues. Elvis Costello caught their show in June and asked them to open for him on his fall tour of Great Britain. Throughout July the Pogues played at least two shows a week. Best of all, Stiff decided to release a Pogues' album. The band spent all of August back in Elephant studios. Stan Brennan was again listed as producer. They also recorded a video of "Waxie's Dargle" in September while rehearsing for the Costello tour.

The Pogues first opened for Costello in Ireland. They were a little apprehensive. Up until then their brand of Irish folk had been played only for Londoners and the displaced London-Irish. They regarded the Irish audience as a much tougher crowd. In addition, they were playing in much larger venues, including Dublin's National Stadium. They should not have worried. Extremely well received, Shane says the Pogues "blew him (Elvis) off the stage" on most nights. Nonetheless, the tour had its share of problems. For one thing, the Pogues opening act income barely met their expenses. Also, their relationship with Costello's band was less than amicable. There were many arguments and a few fights. More than once Costello's musicians tried to convince their boss to drop the Pogues from the bill. The Pogues started most of the rows by drinking all the backstage cold beer while Costello was performing. Overall, the tour was crucial to the Pogues' development. Before it was over, a good portion of the audience were coming to see the opening act rather than the headliner. In the end one thing was clear - the Pogues were no longer a London pub band.

By the end of the year that *Music Week* poll calling the Pogues a band to watch in 1984 was proving prophetic. In October they had expanded their audience considerably on the Costello tour. They had released their first album, *Red Roses for Me*. They had released their second single, another MacGowan original, "Boys from the County Hell." They had released their second video, "Waxie's Dargle." It was all coming together. The increased exposure paid off. *Red Roses for Me* began to sell.

The album, like the single, was produced by Stan Brennan. Stiff would have done well to bring in a more experienced producer. Brennan's approach seems to have been to set up microphones and let a great live band play in front of them in hopes of catching the power of a Pogues' gig on record. The resulting sound is a little flat. Little of the passion and fury of early Pogues' performances survived the process. This is not to say that *Red Roses for Me* is a bad record. The strength of the band and its material come through clearly, especially on the remastered recording released in 2004.

MacGowan has said that the Pogues, who flew Republican banners at their gigs, made a conscious decision not to use any IRA imagery on the album cover. Instead, the band posed around the most Irish of icons, an image that could have been taken directly from above any mantle in County Tipperary: a portrait of John F. Kennedy. It was probably not coincidence that *Red Roses for Me* is also the title of a play by the Irish Republican playwright, Sean O'Casey. And there was certainly no mistaking the music as Irish.

Each cut came from the band's live set. The album has five traditional songs. "Dingle Regatta," an up tempo instrumental that got pub crowds dancing, nicely captures the festive spirit of Dingle's annual boat race. There are three other fast traditional numbers on the record. Each deals in its way with typical Irish themes of poverty and working class conditions. In "Waxie's Dargle" the singer wants to borrow half a crown to attend the candle-makers' annual ball. Later he tries to pawn a pair of suspenders to get "a couple of bob" to spend at the races, before finally being told how to know when he is dying of hunger. The captain in "Greenland Whale Fisheries" is ten times more grieved over the loss of a whale than he is over the loss of five hired hands washed overboard during the hunt. "Poor Paddy" is probably the best of the three. It was a favorite in the Pogues' live set, largely due to its dramatic tempo changes. Alternating between slowed down, indeed almost spoken verses and breakneck speed verses, it relates an Irish immigrant's seven years of drudgery building the English railroad system.

There are only two slow numbers on the album. "Kitty," MacGowan's favorite cut on *Red Roses for Me*, is one. An obscure traditional song from West Tipperary, it boasts a mesmerizing arrangement that the Pogues used in concert to bring crowds that had been swept up into a feverish dance mode back down to earth. It tells the sad story of an Irishman, presumably a rebel, who must leave his darling Kitty or face capture and imprisonment. Much like "And the Band Played Waltzing Matilda," the music builds majestically and dramatically. Shane sings the first verse accompanied only by acoustic guitar and a thin, quavering accordion. Finer's sparse banjo and a tambourine are added to the second verse. It is not until the third and final verse that the bass and tin whistle join in.

"The Auld Triangle" is the album's other slow tune, another pace-changer in concert. Written by Brendan Behan, it was used in the opening scene of *The Quare Fellow*, his play about a condemned man. The song is a tangible link with Irish Republicanism. It is a dirge-like account of life inside the walls of Mountjoy Prison, the facility where Kevin Barry was executed.

Behan was never shy about expressing his feelings for the British living on the Emerald Isle. He told his brother Dominic, "They're the children and grandchildren of murderin' Lords bastard's and cut-throats who bled this very country white until they were forced to get out at the point of a gun. And they changed their mailed suits for Donegal Tweed of the finest cut, and their swords for check books and got back the family estate with the stroke of a pen. What have they lost? Nothing but the hatred of the people. They have all they want and more and behind every grin of a 'Good morning' they hide their dislike of us and their delight in our failures because all their money is in the city of London ready to buy a whip or a cage in whatever part of the world their gilt edge happens to be invested in at the moment."

Behan had done time in Mountjoy himself. Before becoming a wildly popular Irish writer of plays and books in the late 1950s, he had been incarcerated in several prisons for his IRA activities. It was his heritage. His mother's first husband fought in the 1916 Easter Rising. His father was also a Republican. At 16 Behan was arrested in Liverpool for carrying explosives. Three years later he was sent to Mountjoy for shooting a policeman during ceremonies commemorating the 1916 revolt. The bulk of his writing is staunchly Republican. In 1958 he published *Borstal Boy*, a book based on his time in an English boys' prison following his arrest on the Liverpool explosives charge. Later he published *Confessions of an Irish Rebel*. Behan's legacy is based on the quality, not the quantity of his work. A victim of the dual effects of diabetes and alcoholism, he died within ten years after completing his first play. His funeral in 1964 was the largest seen in Ireland since that of Michael Collins.

MacGowan had long been enamoured of Behan. He remembers his Aunt Catherine, a receptionist for the *Irish Times*, telling stories of meeting Behan. When he came round to get paid for stories the paper had published, Behan insisted on cash so he could go out drinking then and there. "I was really into Brendan Behan," MacGowan has said. "We were all into him but I was heavily into him. I think I identified with him because I had a massive drink problem and because I liked his writing and because he was Irish.... He was a writer who really lived, he was in the IRA, he'd been in jail. It appealed to me that he had really been there, that he wasn't making it up."

"Streams of Whiskey," one of seven MacGowan compositions on *Red Roses for Me*, is a bit of an ode to Brendan Behan. The song is built around a dream in which MacGowan meets Behan. The singer asks Behan's philosophy of life and is told that it is to simply be blown about by the wind searching for "streams of whiskey." The idea is not original to MacGowan. Flann O'Brien, a writer he admires, once wrote of a mountain cave with two flowing whiskey streams. Also, the mountain in the old American hobo song "Big Rock Candy Mountain" had streams of alcohol "trickling down the rocks." In MacGowan's hands, however, the whiskey streams evolve from mere convenience into a source of refuge and enlightenment.

Like "Streams of Whiskey," the remaining MacGowan songs are also fast dance numbers. With the exception of the instrumental "Battle of Brisbane," the album gave most Pogues' fans their first opportunity to fully appreciate Shane's lyrics. "Transmetropolitan," for instance, a raucous romp through London, is crammed with cultural and political allusions that were hard to catch in concert. "Sea Shanty" is a song in which MacGowan takes on the persona of a wild, reprobate soldier who puts "a pox and a curse on the people round here/wouldn't give you the price of a half pint of beer." "Down in the Ground Where the Dead Men Go" alludes to the starving populace and rotting corpses of the Irish famine of the 1840s. It includes references to the sand dunes in Sligo where hard pressed famine survivors found it necessary to bury their dead in sandy, shallow graves along the shore. Shane dealt with the same subject more thoroughly in a far superior song called "The Dunes" many years later. "Dark Streets of London," a very early MacGowan tune, touched on traditional Irish themes that were to become MacGowan staples: drink and poverty.

Of all the MacGowan songs on *Red Roses for Me*, "Boys from the County Hell" best hinted at the songwriter he would soon become. Another fast romp, its lyrics are peopled with junkies, drunks, pimps and a landlord who is "the meanest bastard that you have ever seen... a miserable bollocks and a bitch's bastard's whore." The County Hell is MacGowan's pseudonym for London. The "boys" presumably are Shane and company.

The song ends with a warning to stay out of their way because "We've a thirst like a gang of devils, we're the boys of the county hell."

Having been born of traditional Irish music, and particularly of Irish rebel songs, it is ironic that the Pogues felt constrained to play down their Irishness when promoting *Red Roses for Me*. The album's release came at a time when anyone having an Irish accent in England was wise not to be too vocal in support of Irish Republicanism. On October 12, Prime Minister Margaret Thatcher was nearly killed by a delayed-action IRA bomb. She had become the focus of IRA hatred ever since she stood down the hunger strikers in 1981. Thatcher, attending the annual Conservative Party conference in Brighton, was sleeping in her room at the Grand Hotel when the explosion nearly demolished the building. Five people were killed, but not the Prime Minister. The Pogues had played the Top Rank Club, just 200 yards down the street, the week before. In the press coverage surrounding the release of *Red Roses for Me* it was often pointed out that MacGowan was the only Pogue who had actually lived in Ireland for any length of time. MacGowan, for his part, did his best to straddle the fence. He told *Melody Maker*, "The thing is, the people who tar us with this big nationalist thing and the people who beat us up over it are really the ones with the problem. At the same time, I'm not going to sit here and tell you that I don't believe in a 32 county Irish Republic. But that's got absolutely nothing to do with the Pogues, or what happens when we're up on stage. It's nothing at all to do with the music. Yet despite that, we have to run all these risks. The risk of being called posers, the risk of being seen as Paddy parodies, the danger of being labeled some sort of IRA support team. God only knows where people get those sorts of ideas. What we are is a good night out, something that's anti-establishment for sure, and a threat to the new Toryism of the Duran Durans of the world. Musically, we're playing an urban representation of a really brilliant form of music that has been ignored for far too long. And lyrically, it's a form of humanism, expressing the belief in the right of every human being to lead a decent life, without anyone else shitting down on them. And that goes just the same for a protestant Orangeman as it does for a black in Soweto. We are not putting forward any big solution to the Irish problem, because the only people who do that are people who just don't think."

As 1984 came to a close, the Pogues seemed ready to break on a major scale. Their fan base had spread throughout Britain. They were getting frequent media exposure, on television and especially in the printed press. *Red Roses for Me* was beginning to sell. In *NME's* year end critics' poll of the year's best albums it came in at number eleven. It was evident that the Pogues were ready to move on to another level of success. It was also evident that in order to do that they would need a real manager. The MacGowan/Finer tandem was no longer adequate. They chose Frank Murray, a rock business veteran experienced in working with international bands. Murray had worked as a tour manager with Thin Lizzy, Blue Oyster Cult, Elton John and others on world tours. The Pogues had global ambitions.

CHAPTER 5

"I'm an immigrant."

Shane MacGowan

It is fitting that the Pogues spent the first moments of 1985 on stage. It was where they would spend most of the next seven years. As the clock struck midnight that New Year's Eve the band led the crowd at London's Institute of Contemporary Arts in "Auld Lang Syne." Moments earlier it was announced that Pete Kendal was the lucky winner in the night's raffle. His prize was dubious at best. He won a weekend with the Pogues. He must have spent a good part of it cramped in the crowded van the band was still using to travel from gig to gig.

Frank Murray had begun booking the Pogues as often as possible and in just about every venue that would have them. Years later MacGowan recalled confrontations over Murray's managerial style, implying that Murray's 20% of the gross concert receipts caused him to be less concerned about keeping the Pogues happy and well than he was in keeping them onstage. If the 20% figure is accurate, Murray was making considerably more on every show than any of the band members were. In such a case a certain amount of resentment is nearly unavoidable, but in fairness it must be said that Murray was doing his job quite well. The Pogues were very busy, they were in the public eye, and their audience was growing exponentially. The word was out: the Pogues were the band to see if you were out for a rowdy, good time.

The band's appeal was not lost on MacGowan. "People like going out and having a good time," he said. "I don't mean going out and posing in cafes and stuff, I mean actually going out and going bloody nuts. It's great getting pissed out of your head, draining yourself of every ounce of energy in your body. That's why people take drugs, that's why people go to football matches, that's why people go to pop concerts. It's all about letting go." They finished that winter playing in England, Scotland, and Ireland while Murray was finalizing details for their first real European tour.

In January they had re-entered Elephant studios to record their third single, "A Pair of Brown Eyes." During that and a subsequent session they also recorded "Muirshin Durkin," a concert staple since their earliest shows; "Sally MacLennane," a MacGowan original that had recently been added to their live set; and "Whiskey You're the Devil," a traditional number. "A Pair of Brown Eyes," released in March, is arguably MacGowan's first masterpiece. A slow ballad, it does not tell a story as much as it vividly recreates a few depressing moments in a bar. The singer, trying to drink away the memory of a brown-eyed ex-lover, is subjected to the ramblings of a drunken veteran of the Great War. The old-timer graphically relates how he endured the horrors of battle ("In blood and death 'neath a screaming sky, I lay down on the ground. And the arms and legs of other men were scattered all around") only to return home and find that his own brown-eyed girl had not waited for him. Following the time honored folk process, MacGowan set his lyrics against a backdrop of traditional Irish music. He's explained, "I could write, compose Irish tunes, in the Irish tradition. And write lyrics in the Irish tradition but make them about modern subjects. And I could also arrange old Irish tunes... well, in the slower and mid-tempo numbers that's where I was doing it the way (Sean) O'Riada did it. By arranging. By mixing up old airs to form a new air, things like that."

"Whiskey You're the Devil" made the B-side. "Muirshin Durkin," an Irish pub favorite about emigrating to America, was included on the twelve-inch pressing of the single. "Sally MacLennane" remained on the shelf until June when it was released as the Pogues' fourth single. Its flipside was "The Wild Rover," a cover of a classic from Dubliner Luke Kelly's traditional repertoire. The twelve-inch version included "The Leaving of Liverpool," a traditional sailor's lament about the pain of separation during transatlantic voyages. Bob Dylan appropriated its lovely melody for his song "Farewell" in 1963. "Sally MacLennane" is a full throttle dance number that quickly became a favorite in concert. Until the lyrics became decipherable in printed form, it is unlikely that many fans knew just how good it was. The song is about a neighborhood pub and the characters that frequent it. Calling the place "the pub where I was born," MacGowan has said that he had his Uncle Frank's pub in Dagenham in mind when he wrote the song. While the song is not specifically about emigration, the central character, Jimmy, moves "far away." Many years later tales in the pub have Jimmy making good money in his new location.

Emigration for economic reasons, particularly Irish emigration, had become and would remain an important theme in Shane MacGowan's work. The first time Terry Woods (who would join the band later in the year) heard the Pogues play he was struck by the fact that MacGowan was writing songs from what Woods called "an emigrant's point of view." Historically, Ireland's emigration rate has been the highest among European nations. It has been estimated that more than half of the people born in Ireland have left the country. It is ironic, yet understandable, that Irish Republicanism and Irish emigration are related in Ireland's collective consciousness. There is no Gaelic word for emigration, with its neutral, voluntary connotation. The word most commonly used is *juree*. It means exile or banished one.

Irish immigrants were among the first to colonize America. At first most of them were the Ulster Irish, the majority of Scottish descent. Their families, having been displaced from their land in Scotland by their British overlords, were used to colonize Northern Ireland. Most of them were Protestant, but they had at least two things in common with the Catholic Irishmen who would follow them to America years later. Their music was similar, and they hated the British for taking over their homeland. That hatred was essential to the success of the American Revolution. Irish immigrants were transformed into American patriots. There were over 250,000 Irish in the colonies by 1776, and they were anxious to fight the British. One of the five patriots killed at the

Boston Massacre was Irish. Three signers of the Declaration of Independence were born in Ireland, five more were of Irish descent. It's estimated that up to one third of Washington's Army had Irish blood. Twenty-six generals and 14,092 officers were either of Irish birth or descent. When one of them, Andrew Jackson, was elected President in 1828, Irish immigration increased.

The first massive wave of Irish emigration took place in the late 1840s. Between 1845 and 1860 one third of Ireland's people left the island. They risked their lives to do so. They crowded onto old "coffin ships" for cheap passage across the ocean. The ships had been designed to carry African slaves to the New World in the smallest amount of space possible. They had been unused for years. Over 50,000 Irish died on the trans-Atlantic voyages. Schools of sharks circled the ships as they made the passage, waiting to devour the next casualty. Most American school children have been led to believe that the desperation at the root of Irish immigration was the result of the "Irish Potato Famine." In Ireland the period is more often referred to as the "Great Hunger." The difference in terminology is not insignificant. It is true that in the summer of 1845 a fungus arrived in Ireland causing a blight that wiped out the potato crop within two years. However, the same potato blight had hit America and Europe around the same time. Famine was never a consideration in the United States and Europe due to the availability of other food crops. Millions began starving in Ireland because, apart from potatoes, they had little if anything else to eat. Most held the English directly responsible for their dilemma. Some went beyond finger pointing and took up arms. The Young Irelander Rebellion, also called the Famine Rebellion of 1848, took place in a village called Ballingary, County Tipperary, just a few miles from MacGowan's home in Carney Commons. Rebels led by William O'Brien pinned down 46 policemen who had taken refuge in a farmhouse until reinforcements from Cashel arrived. O'Brien was tried for treason, convicted, and sentenced to be hanged, drawn, and quartered. Ultimately, he was exiled to Tasmania after 80,000 people signed a petition asking for clemency.

The problem went back to at least 1556 when the British began large-scale land reallocation. Farms were confiscated and given to new settlers. The English gentry ended up with many Irish plantations. In the 1640s a serious revolt broke out and several of the usurping planters were murdered. England sent Oliver Cromwell to restore order. His army of 20,000 men did just that, massacring the populations of Drogheda and Wexford in the process. Cromwell also instituted another massive land grab, evicting Irish landowners from their property. Those who would not leave were executed. The now landless farmers, most who had been struggling against poverty *before* Cromwell's arrival, had little choice but to hire out as farm laborers to their new English landlords. As often as not they worked on land that had until recently been theirs. These displaced Irish farmers were forced to rent back small patches of land to live on. Invariably it was poor, barely arable land. They worked the landlords' land all day for a wage hardly able to meet the rent. In what little time was left to them, they tried growing a little food on their small, unfertile plots. They discovered that potatoes gave the best yields, and potatoes became entrenched as the Irish poor's staple food.

When the blight peaked in 1847, that food was gone. Tragically, Ireland's poor began to starve. Over one million died and many thousands more were evicted from their homes. More tragic still, the Irish suffered while thousands of tons of Irish grown crops were exported annually to fill wealthy English tables. Rather than respond to the plight of the Irish by sending over aid, the English instead sent troops to ensure that those exports were not interfered with by starving Irish peasants.

That's not to say the British were not sensitive to the Irish plight. They appointed Sir Charles Trevelyan to be the British Director of Irish Relief Efforts. The appointment was like asking George Wallace to help Martin Luther King develop a strategy to boycott busses in Montgomery, AL. Trevelyan saw the famine as a godsend that would help eliminate Ireland's "surplus" population. Displaying an uncanny ability to read his creator's mind, Trevelyan told Parliament, "The judgment of God sent the calamity to teach the Irish a lesson. That calamity must not be too much mitigated. The greater evil with which we have to contend is not the physical evil of the famine, but the moral evil of the selfish, perverse and turbulent character of the Irish people."

Understanding the role of British government officials like Sir Charles Trevelyan helps one understand the blurred distinction between Irish songs of rebellion, emigration, and poverty. A case in point is "The Fields of Athenry," the song most often cited as a favorite rebel song during my informal surveys at Ryan's, the pub just down the road from Shane MacGowan's old farmhouse in Carney Commons. One of the most popular songs in pubs throughout Ireland, "The Fields of Athenry" is as much a love song as it is a rebel song steeped in poverty, famine, and injustice.

By a lonely prison wall
I heard a young girl calling
Michael they are taking you away
For you stole Trevelyan's corn
So the young might see the morn.
Now a prison ship lies waiting in the bay.

Low lie the Fields of Athenry
Where once we watched the small free birds fly.
Our love was on the wing we had dreams and songs to sing
It's so lonely 'round the Fields of Athenry.

By a lonely prison wall
I heard a young man calling
Nothing matters Mary when you're free,

Against the Famine and the Crown
I rebelled, they ran me down
Now you must raise our child with dignity.

The Great Hunger caused Ireland to hemorrhage people. Nearly two million Irish emigrated to America and Australia by 1855. They represented about 10% of the United States' population. More Irish lived in New York City than Dublin or Belfast. Another 750,000 Irish emigrated to England. They were not always welcome in their new lands. In New York it was not uncommon for 19th century landlords to post signs reading "No negroes, actors, or Irish." One of the most popular songs in America in the 1870s was called "No Irish Need Apply." Irish emigration ebbed and flowed in subsequent years, but the Irish kept coming. The first immigrant to pass through Ellis Island when it opened on New Year's Day in 1882 was Annie Moore, an Irish girl from County Cork. As she set foot in America she was handed a ten dollar gold piece for being the first to arrive on Ellis Island. For 15-year-old Annie it was, as it was for millions of other Irish arriving in America, a new beginning that held the promise of a limitless future. Seven years later, Catherine Coll, a girl from the village of Knockmore near the town of Bruree, County Limerick, walked down an Ellis Island gangplank. Penniless, she had left her family's one room, mud walled, thatched cottage with only a letter to her aunt in Brooklyn. Three years later she gave birth to one of Shane MacGowan's heroes: New York born Eamon de Valera, Ireland's most important political figure in the 20th century.

De Valera wasn't the only thing the Irish Americans contributed to Irish Republicanism. During the Irish Revolution, the Irish Civil War, and all throughout "the troubles" they sent vast amounts of money to support the cause. Some went further than that. Thomas J. Clarke, a naturalized American citizen, was the first to sign the proclamation of Irish independence read from the steps of the GPO during the 1916 Easter Rising. Moreover, when the British captured the GPO, Clarke was the first rebel they executed. A half-century earlier Cork born Tom Sweeney took up arms against the British Empire on Ireland's behalf. Sweeney came to America in 1832 and promptly joined the army. He lost an arm in the Mexican War. During the American Civil War he rose to the rank of Brigadier General. In 1866 he raised an Army of Irish immigrants and led a Fenian invasion of Canada, intending to hold the British Dominion hostage until the English left Ireland. He failed miserably, but gave it another shot four years later. He failed again.

At the time Shane MacGowan was born nearly all Irish music on record came out of the Diaspora, most of it recorded in America by Irish expatriates. In poverty stricken, pre-Celtic Tiger Ireland, there wasn't much of a recording industry to speak of. The recording of Irish music began in America in 1916 when Ellen O'Bryan, a Cork-born music seller and travel agent convinced Columbia Records to record James Wheeler and Eddie Heborn, an immigrant banjo and accordion duo. The initial 500 discs sold out overnight, and the Irish-American recording industry was off to the races. Many of Ireland's best musicians emigrated to the States. Unable to make a decent living playing music at home, they found that in America they could be professional, full time musicians playing on the vaudeville circuit and in concerts promoted by the Gaelic League and other Irish cultural organizations. The Flanagan Brothers, Tom Ennis, Patsy Touhey, and especially Sligo fiddler Michael Coleman did quite well. Moreover, the Diaspora had a profound influence on the Irish music played in Ireland. Coleman's American recordings were widely circulated in Ireland and had a homogenizing effect on the regional styles in Irish fiddle music. The first mass produced LP recorded in Ireland was probably *All Ireland Champions*, a 1959 anthology of great fiddlers from around the country, which documented the dwindling regional influences.

MacGowan's use of emigration themes affirms, celebrates, and invigorates Irish musical tradition. He grew up at a time when the kitchens of West Tipperary rang with songs of the Diaspora. There were songs written from the point of view of people thinking about leaving Ireland. There were songs about the long voyage to a new country. There were songs about living in that new country, and the longing for the homeland and loved ones left behind. And, of course, there were songs written from the point of view of those left behind. The ritual of the American wake can give some insight into the passions surrounding emigration that led to it becoming so much a part of Irish folk music.

The American wake was a traditional departure ritual held for Irish emigrants leaving for America. Those emigrating to Canada, Australia, and New Zealand were also included in the ritual which was sometimes called a live wake, a parting spree, a bottle drink, a convoy, a feast of departure, or a variant of these names. The concept of the wake, the period of time when friends and family gather together preceding a funeral, seems far more appropriate than that of a feast. By any name, the event was a community wide affair paid for by friends and neighbors. As hard times and emigration went hand in hand, whole communities had to chip in to make an American wake possible. Even so, edible refreshments were meager. There were three things that every American wake had in abundance: music, dance, and drink. At least two musicians, usually a flute player and a fiddle player, provided the music. An accordion, a concertina, or pipes were a welcome addition when available. The dancing, in a room cleared of tables and chairs, was always lively. To make sure things stayed lively there was always a barrel of porter for the men. An ample supply of wine and tea was available for the women. Fights, likely the result of too much porter on an empty stomach, were pretty much a given.

The wake was always held the night before departure. Often the wheels were set in motion when money from a relative in America arrived. It is estimated that Irish immigrants in America sent $260,000,000 back home in the 19th century alone. Much of that money was used to enable another family member to emigrate. That member was nearly always young, someone in their late teens to early twenties. Someone that was old enough to look after themselves, but young enough to have their whole future in front of them. Almost immediately there would be uneasiness around the house. The young person began to get things in order, making preparations much like an old person preparing to die. There was finality to it. There was the realization that this youngster would not likely be seen again. It was traumatic for everyone involved.

An American wake started at sundown and generally lasted until the emigrant was led to the cart, car, train, or boat that would take him away at sunrise. Like a wake for the dead, it was as much as anything a sad party. Most of the songs sung that night were about the dark side of emigration. Oddly enough, the soon-to-be-departed was comforted with songs about the difficult voyage and the possibility of shipwrecks. Other songs told of the hard work and health problems anyone surviving the ocean crossing could expect to encounter in America. The bulk of the songs, however, seemed to center around the grieving loved ones left behind. Songs about heartbroken mothers, particularly mothers losing their only or youngest or last living sons, were especially prevalent. As often as not the last tune of the evening was "The Farewell Reel," slowed down to make it sad.

During the second half of the 20th century emigration patterns shifted from across the ocean to across the Irish Sea, and the wake ritual faded out. People emigrating to England were more likely to return home, if not to live in Ireland then at least to visit. Emigration to England reached new highs in the 1950s and 1960s. While widespread starvation was not a factor during those years, a pervasive poverty popularly attributed to centuries of British occupation remained a root cause of Irish emigration. It was employment opportunity that brought Maurice MacGowan's family to England. Perhaps he was exaggerating, but Shane has said he has "thousands" of cousins "scattered all over the world."

Another Irishman in England, Phil Chevron, joined the Pogues in the spring of 1985. Chevron had more than Ireland in common with MacGowan. He too had experienced hard times there, but like Shane, Chevron holds mainly good memories of "not being so bad off." His family was of a long line of city dwellers living in what passed for the middle class in Dublin at the time. It couldn't have been much better than being broke in idyllic Tipperary. Like MacGowan's, Chevron's family had strong Republican convictions. His grandmother was a member of *Cumann na mBan,* a woman's organization founded in Dublin in 1914 to support the men of the recently formed Irish Volunteers. The group's stated purpose was to "advance the cause of Irish liberty." Forty of the women took part in the 1916 Easter Rising, fighting alongside the men holding down the General Post Office and most of the other rebel strongholds throughout Dublin. Several died in that revolt. During the Black and Tan War, Chevron's grandparents ran a safe house, and his grandmother smuggled guns in a baby carriage because the Black and Tans wouldn't look there. *Cumann na mBan* voted to reject the Anglo-Irish Treaty that ended the Irish Revolution in 1922, choosing to support Eamon de Valera's anti-treaty Republican forces in the Irish Civil War.

Chevron came onboard to fill in on banjo for Jem Finer, who was home on maternity leave. The Pogues were in Germany on their first tour outside of the UK. It was MacGowan's first trip abroad since he'd been to France as a teenager. He marked the occasion by partying continually, drinking heavily, and sleeping sporadically. He was hospitalized after the Hamburg show when he passed out after an all night drinking binge in an Irish bar on the edge of the Reeperbahn. By the time the German tour was over, Shane had already begun his aversion to touring, telling a reporter, "I'm getting pretty sick of it now and looking forward to going home."

When Finer returned, Chevron stayed on. Banjo duties returned to Jem. Chevron took over the Pogues' rhythm guitar spot. As it turned out, MacGowan apparently hadn't thought of stepping down from that spot. Shane had played rhythm guitar from the start. As in many areas of his history with the band, there's some controversy as to how the whole move came about. It's been suggested that Shane's playing wasn't up to snuff. It's been suggested that Shane needed to concentrate more on singing than playing the guitar. It seems fair to say that Shane had no problem with Chevron joining the band, but did have two points of contention. First, he considered himself a damn fine Irish rhythm guitar player. Second, he didn't want to just stand in front of the band singing, and he said he, "…didn't want to do all rock and roll poses and jump around either."

And the band played on. The Pogues toured Scandinavia. They returned home to play to bigger and bigger crowds in England, Scotland, and Ireland. The crowds' size grew in proportion to its reaction. The frenzied fans brought ever increasing press attention, and an enthusiastic rock press brought some television appearances. Through it all, MacGowan tried to find something to replace his guitar on stage. He tried some banjo, broke several bodhrans, and even did a little improvised Irish dancing called "battering." He's described it as, "furious tap dancing, where you batter your feet on the floor." After a long period of trial and error, MacGowan found just what he needed to forevermore occupy his hands in lieu of the guitar: a cigarette and a drink.

Along with the increasing press adulation came an increasing press infatuation with the Pogues' drinking habits. The band members felt the press went overboard, which is what the press generally does. In truth, the Pogues did nothing to dissuade journalists from reporting their drunken excesses apart from dismissing or trivializing them. In 1987 MacGowan told a reporter, "There's been a long history of the drink angle being concentrated on. The fact is, we don't drink any more than any other band, you know. When we started we were playing in bars. We had short hair and suits and we drank on stage, right? We regarded ourselves as a dance band, an Irish dance band basically that also did slower numbers with more feeling. Because we drank on stage, which lots do, and because our audience had a good time and got drunk and generally looned around a bit, that's where all that thing came from." What Shane says may have some truth in it, but the incident involving an Irish bar and a Hamburg hospital was not an isolated case. On the same tour, after doing a good bit of throwing up on stage, Phil Chevron was hospitalized in Finland. Spider Stacy got too drunk to perform at a gig in Scotland. Excessive drinking was beginning to take its toll on the band, and in particular, on Shane.

For the time, however, things were looking really good for the Pogues. That summer of 1985 they recorded and released their second album, *Rum, Sodomy, and the Lash*. It was produced by Elvis Costello, already an important figure in the English, and even the world's, pop scene. Costello had become infatuated with the Pogues' bassist, Cait O'Riordan. He decided to come along when the Pogues hit the road in support of their new release. Costello did guest spots at the Pogues' gigs, attracting attention to the band that went beyond their rapidly growing fan base. Many people who came to the shows as Elvis Costello fans left as diehard Pogues fans. They were selling out everywhere they went.

The Costello connection was undoubtedly good for the Pogues, but Elvis' time with the band wasn't always pleasant as far as MacGowan was concerned. There seems to have been a good deal of resentment, some "who's in charge here?" going on. Some of that is inevitable when two frontmen share a stage. Some of it may have gone back to the previous year when as an opening act for Elvis, the Pogues routinely drank all the backstage alcohol before Costello's band finished their set. At times, some of it was evident in the studio, with songwriter Shane and producer Elvis arguing whether an arrangement needed an oboe or a trumpet. No doubt a good bit of it stemmed from an incident on the Pogues first American tour that winter. For reasons still unexplained, Elvis arranged for Cait to be snuck out of the band's hotel, driven to the airport, and flown back to England leaving the Pogues high and dry.

But that was still five months off. Presently, the Pogues were tearing up stages all over Europe. In September they added another native Irishman, Terry Woods, to the line up. Woods, an old music business friend of Frank Murray, played nearly anything with strings on it. The multi-instrumentalist was well-respected in traditional Irish folk music circles. He had been in Sweeney's Men, one of the first British folk music bands. From there he went to Steeleye Span, one of the genre's most successful. Ultimately, he put out a few fine albums as a duo with his wife Gay before giving up the professional musician's life in favor of the quiet, stable existence of an Irish factory worker. When he joined the Pogues, Woods' only musical endeavor was playing folk music for pints in Irish pubs with a group he called the Gartloney Rats. With Woods, the Pogues were solidifying their Irish sound. James Fearnley said of Woods, "There was that sense that he brought the whole burden of Irish history with him." His first show was a barn-burner in that hotbed of Pogues fanaticism, the Barrowlands in Glasgow, Scotland. For Woods' part, the history of his new band did not escape him, "...they (the Pogues) opened up the avenue of emigrants' music and it gave me an understanding of how it felt for the Irish in particular being elsewhere."

By October the growing crowds warranted the band's first tour bus. They traversed Europe in style watching movies and listening to music. The gangster classic, *Once*

Upon a Time in America, was a favorite. Tom Waits' newest release, *Rain Dogs*, played continually. As the crowds grew, so did interest in traditional Irish folk music. Apart from the occasional novelty record, Irish music hadn't seen much chart success since the Clancy Brothers. In a classic "bite the hand that feeds you" mode, traditional Irish folk music purists began to criticize what they viewed as the Pogues' bastardization of the tradition. The band was invited to appear on television panel discussions to defend their approach to the songs. MacGowan was anything but defensive. "I think purism stifles creativity," he argued. "I just mix it all in. You have to go backwards to go forward. I'm regressive. That's what the Rolling Stones did. They went back to Robert Johnson. That's what I did with Irish music, but I'm not into all that purist shite." Reflecting on the purists versus the Pogues debates years later, Phil Chevron told Martin Roddy, "There was a certain group of people who were opposed to whatever we were trying to do because we were plastic paddies. 'We had no love for Irish music' because we hadn't learned the Uillean pipes for fifty years in the *Gaeltaicht*... To me, it was strange that anyone should think that we were doing anything else but advancing Irish music, adding something to the tradition by giving it a kick under itself. All good traditions need to be shaken up a bit now and again. Someone needs to come along, be it in the cinema, literature or music, and say 'this is going in the wrong direction, but I know where it can go.' Shane was very much the person most of all that understood that."

By the end of the year the touring pace had again gotten the best of Shane. In November he was hospitalized in Sweden, this time for pneumonia. That night the band went on stage without him. Spider Stacy and Elvis Costello filled in on vocals. By all accounts, the Shaneless Pogues were not the same. Spider Stacy recalled, "It was a complete mess because our attitude was 'What the hell?' We were quite a shambles that night, we got totally looped before we went onstage." The next day they cancelled the tour's remaining dates. It would take another five or six years before the Pogues mistakenly thought they could carry on fine without Shane MacGowan. He returned in time to complete a 21-show whirlwind UK tour of large venues just before the year ended. *Melody Maker* named MacGowan 1985's "Man of the Year."

No doubt Shane's songs on *Rum, Sodomy, and the Lash* had a tremendous impact on those choosing on whom to bestow such an honor. The album title came from Winston Churchill's famous quote describing life in the British navy. In addition to "A Pair of Brown Eyes," and "Sally MacLennane," recorded in January in the singles session, the LP included two more MacGowan classics: "The Sickbed of Cuchulainn" and "The Old Main Drag."

Replete with allusions to Irish history and culture, "Sick Bed" is a MacGowan tour de force with references to the mythical Irish hero Cuchulainn, Irish singers John McCormack and Richard Tauber, Irish Republican Frank Ryan, and Cloughprior cemetery where most of Carney Commons' Lynch clan are buried. Padraic Pearse, a leader of the 1916 Easter Uprising, was as keen on Cuchulainn as MacGowan. In his pre-revolution days as Headmaster of a private school, Pearse had a mural of the Irish hero painted on the wall. The caption read, "I care not if my life has only the span of a day and a night if my deeds be spoken of by the men of Ireland." Despite its allusion, MacGowan's song is not specifically about Cuchulainn. "It's about Frank Ryan, who was a leader of an Irish contingent in the Spanish Civil War," MacGowan has said. "It's about an old dosser dying. You always get old dodgers dying in the street, but the people don't think that they lived through a whole century and was at war and all. The first verse is self-explanatory, then he gets on the death train. He's in Germany, in Cologne. The second verse is more real life. Me and my Dad were drinking in the Euston Tavern and a small wiry Irish guy walks in. You know the kind, a really pissed up Irish guy, really small, small but well built, black greasy hair. Very determined, very angry, and very drunk. They wouldn't serve him. He was actually offering to buy the bar a round of drink. Then he jumped into the bar and started smashing up all the bottles. It took four big, fat, English bastards to drag him outside and kick him senseless. We could hear the thumps outside. And then they came back in sort of clapping their hands, you know, 'A job well done!' And then he comes banging through the door again and kicks the hell out of them."

"The Old Main Drag," a slow poignant number, is a seamy slice of life tale of a 16 year old immigrant's attempts to cope with London's underbelly. MacGowan has claimed that the song isn't autobiographical, not surprising given the teenager's involvement with male prostitution, but much of the lyrics' power is surely born of experience. MacGowan told a reporter, "Trash is what we're really all about. I've always lived around the Soho part of London. The side that's full of pimps, whores and junkies and New York must be the same, but every fucking record you hear on the radio is the sound of California. There are no records that really capture the trashiness of London." At least there wasn't until *Rum, Sodomy, and the Lash* was released. Nearly 25 years after its release "The Old Main Drag" had lost none of its power and has remained a concert favorite.

Rum, Sodomy, and the Lash contains several other fine tracks. A traditional Scottish song, "I'm a Man You Don't Meet Everyday," featuring Cait O'Riordan's finest recorded vocal, is one. MacGowan's vocals on three cover tunes, however, are even better. "Navigator," an excellent song about immigrants building the railroads was written by the Nips' manager Phillip Gaston. "Dirty Old Town," the Ewan McColl classic, is nearly perfect. But best of all is MacGowan's flawless interpretation of Eric Bogel's anti-war masterpiece, "And the Band Played Waltzing Matilda." Otis Redding once said that Aretha Franklin stole his song, "Respect." Indeed, most fans associate the song with Franklin despite Redding's outstanding recording. The same can be said of "And the Band Played Waltzing Matilda." Bogel's version is fine, but with the release of *Rum, Sodomy, and the Lash* the song became MacGowan's.

With *Melody Maker's* Man of the Year award under his belt, Shane was quick to deliver two more of his finest songs in January of 1986: "A Rainy Night in Soho," and "Body of an American." They were released in February on the *Poguetry in Motion* EP.

"London Girl," another MacGowan song, was also included as was Jem Finer's "Planxty Noel Hill," an Irish instrumental jab at Noel Hill, a member of the traditional band Planxty. Hill was particularly hard on the Pogues during the folk purists versus the Pogues debates. MacGowan's take on the Lovin' Spoonful's "Do You Believe in Magic" was also recorded during the EP's sessions, but it was left on the shelf.

While "London Girl" is a serviceable rocker, "A Rainy Night in Soho" and "Body of an American" are two reasons MacGowan's music will live on long after the songs of more famous contemporaries like Elton John have disappeared down the yellow brick road. "A Rainy Night in Soho," perhaps MacGowan's finest love song, is elegant in its simplicity. It achieves every poet's dream, a new and better way to say "I love you," with the line "You're the measure of my dreams." "Body of an American" is a masterful twist on one of MacGowan's primary themes, emigration. Filled with allusions to Irish culture, the song is set at the raucous wake of Jim Dwyer, an Irish emigrant who has returned from America one last time to be buried in Irish soil with his forefathers. Shane says that much of it is based on childhood memories. "You may not believe this but 'Body Of An American' was the result of me thinking of the line 'Everyone there was pisskey.' I got obsessed with the idea of a song with that line in it. Pisskey means pissed, yeah? Then I thought of various stories from Ireland in my formative years, like the Cadillac outside the house, the American coming home dead, the boxers....they're all mixtures of people and things."

Before setting off on their first tour of America in February, the Pogues did a few dates in England and Ireland. One must have been a great night for Shane; they played Kennedy's pub in Pecaun, a few miles down the road from the farm in Carney Commons. There hadn't been as much excitement at Kennedy's since Gene Kelly stayed there decades before. There wouldn't be as much excitement again until the next millenium when Shane, in town for a funeral, returned to the pub and swapped songs with old friends and locals.

Making it in America, if for nothing more than financial reasons, is a very big deal for European bands. There is a lot riding on a band's first American tour. The Pogues' first crack at the states was not overly ambitious; they concentrated on the East Coast where the huge Irish-American populations in New York and Boston were likely to be receptive. In New York, to be on the safe side, they did three solid days of press and promotion. MacGowan, never enthusiastic about being interviewed, said that he found America journalists more knowledgeable than those in the UK.

The Pogues needn't have worried. They were the toast of the town in Manhattan with celebrities like Matt Dillon, Jack Nicholson, Robert DeNiro, Bruce Springsteen, Christopher Reeves, Steve Buscemi, and Iggy Pop in the audience every night. To put it mildly, the band blew audiences away show after show. The press was ecstatic about them. The Pogues had exceeded everyone's expectations. There was, however, one serious hitch on the tour. Cait O'Riordan skipped out of the band's New York hotel with the help of an accomplice provided by Elvis Costello. The pair proceeded to the airport where Costello had tickets to London waiting. The band, especially Shane, was furious. The Pogues were left without a bass player – almost. Darryl Hunt, a long suffering member of the Pogues' road crew, filled in admirably. A few months later, when O'Riordan quit the band to marry Costello, Hunt became a permanent band member. His relationship with the Pogues has lasted far longer than Cait's relationship with Elvis. They split up in 2002.

By March the Pogues were back in England playing some shows and preparing for a German and French tour. Things changed the night MacGowan had dinner with Alex Cox, who had been brought in to direct the promotional video of "A Pair of Brown Eyes" soon after his movie *Repo Man* established him as an important young film-maker. The tour plans came to a screeching halt, unlike the taxi-cab that hit Shane, as he and Cox left a London restaurant. The accident left MacGowan in no shape to tour. During a month long convalescence, he wrote two songs that remain prominent in his catalogue: "The Broad Majestic Shannon" and "The Turkish Song of the Damned." The Pogues also took the opportunity to finish up a project they had been working on with Cox: the soundtrack to *Sid and Nancy*, his film about the doomed love affair between the Sex Pistols' bassist, Sid Vicious, and the American groupie, Nancy Spurgeon. The soundtrack included MacGowan's "Haunted." Despite some uninspired lyrics ("You were so cool you could have put out Vietnam"), "Haunted's" haunting melody puts it among MacGowan's most memorable tunes. Originally recorded with Cait O'Riordan's solo vocal, the song realized its full potential when MacGowan and Sinead O'Conner recorded it as a duet on MacGowan's post Pogues CD, 1994's *The Snake*.

Once MacGowan had recovered from the taxi accident, the Pogues were back on the road. The crowds were getting even larger. The venues included festivals and, in May, Live Aid's international showcase. They toured France, Finland, and for the second time, America. This trip to America included the East Coast again but was expanded to include Chicago, Detroit, Los Angeles, and Canada. Although they were received well everywhere they played, the Pogues never got the reception they enjoyed in New York and Boston. At Chicago's Vic Theater they were saddled with a comic duo for an opening act whose set included one of them singing "Old MacDonald Had a Farm" while hitting himself over the head with a large, empty, plastic water jug. Reviewing the tour's final gig, a reporter who apparently wasn't very impressed with the show said Shane MacGowan had the "potential to become a Joe Strummer-like figure."

Back in England for the summer, the band went back to work with Alex Cox, working on the soundtrack for his next film, *Straight to Hell*. MacGowan wrote some good songs during this time, including "Rake at the Gates of Hell," "Fiesta," "If I Should Fall from Grace with God," and later shooting the film on location, "Lullaby of London." Having been offered parts in the film, the Pogues finished up a round of festivals in France before heading to Almeria, Spain, to shoot it. Almeria, located on Spain's southern coast, was selected because it still had useable sets left over from Sergio Leone's classic spaghetti westerns, *The Good, the Bad, and the Ugly* and *A Fistful of Dollars*.

A huge movie fan, MacGowan was delighted at the prospect of becoming a celluloid hero. Being in a western must have been especially appealing. He greatly admired John Ford, the American director who made his reputation with a string of classic westerns. Ford had Irish roots. His father was was born in Spiddal, County Galway, in 1854. One of his most beloved films, *The Quiet Man*, is about an Irish American moving to Ireland to settle down. Two others, *The Informer* and *The Rising of the Moon* involve the IRA. MacGowan, who loves violent films (a predilection he says his mother influenced when he was a boy), credits Ford with bringing a sense of realism to film violence.

Straight to Hell is far from a highlight of the Pogues' career. Shot in less than a month, it was roundly trashed by critics at the time of its release. Much like Ozzy Osborne and Iggy Pop, the film's reputation has been enhanced by age. Today, some consider it a cult classic. Longevity be damned, it was and remains an awful piece of movie-making. Still, having committed the likes of Joe Strummer, Elvis Costello, Courtney Love, and the Pogues to the big screen, it is worth seeing. While promoting the film, Alex Cox was widely quoted in the press as having spent only three and a half days writing the script. Most reviewers wondered why it took him so long.

Promoted as a spoof of spaghetti westerns, much of the dialogue seems improvised. At times Cox seems to be aiming at a Monty Pythonesque feel, but it is never achieved. The plot, what there is of it, involves a gang of bank robbers who head for the desert town of El Blanco where they clash with the violent, caffeine addicted McMahon gang, played by, among others, the Pogues. The highlight of MacGowan's performance comes early in the film. As Bruno McMahon he and Spider Stacy stand outside a bar where the bank robbers, including Joe Strummer, are drinking. As Shane and Spider call them out to fight, Shane's famous laugh is used as a sinister embellishment to the challenge. During the film's shootout finale Shane manages to shoot Joe Strummer, but the wounded Strummer shoots MacGowan dead. The film's highlight is the Pogues' soundtrack. Cait O'Riordan's acappella version of "Danny Boy," while incongruous in its setting, is very nicely done. Better still is "Rake at the Gates of Hell," which is used during the closing credits.

"It was fun to make, but it was much harder work than I ever thought," Shane said at the time. "I thought it would just mean putting on the guns and so on, but it wasn't like that at all. We did have our three weeks in Spain, which was great, but we had just finished a long tour and then had to get up really early every morning. We were dragged out of bed at five and sent out onto the heat of the desert while the Spaniards were staying in the shade."

That fall, with the film in the can, the Pogues were back on the road. Cait officially quit the group in October and set off with Elvis Costello. MacGowan was reportedly furious, but most of the band was less than sorry to see her go. She was, at best, a mediocre bass player. Moreover, there seemed to be a good bit of friction between her and the boys. MacGowan wanted to replace her with another female, his old flame and Nips' band-mate, Shanne Bradley. Ultimately, the band opted to make long-time roadie and fill-in bass player Daryl Hunt a permanent Pogue. With the new line up in place, the band hit the stage with a revamped set, adding "If I Should Fall from Grace with God," "Rake at the Gates of Hell," "Lullaby of London," "Turkish Song of the Damned," and the magnificent "Broad Majestic Shannon."

Before the month was out the Pogues were in the studio recording four tracks for the upcoming Dubliners' 25th anniversary album. MacGowan was delighted to work with the Dubliners, a band he had grown up with via his father's record collection. The session proved to be more than a once in a lifetime opportunity for Shane to work with some of his childhood heroes. It was the beginning of a lasting and fruitful relationship. One track from the session, the traditional "Irish Rover," topped the Irish charts and made it to #8 in the UK. In November the Dubliners made a few guest appearances with the Pogues as they wound up 1986 with a 23-gig whirlwind tour of continental Europe before, after just a 36-hour break, doing a December tour of England, Scotland, and Ireland that didn't end until Christmas.

By the time the New Year began just about everybody in the band was getting pretty sick of touring. They cut back a bit, doing some select shows and making some television appearances, including a special celebrating the Dubliners' 25th Anniversary. MacGowan took another stab at the movies. He, Spider Stacy, Terry Woods, and Frank Murray took small parts in *Eat the Rich*, Peter Richardson's black comedy about a London restaurant that serves murdered English aristocrats to unsuspecting diners. Hardly a film for the ages, *Eat the Rich* does fare better than *Straight to Hell*. While Shane and the boys are not on screen nearly as much as in their film debut, they are more suited to their new roles as tough street punks.

Meanwhile, Frank Murray had been busy trying to extricate the Pogues from their relationship with Stiff Records. Stiff, after having shown tremendous promise early on, was having a difficult time making ends meet. The label's financial problems played a part in the Pogues not releasing a new album for nearly three years. Murray managed to line up a new deal with WEA (Warner/Elektra/Asylum) Records and the band went into the studio to begin recording a new album that May with Steve Lillywhite producing. Since the situation with Stiff had not yet been completely resolved, Murray and the band paid for the sessions themselves to ensure that Stiff had no claim on the recordings.

Throughout the summer the band worked in the studio during the week and played lucrative concerts on the weekends. They were playing to their biggest crowds yet, opening for U2. Considering the size of the shows they played that summer, there was growing anticipation for the new album. In July they played Dublin's Croke Park where 67 years earlier the British Auxies and Black & Tans had opened fire on an Irish crowd enjoying a Tipperary football match. In August they played before 70,000 people in

Wembley Stadium. By September they were opening for U2 in America playing stadiums in Boston and other cities and New York's Madison Square Garden.

On the surface things couldn't have been better. The Pogues were on the verge of super stardom. Shane later said of this period that he was "on top of the world… making loads of money" and experiencing "non-stop excitement" and "constant creative expression." Just below the surface some as yet undetected problems were birthing. Rifts that would one day contribute to the Pogues' demise. For one thing, MacGowan had mixed feelings about playing stadiums. Deep down, he loved fronting a pub dance band. It was clear the Pogues were becoming something else entirely. And then there was the idea that this was a democratic band of equals. It was clear that to Pogues' fans, and even more so the press, some of the Pogues were more equal than others. When the band played Ireland's Trallee Festival that August the promoter billed them as "The Unique Shane MacGowan and the Pogues." Finally, most of the rest of the band were intent on distancing themselves from the image of an Irish band steeped in traditional Irish themes, especially Irish Republicanism. They probably cringed that August when MacGowan told a reporter from the *Sunday Tribune*, "I'm not going to start preaching about Irish politics, but at least Haughey confronts the issue that a certain amount of the country is occupied by a foreign power."

CHAPTER 6

**"I won't sit in a fuckin' bus for the whole of my life,
going from one shitty gig to another."**

Shane MacGowan

The Pogues finished 1987 doing a short tour of the USA and Canada with Joe Strummer filling in for Phillip Chevron. Chevron's ulcer had landed him in the hospital. Not having released an album in three years, the tour provided them with much needed money. Although, as Shane put it, they were making "loads" of money, they were reportedly living on individual allowances of $250 per week. That was about to change. In late November they released "Fairytale of New York," which became a huge hit that Christmas.

If I Should Fall from Grace with God, the band's third album, was released on January 18th. Foreshadowing the lyrical magic within, the album's cover showed the boys posing with Irish literary giant James Joyce. The album was an immediate hit, racing up the charts to #3 where it remained for 16 weeks. In support of their new release, the Pogues set off on a tour of Australia and New Zealand.

The concerts mixed material from the new record with songs from *Red Roses for Me* and *Rum, Sodomy & the Lash*. They even threw in a few as yet unrecorded tunes like "Boat Train." The shows garnered excellent reviews and an ever-increasing number of fans. Along with the fame came more money, lots more money. Along with the money came more pressure, lots more pressure. That pressure was beginning to take its toll on MacGowan.

Years later Phil Chevron told Martin Roddy, "During the period that we did most of our work, from '85 to '89, Shane worked furiously hard. You would be walking past his room at three or four in the morning and you would hear this ineloquent guitar playing and you could hear him muttering the melody with sheets of paper everywhere. His process was that whatever it took and whatever frame of mind he was in the songs would come out in a certain way. Very often you would see him on the tour bus or on the van, you would see him there very concentrated and tapping his foot and hands, then you knew that he was working out the tune and maybe the secondary tune that would be the whistle or something. So, quite often he would have the song worked out to that extent. He would quite often come to rehearsal with the full song, but as often as not there was times when stuff didn't quite land right and required tweaking or adjusting. If something felt like it could be stronger someone would say 'how about just putting in that chord or this chord.' That's not to take away from the fact that Shane was responsible for the main body of the song in almost all cases."

In New Zealand he went off the deep end. As usual he was drinking heavily. In order to keep up with the pace he added amphetamines to his daily routine. At times MacGowan was barely capable of performing, but the audiences still loved it. Not everyone did. Paul Scully, a longtime roadie, had seen enough after a particularly bad performance. Backstage he let into the band for just sitting back and allowing MacGowan to, as he put it, "die in front of your eyes." The following morning Shane was even later than usual in making his appearance. When he was found in his room he refused to come out. During the night he had painted himself blue and written all over the hotel room walls. He claimed that the hotel had been built over a Maori graveyard and the spirits of the dead Maori had told him to do it.

Still, the Pogues were riding high. In February they released the title cut from *If I Should Fall from Grace with God* as a single. The release hinted that MacGowan was losing his grip on the band as well as on reality. He argued against it, insisting that "Broad Majestic Shannon" should be the single. Perhaps management and the other Pogues felt justified in rejecting the advice of a singer/songwriter who was goaded by dead Maori tribesmen into painting himself blue and trashing a hotel room. They shouldn't have. The musical instincts of the man who had led them to stardom were, as usual, on the money. Instead of releasing a MacGowan masterpiece, they chose a single that failed to capitalize on the album's success, stalling at #58 on the charts.

MacGowan has said that the Pogues "peaked" with *If I Should Fall from Grace with God*. That would be a hard point to argue against. Produced by Steve Lillywhite, the album is an intoxicating blend of musical styles. It manages to maintain a sense of the band's Irish roots while incorporating Mideast sounds, jazz, and of course rock and roll into its eclectic mix. Years later MacGowan complained that the Pogues began to lose their way when, through a democratic process, the band began to stray from its Irish foundation and started to infuse other musical styles into their sound. That's an ironic position for him to take since the musical fusion began with *If I Should Fall from Grace with God* while Shane still held the Pogues' creative reins. Of the albums eleven non-traditional tracks, he wrote or co-wrote nine of them.

Lillywhite was instrumental in expanding the Pogues' sound. By all accounts Shane got on better with the new producer than he did with Elvis Costello. Lillywhite moved the recording sessions to RAK Studios, a vast improvement over Elephant, the smaller, darker studio where the band had recorded up until that time. Lillywhite suggested abandoning Andrew Rankin's stripped down drum kit for a full drum set, immediately giving the band a bigger sound. He also brought in more horns and string arrangements.

With an album as strong as *If I Should Fall from Grace with God* it is difficult, if not foolhardy, to try to single out a single track as the record's highlight. That said, for my money, "The Broad Majestic Shannon" is a contender. MacGowan has said that he wrote the song for fellow Tipperarian Liam Clancy and Tommy Makem. Over two decades later, after Liam's death in 2009, each night in concert he dedicated the song to Clancy and Makem. The simple beauty of the lyrics earned the song a place in a 2005 anthology called *The Best of Popular Irish Poetry*. The song is a sentimental reminisce of County Tipperary as MacGowan remembered it from his childhood. "The widest part of the Shannon is just down the road from where I live," he has said. "All the places in the song are local places."

If the album has a better track than "The Broad Majestic Shannon," surely it is "Fairytale of New York." The title comes from J.P. Donleavey's novel of the same name. The book is about Cornelius Christian, an American expatriate returning to his native New York City from Ireland with his Irish wife who dies on the voyage. In MacGowan's song both the husband and wife are Irish immigrants to the Big Apple. Both the book and the song touch on the elusive nature of the American dream. While the novel was written in the 1960s, a period when Irish emigration to America had waned, the song was written during a peak period of a new wave of Irish arriving in the USA. MacGowan shared writer's credits with Jem Finer.

"We decided that we wanted to do a male-female duet, a Christmas song," MacGowan said years later. "And I was told to go and write one. All I had was a little riff from Jem, right, which was ripped off from my own song 'The Broad Majestic Shannon' anyway. And it just came in a blinding flash of inspiration." It is a Christmas song like no other. The husband, past his prime, spends Christmas Eve in the drunk tank. His wife is apparently a junky hooked up to an intravenous line in a hospital bed. Obviously, they've seen better times. The husband is optimistic for their future, but the wife, who accuses him of stealing her youthful dreams, is having none of it. At one point she chastises him with the classic line, "You scumbag, you maggot, you cheap lousy faggot. Happy Christmas your arse, I pray God it's our last." It's a Christmas story only Shane MacGowan could tell.

He once told an interviewer, "I think Christmas is a beautiful religious holiday if it is taken in the right spirit because it's Christ's birthday and Christ was a wonderful man. I think everyone should get drunk and have a good time and give each other presents if they really want to, although I think that's just turning it into a consumer-load of rubbish. I never believed in Father Christmas because, in Ireland, they didn't have him, not in the house I was brought up in. They didn't insult my intelligence by expecting me to believe that a guy all the way from the Arctic Circle came along with flying reindeer and a carriage and came down the bloody chimney and shoved an effing clockwork mouse in my sock, you know what I mean? Christmas never used to be that big a deal in Ireland when I was a kid. It was a big religious festival, with midnight Mass as the highlight. That was a very beautiful thing, watching all the drunks trying to stand up."

"Fairytale of New York" was over two years in the making. It began with an idea Jem Finer and his wife conceived. By Finer's own admission, their beginning was a rather typical, sappy Christmas piece. It took MacGowan's unique perspective to transform the Finers' beginning. "We decided to make it about two Irish immigrants on their way out," Shane says. "They'd had their glory days." He completed the lyrics in Scandinavia, delirious from a bout with pneumonia. Musically, it achieved a level of sophistication the Pogues had never approached in the past. It sounds like a mini symphony. James Fearnley, whose solo piano opens the song, has said that the haunting introduction came directly from Ernio Mariconi's score for *Once Upon a Time in America*, the mob film the Pogues watched incessantly as they toured America by bus.

The female part was originally intended for Cait O'Riordan to sing. When she quit the band to marry Elvis Costello, producer Steve Lillywhite suggested his then wife, Kirsty McColl, duet with Shane. McColl, daughter of "Dirty Old Town" author Ewan McColl, had begun her career with a punk band called Drug Addix. She left that group to record as a solo artist on Stiff records, scoring a hit with "There's a Boy Down the Chip Shop Swears He's Elvis." At the point she was recruited to sing "Fairytale of New York," she was doing a good bit of session work. McColl was the perfect foil for MacGowan. "Kirsty was the magic thing that happened there," Shane said in 2006. "The final thing was getting Kirsty into the studio and like saying 'well I'll have a crack at doing this,' the way she did that vocal really put the stamp on the song. Fairytale was a proud moment, but it's to do with the whole band plus Kirsty."

"The Broad Majestic Shannon" and "Fairytale of New York" were enough to make *If I Should Fall from Grace with God* a classic album, but there was more. Much more. "Lullaby of London," "Turkish Song of the Damned," and the title cut are all strong enough tracks to remain on the Pogues' live set list more than two decades after their release. "Lullaby of London" is a slow, sad, beautiful song evoking images of the town MacGowan loves to hate so well. "Turkish Song of the Damned" (co-written by Finer) and "If I Should Fall from Grace with God" burst with visions of death and religion. The former is reminiscent of 19th Century English poet Samuel Taylor Cooleridge's opium-fueled epic *The Rime of the Ancient Mariner*. The music has an infectious Mideastern feel. The later brings MacGowan's nationalist passion forward with the lines "This land was always ours, was the proud land of our fathers. It belongs to us and them, not to any others." Certainly not to the British.

Republican sentiments are even more up front in one of the album's traditional cuts, "Medley." The piece is a merger of three songs, "The Recruiting Sergeant," "Rocky Road to Dublin," and "Galway Races." MacGowan shares the vocals with Terry Woods in "The Recruiting Sergeant" portion of the track. It's about British attempts to recruit Irishmen to fight with England in World War I. The would-be recruits decline saying, "There's fighting in Dublin to be done," a reference to the 1916 Easter Rising that kicked off the Irish revolution against the British. That reference is a mild dose of anti-British sentiment compared to the album's other MacGowan-Woods collaboration.

"Streets of Sorrow/Birmingham Six," is technically a medley as well. "Streets of Sorrow," written and sung by Woods, is a soft, reflective piece about the sorrow, pain, and death caused by terrorism in the streets, presumably the streets of Belfast. It is a perfect lead in to MacGowan's more virulent "Birmingham Six." The Birmingham Six were Hugh Callaghan, Patrick Joseph Hill, Gerard Hunter, Richard McIlkenny, William Power and John Walker. Five of the men were born in Belfast, one in Derry. All six had lived in Birmingham, England, since the 1960s. They were arrested in November of 1974 while attempting to travel to Ireland the same day IRA bombs rocked two Birmingham pubs. All six Irishmen were convicted and sentenced to life in prison for carrying out the bombings. The terrorist attacks were the most deadly in England up until that time. Twenty-one people died and 162 were injured. The six were convicted of the crime on August 15, 1975. When they appeared in court again some three months later, all six were badly bruised and showed signs of having been brutalized in jail. Fourteen British prison officers were charged with assaulting the prisoners, but all were acquitted. MacGowan's song also referenced The Guilford Four (Gerry Conlon, Paul Hill, Patrick Armstrong, and Carole Richardson), convicted of IRA bombings targeting pubs popular with British Army personnel a month before the Birmingham explosions. Four soldiers and one civilian were killed in those attacks. Sixty-five people were injured. The Guilford Four's convictions were based on confessions that they claimed were extracted through torture. They too were sentenced to life in prison. The judge lamented that they had not been charged with treason so that he could have imposed the death penalty. "Birmingham Six" was not limited to decade old incidents. The final verse references eight IRA men who had recently been "kicked down and shot in the back of the head" by the British in Armagh, Ireland.

MacGowan's lyrics pulled no punches. He called the British prosecutors "filth," accusing them of framing and torturing the convicted "for being Irish in the wrong place and at the wrong time." For good measure he referred to the British authorities as "whores of the empire" and hoped they would "rot down in hell." The "whores" were not amused. "Birmingham Six" became the first song to fall victim to a government ban on broadcasting statements by terrorists or their supporters. Television and radio stations were told not to the play the song. Even before the official ban was announced, the song was cut from an edition of *Friday Night Live*. A government spokesman said the song contained "lyrics alleging that some convicted terrorists are not guilty and that Irish people in general are at a disadvantage in British courts of law. We think these allegations might support, solicit or invite support for an (terrorist) organization." It's not surprising that the British were concerned about anything that might invite support for Irish terrorists. Just two months before the release of *If I Should Fall from Grace with God* the Provos bombed a Remembrance Day Service at a war memorial in Enniskillen, County Fermanagh. Eleven people died and sixty were injured.

The same month that *If I Should Fall from Grace with God* was released Chief Justice Lord Lane, after a six-week appeal hearing, upheld the Birmingham Six convictions. Over the next three years newspaper articles, television documentaries, and books brought forward new evidence to question the conviction while campaign groups calling for the men's release sprang up across Britain, Ireland, Europe and the USA. The Pogues got involved raising money for the prisoner's families.

In October of 1989 the Guilford Four's convictions were overturned on appeal. The appeals court ruled that the confessions were obtained through torture and that the police had withheld evidence clearing the four. They were released after spending 15 years in prison. Shortly thereafter, Gerry Conlan of the four was being introduced onstage as a special guest at Pogues' gigs. Two years later a British court of appeals agreed that the Birmingham Six had indeed been framed and they were released after serving 16 years for a crime they didn't commit. In 2001, a decade after their release, the six men were awarded compensation ranging from $1.2 to $1.8 million. MacGowan and the Pogues received no apology.

If I Should Fall from Grace with God also contains the expected allotment of Pogues' rave-ups. "Bottle of Smoke" and "Fiesta," like so many of the album's numbers remain staples of the band's live set more than two decades later. "Bottle of Smoke" reflects the Irish passion for horse racing, a passion nurtured in MacGowan by his Aunt Nora when he was just a pre-schooler growing up on the Lynch homestead in Carney Commons. A far cry from "Old Stewball," the steed in "Bottle of Smoke" comes in at "Twenty fucking five to one" causing the "Priests and maidens, drunk as pagans" to celebrate. "Fiesta," co-written by Finer, was inspired by the fiesta that took place outside the Pogues' hotel while they were filming *Straight to Hell* in Spain. Most of the cast hated the noisy fiesta after a long day on the film set, but Shane loved it. He once said, however, that he hated the song calling it one of the "arty" things he had to do in the Pogues but "won't be responsible for." Few Pogues fans would agree. Over the years it has become the standard live showstopper, the last song of the night, whipping the crowd into a frenzy as a machine showers them with colorful confetti. MacGowan has called "Sit Down by the Fire," another full speed ahead number, "a typical Irish bedtime story." If that's true, nightmares must be rampant in Ireland. The lyrics tell of creeping things in the night suggesting that "if ever you see them pretend that you're dead, or they'll bite off your head. They'll rip out your liver and dance on your neck."

The album also contains the hands down best non-MacGowan Pogues' composition in the band's repertoire. Phil Chevron's "Thousands Are Sailing" is absolutely brilliant. The perfect song of Irish emigration to America, it manages to include all the expected immigrant references without ever sounding cliched. Paddys working on the railroad and the police force, coffin ships, escaping poverty for the "land of opportunity," famine, the old songs from home – they're all here. On the record, MacGowan's vocal is the perfect vehicle for bringing Chevron's lyrics to life. Shane's live performances of the song, however, are relatively rare. The reason, I suspect, is due to the line "in Brendan Behan's footsteps I danced up and down the street." That lyric refers to Behan's first visit to New York. MacGowan never liked the line, contending that Behan would not dance either up or down Manhattan's streets, even though the song has the singer rather than Behan doing the dancing. On the album Shane says he sang those words "so viciously that it's obvious that he was kicking windows in at the same time." In concert during the months following the album's release Shane changed the words to pissed, puked, crawled, shat, or spewed up and down the street. Reportedly, this annoyed Chevron to no end. Before the year was out Chevron was singing his masterpiece himself onstage.

The band toured the UK in February and March. The Saint Patrick's day show, as usual, was terrific. Fortunately, it was videotaped and released commercially as *The Pogues Live at the Town & Country*. It stands today as a vital document of a great live band in its prime. American singer/songwriter Steve Earle was a guest on four of the tour's shows. He sat in with the Pogues on "Johnny Come Lately," a song of Earle's that the band has covered. They also backed Earle up on the song when he recorded it for his *Copperhead Road* album. That's when Earle, a self-proclaimed MacGowan fan, got his first taste of how difficult it can be working with him. Shane was four hours late for that recording session. During the subsequent tour, Earle recalls the Pogues drawing lots to see who would have to get Shane out of bed each afternoon.

The Pogues continued to tour throughout the year playing to larger and larger crowds in bigger and bigger venues. During the summer months they played massive outdoor festivals. The Pogues had arrived. They were huge. Shane MacGowan had gotten what he wanted. He was a star. He was also the embodiment of the old cliché, "Be careful what you wish for."

The pressure he felt was intense. As the band's front man and primary singer and songwriter he was generally the focus of media and fan attention. Unfortunately, increasing fame brought with it increasing egos, and the other band members often resented the attention lavished on Shane. That resentment was not eased by the fact that, quite frankly, Shane MacGowan could be a real pain in the ass to work with. For his part, MacGowan felt responsible for providing the band with quality material, but he also felt constrained by the band's democratic structure. His mates wanted more say in the band's direction, leaning ever farther away from its Irish roots toward a more eclectic pop sound. Moreover, they wanted to do more of the writing in order to share in the lucrative royalties. MacGowan's songwriting royalties would have made it possible for him to live well while touring less, but the rest of the band wanted and needed the income concerts brought in.

There were mounting signs that Shane was going off the deep end. During a tour of Spain he was found wandering around Barcelona with a Samurai sword. In Dublin, having once again painted himself blue and swallowing a handful of Ecstasy, he was thrown out of a pub. His "handlers" decided to take him to his cousin's home. He tried to jump out of the car on the way. The incident prompted his cousin and sister to get him admitted to St. John's of God rehab facility, reportedly against his will. Two days later he left St. John's intending to fly London. He arrived at the airport drunk and rearing to go, only to find that his flight was delayed. While he waited he continued drinking until he got into an altercation with a stranger. The stranger claimed that MacGowan had attacked him. Somehow, a woman who had up until then not been involved in the commotion was bumped into and knocked down. Shane was arrested. He was given the choice of going to jail or returning to St. John's. He chose the latter.

It was around this time that what has become known to Pogues' fans as the "Beach Boys LP Affair" took place. Years later Victoria Clarke, MacGowan's long time girl-friend, described the incident in detail in a television show called *Rock Wives*. "I was called from my bed many years ago by the landlady of my boyfriend, Shane MacGowan. She had heard strange noises coming from his flat at the top floor of her respectable townhouse." Clarke went on to explain that when the landlord tried to enter Shane's apartment, he confronted her at the top of the stairs. Bleeding profusely from the mouth and holding half a Beach Boys album, MacGowan threw an acoustic guitar at the woman forcing her to retreat back down the stairs. When Clarke arrived on the scene "to sort things out," as she put it, Shane calmed down enough to explain what was going on. "He told me that he had taken 15 or 20 tabs of acid earlier in the evening," she said, "and had become convinced that the third world war was taking place and that he, as the leader of the Irish Republic, was holding a summit meeting in his kitchen between the heads of state of the world superpowers: Russia, China, America and Ireland. In order to demonstrate the cultural inferiority of the United States, he was eating a Beach Boys album." If it's true that veracity is detected in the details, it may be worth noting that the album in question was *The Beach Boys' Greatest Hits, Volume Three.*

Through it all, popularity swelled for both MacGowan and the band. "Fiesta" was released as a single that summer and did quite well. They finished the year with a December UK tour. When it was over, MacGowan was rushed to a Dublin hospital after keeling over. His collapse was attributed to "nervous exhaustion." Before the year ended the Pogues released a new single, "Yeah, Yeah, Yeah," which sounded a good bit like the early R&B steeped Rolling Stones. The flip side, an Irish traditional song called "Limerick Rake," was a perfect vehicle for MacGowan.

At Christmas, "Fairytale of New York" was all over the radio for the second year in a row. The record had made Shane MacGowan and Kirsty McColl household names in Britain. The song charted at number two the previous Christmas, being edged out by the Pet Shop Boys' cover of Elvis Presley's "Always on My Mind," causing MacGowan to quip, "We were beaten by two queens and a drum machine." "Fairytale of New York" has since been named the world's fifth most popular Christmas song of all time. In a 2003 poll it was named the most popular Irish song *ever*. Year after year MacGowan and McColl's duet dominates Britain's Christmas airwaves. The BBC has actually produced a half-hour documentary investigating where the song came from and why it means so much to so many people. Apart from the classic Christian hymn "Amazing Grace," it's the only song I'm aware of to have been honored with a television special. In 2007, BBC Radio One decided to bleep the word "faggot" after it had been played uncensored for 20 years. They backed down after being besieged with complaints. At the time Shane said, "that says more about Radio One than about me or about anyone else. It's probably a good thing really, because everyone will want to know what the bleeps are. It's just a pop song at the end of the day." Ironically, Kirsty McColl herself sang "you scumbag, you maggot, you're cheap and you're haggard" when she performed the song on British television.

A week before Christmas 2000, the unthinkable happened. Kirsty McColl was killed before her children's eyes in Cozumel, Mexico. She was 41 years old. She had taken her two sons, Jamie, 15, and Louis, 14, there as a getaway for one of the boys who had just lost a close friend. She had always put her kids before her career. Her attempt to ease the boy's loss ended up adding to it. Steve Lillywhite, Kirsty's ex-husband, flew down to Mexico to retrieve the boys.

Kirsty and her sons were swimming when she was struck by a speedboat's propeller, nearly cutting her in two. An experienced diver, McColl was introducing the boys to the wonders of Chankanaab reef, one of the most popular dive sites off the Yucatán Peninsula. They had just surfaced after spending half an hour marveling at a huge lobster, a massive eel, and scores of fish and corals. Suddenly a $213,000, 31-foot boat sped into the restricted diving area. Kirsty pushed one of her sons out of its path. Ivan Diaz, their dive guide, grabbed the other boy and managed to get him out of the way.

The boat was owned by one of Mexico's richest men, Guillermo Gonzalez Nova, a supermarket magnate with close ties to the government. It was in a restricted diving area where it was not allowed to be. Nova was on board along with two sons, a daughter-in-law, and a granddaughter. In court they claimed the driver was Juan Jose Cen Yam, the powerful businessman's employee. Cen Yam got 3 years but the sentence was commuted after he paid a $180 fine, one peso for each day of jail time. He was also required to pay Kirsty MacColl's sons a reparation of 25,280 pesos (about $2,300), an amount based on the minimum wage in Mexico. Several eyewitnesses testified that Yam was not at the boat's controls. Diaz testified he saw him in the back of the boat, leaping forward to help during the emergency. Local newspapers reported that after coming ashore, Gonzalez Nova, the only one onboard licensed to pilot a boat that large and powerful, admitted he had been at the helm.

Kirsty's mother, Jean, began seeking justice in the case shortly after the accident. According to her, "We do know that a witness saw Cen Yam a day or so after the accident. He had got very drunk in the pub and was celebrating, and he said that his boss had asked him to take responsibility for the accident and if he did he would give him a good lot of money. So he was going to buy himself a new house. I don't know if he's bought a new house because I can't find him." Jean McColl launched the Justice for Kirsty campaign to pressure the Mexican judicial system into investigating the case more thoroughly. She rallied outrage and anger at the accident, and raised funds to pay for lawyers, and to approach governments at the highest levels. Her efforts compelled Mexico to re-open its inquiries after pressure from the campaign and the British government exposed the clumsy cover-up that followed the accident.

After the accident, MacGowan told the *Irish Post*, "She (Kirsty) was always brilliant. She lit up a room. She was an amazing woman. Funny and intelligent. She had a lot of demons in her life, but she never put it on to others. She was always up and raring to go and enjoy life. I first got to know her properly when her husband was trying to produce *If I Should Fall From Grace with God*. We had a long chat down the studio when she was as out of it as I was, and it turned out that the shy, frightened looking girl with classical red-haired Gaelic beauty was funny, charming, intelligent, and a real gas to talk to. We became good friends and she was soon boosting my ego and hypocritically lecturing me about my excessive drinking while keeping me up all night slugging champagne." At Christmas in 2005 the Pogues re-released "Fairytale of New York" and donated profits to Jean McColl's campaign to bring Guillermo Gonzalez Nova to justice. "We're doing everything we can," MacGowan said. "It's really down to Kirsty's mother, Jean, and her children about what happens next. But, I mean, we gave a massive injection of bread into taking the guy to court. You must have read about the owner of the boat and all that. I think they can get it sorted out." In the end, they didn't. Late in 2009 the Mexican government announced that it had closed their case file on Kirsty's death and regarded that as the end of the matter. They said they had taken statements and affidavits from many witnesses and had exhausted all avenues of investigation, none of which implicated anyone other than the boat hand Cen Yam, who had already been convicted of causing the accident.

"Fairytale of New York" remains a treasured song in the Pogues' repertoire. Before each concert tour there's considerable speculation and concern as to who will sing Kirsty's part. In 2006 MacGowan said, "When we do the song live these days, there are people in and around the Pogues who nominate guest singers for the Kirsty part. I leave it to them to argue it out. I can't be bothered with the politics any more than Machiavelli could. To say I have any favorites for that role other than Kirsty is to sully her name. I'm old fashioned like that. Besides, it's hearing the original group playing it that keeps me happy....The role, and it is a role, frequently goes to Ella Finer, daughter of Jem in the band who co-wrote the song with me. It works fine with Ella, partly as it keeps it in the family, and partly because "Fairytale" is meant to be a song from an older man to a younger woman. And I knew her before she was born."

CHAPTER 7

**"I feel like I've spent the last five years of my life on the road...
the more you travel, the wilder the things that keep happening to you."**

Shane MacGowan

At 31 years of age Shane MacGowan greatly preferred Thailand's beaches to the world's concert stages. He had fallen in love with the country on Far Eastern retreats with Victoria Clarke. None the less, 1989 began just as the last several years had begun for Shane MacGowan and the rest of the Pogues: on the road. They began the year in Europe and then headed into the studio to begin working on their fourth album, *Peace and Love*. Once it was in the can, it was back to the stage. By year's end they had toured Australia and the United States.

Peace and Love was released in July. Naturally, Frank Murray wanted to tour extensively in support of the new release. Shane was anything but enthusiastic. By that time he was getting quite vocal in the press concerning his loathing of concert tours. In interview after interview he vented about hating touring. He told a reporter from *Hot Press*, "I'm sick of performing live. I've done too much of it. Over the last while, it's gotten to the stage where we're doing it every night, week after week, it's too much. It's very hard to put as much into it and you really have to work at psychin' yourself up, getting' drunk enough but not too drunk to fuckin' enjoy it and be good. You have to do it, so you do it, but it's a bit like screwin' for a living. Screwin' is only good if you're an amateur or a part-timer. Old whores don't have much fun."

It's likely that MacGowan's aversion to getting on stage was compounded by something that took place the previous month during a concert at St. Andrew's football stadium in Birmingham. While the Pogues were performing, rowdy fans broke down a barrier and rushed the stage. There were more than 100 injuries. The incident undoubtedly brought back horrid memories of an infamous incident that had taken place just two months before at a stadium in Sheffield. During an FA Cup semi-final match, 96 Liverpool fans were crushed to death and an additional 730 were injured in a stampede that the press dubbed the Hillsborough Disaster. Daryl Hunt and Phil Chevron were at the match that day. The Pogues subsequently dedicated *Peace and Love* to the fans who died that day. When a reporter asked MacGowan to comment on the incident at the Pogues' Birmingham concert in light of the Hillsborough Disaster he was visibly upset, replying, "If a bunch of people got killed at one of our gigs, I wouldn't play ever again. I'm not interested in causing a single piece of human suffering just for the sake of a fucking pop concert."

If Pogues shows were potentially dangerous for their fans, they were even moreso for their front man. The pressure of touring and the increasing disatisfaction with the direction the band was beginning to go continued to take a toll on MacGowan. It was clear he wasn't happy with *Peace and Love*. In an interview intended to promote the new album he told a reporter, "I don't control anything I do now. Too many people have influence over me for my liking." According to the Pogues tour manager, Joey Cashman, "There was an underlying sort of resentment against Shane in the band because all the media would want to speak to Shane… they liked to think about themselves as a nine (sic) piece band where everybody had an equal input and equal importance, so sometimes I felt that people were objecting to his opinions not based upon his actual opinions but simply because they just got fed up with it being Shane, Shane, Shane."

The Pogues seemed to be trying to expand their audience with *Peace and Love* through a fusion of various musical styles. One can make the argument that the fusion began with *If I Should Fall from Grace with God*, but with that release MacGowan was still in control and the album worked. *Peace and Love* was more like the Beatles' *White Album* in that several individual songwriters were recording their material in the way they wanted. The difference was that the Beatles had two, maybe two and a half, gifted songwriters. The Pogues had one. On a good day, maybe one and a half.

MacGowan penned just six of the album's fourteen songs. Finer, Woods, Chevron, Rankin, and Hunt all contributed material. Part of the problem was that MacGowan was not part of the fusion process on the other Pogues' songs. Whereas Shane and Finer had co-written songs on previous albums, when Jem collaborated on *Peace and Love* it was with Andrew Rankin. Phil Chevron co-wrote one of the album's tracks with Daryl Hunt. Terry Woods collaborated with fellow Irishman Ron Kavana. "I couldn't play what I wanted," MacGowan said in an interview. "On the Pogues' best album, *If I Should Fall From Grace with God,* me and Jem wrote every note, apart from the traditional numbers which I arranged… but after that, things changed. On *Peace & Love* I had one last go, then I gave up." Years later he told Victoria Clarke, "They were trying to turn it into progressive rock. It was getting louder and louder, and more electric. More sort of rock solos in it. Songs the others were writing, we were doing more of them, and they didn't have anything to do with the basic Irish roots of it… They were trying to divorce themselves from the Irish thing. They saw it as a limitation." He was less diplomatic in an interview in the *Guardian*: "We'd stopped playing Irish music, basically. It was all that fusion shite, and there was no emotion left in the songs."

In defense of the other Pogues, they were dealing with the classic vicious cycle. It was probably true that there were substantial disagreements in the scramble to secure songwriting royalties. On the other hand, Shane's substance abuse had effected his creative output. He was taking prodigious amounts of acid. He claims to have taken 15 to 50 tabs a day. "Once you go over a few tabs that's it," he claimed. " It doesn't have any further effect. And you get used to it. You can function on it. But very few people have the constitution for it." And that was in addition to his drinking. One doctor told him that if he didn't stop he'd be dead in two years. The MacGowan songs that did make it on to *Peace and Love*, while they are surely among the record's best, are hardly

Shane's best. Those that didn't make it were probably discarded with good reason. One song the band rejected was an Acid-House, rave inspired, 24-minute dance tune called "You've Got to Connect Yourself." Years later Phil Chevron gave his perspective on the selection of *Peace and Love's* songs. "One thing that Shane forgets when he talks of us trying to sideline Irish music is that he was the one trying to do that," he told Martin Roddy in 2004. "He was the one saying that he wants to do this twenty minute acid house experimental track called 'Contact Yourself.' This was a big bone of contention on the *Peace And Love* album. None of us were going to walk into Warner Brothers and say 'here is our new album, and by the way one whole side is a jazz acid house contraption called 'Contact Yourself.'"

MacGowan's best songs on *Peace and Love* are probably "White City," "Down All the Days," "London You're a Lady," and "Boat Train." "Cotton Fields" and "USA," both written while the Pogues were touring America, do little to enhance Shane's reputation as a top songwriter. While both songs deal with the States, neither touch on Irish immigration, a theme he handled so deftly on previous albums. Instead, he seems to focus on inner turmoil, perhaps brought on by dissatisfaction with the direction the Pogues were taking. A sense of martyrdom is apparent in "Cotton Fields'" when Shane sings the refrain, "They're gonna crucify you." In place of allusions to Irish history or culture, the tracks have references to an old American folk song and "The Battle Hymn of the Republic." If there is a redeeming factor to the pair of songs it's Shane's vocal.

"White City" fares better. The song is about urban development, particularly the razing of a London Greyhound dog-racing track where Shane's father Maurice sometimes gambled. Today the White City tube station and the song are about all that's left of it. MacGowan has said that he wrote the song while waiting to film *Top of the Pops* in the BBC studio that was built over part of the area where the track used to be. Admittedly, there's no magic in the lyrics, but the track rocks along nicely and Shane's vocal is excellent. "White City" is one of the few tracks from *Peace and Love* that survived on concert set lists beyond the year or so that the Pogues toured in support of the album.

"Down All the Days" is about Christy Brown, the Irish novelist who died in 1981. Brown was born with cerebral palsy, which left him unable to control his limbs, except for his left foot. Amazingly, he learned to write and eventually to type with it. His first book, an autobiography called *My Left Foot*, was published in 1954. Sixteen years later he expanded it into *Down All the Days,* a novel embracing Dublin culture. It became an international bestseller translated into 14 languages. A 1989 film version of the autobiography received five Oscar nominations, including Best Picture. MacGowan's song was intended for the movie but was not used. Perhaps the line "I type with me toes, I suck stout through me nose," something Brown didn't do, was the reason the song was turned down.

On first listen "London You're a Lady" holds out a tremendous promise that it never fully delivers. MacGowan's vocal is excellent. The lyrics expose his love-hate relationship with the city in an extended metaphor that at times reaches fine heights. The pulsing "heart" of the city and the streets and or buildings compared to "scarred up thighs" work nicely. The metaphor is especially effective when referencing the Lady's apparel with the lines "Red busses skirt your hem. Your head dress is a string of lights." Unfortunately, the lyric's beauty evaporates quickly in the last verse when Shane sings "Your piss is like a river. Its scent is beer and gin." Musically "London You're a Lady" brings to mind several Irish flavored MacGowan classics, particularly "Broad Majestic Shannon." The elegant, striding tune soars confidently towards what listeners feel sure will be a classic bridge, but it never materializes. Overall, the track has the feel of a nearly great song that was finished too quickly. James Fearnley has said that although it has an unbeatable melody, some of the Pogues agreed, "he could have had another pass at the words."

My favorite track on *Peace and Love* is "Boat Train." It's hard not to appreciate a song that begins "I met with Napper Tandy and I shook him by the hand. He said 'Hold me up for Chrissake, for I can hardly stand.'" Despite the reference to Napper Tandy, a leader in the Irish Rebellion of 1798, the song is not nationalistic. It's about the ferry, or boat train, that runs between Ireland and England for about $125.00 round trip. It's a joyful, up-tempo romp about drinking, gambling, and generally carrying on during the voyage across the Irish Sea. It's a topic Shane knew very well. "I love the boat. You don't get treated like a piece of shit like you do on an airplane," he told documentary filmmaker Sarah Share. Her film shows him boarding the boat train and immediately ordering a double gin and tonic with a slice of lemon, sitting in the lounge discussing Van Morrison with Joey Cashman, singing along to an old rock and roll song, and signing autographs with a women's club from Dublin. Obviously, he was enjoying himself on a crossing he'd made before. His love of the ferry is palpable in "Boat Train."

Peace and Love does contain a song about Irish nationalism, but it wasn't written by MacGowan. "Young Ned of the Hill," co-authored by Terry Woods and Ron Kavana, concerns the Irish fight against Oliver Cromwell's invading English army in the 17th century. Woods, who teamed with MacGowan on "Streets of Sorrow / Birmingham Six" and "The Recruiting Sergeant" comes closer to matching Shane's anti-British sentiments than any of the other Pogues. Kavana, who rumor had it was once considered as an addition to the Pogues, put out a double CD in 2006 called *Irish Songs of Rebellion, Resistance, and Reconciliation*.

In addition to the six songs MacGowan wrote for *Peace and Love*, he put his stamp on two more of the album's tracks. He did the vocals on "Night Train to Lorca" and "Misty Morning, Albert Bridge," both written by Jem Finer. Of the two "Misty Morning, Albert Bridge" is easily the better. It has an Irish feel that brings to mind some of the Pogues' best slow numbers. In 2002 the song was featured in an episode of an American TV show, *American Embassy*, about the US embassy in London.

Actually, the bands' decision to take the musical fusion up a notch at the expense of their Irish roots and MacGowan's preferences was commercially successful. *Peace and Love* may have alienated Shane, but the broadening of the Pogues' musical styles continued to increase their appeal well beyond the limited audience that their Irish folk styles initially attracted. *Peace and Love* debuted in the UK at number five and spent two months on the charts. One reviewer actually wrote that *Peace and Love* was superior to the *Poguetry in Motion* EP, which included "A Rainy Night in Soho" and "Body of an American," surely two of MacGowan's best works. To put that reviewer's commendation in perspective, it should also be noted that he raved about "My Blue Heaven," a sappy Phil Chevron/Daryl Hunt pop song on *Peace and Love* that MacGowan has justifiably called "rubbish." Even Chevron agrees with Shane. "Believe it or not, 'Blue Heaven' was a really great idea that went horribly wrong in the studio," he said in 2004. "I agree with Shane when he says it was rubbish." Despite the positive public response in 1989, eventually even the Pogues themselves seemed to have realized the album's shortcomings. While they performed most of the record's songs in subsequent tours to support the release, within a year the only non-MacGowan song from *Peace and Love* left in the live set list was "Young Ned of the Hill." When the reunited Pogues toured in 2009, their 22-song set contained 16 songs from *Red Roses for Me*; *Rum, Sodomy, and the Lash*; *Poguetry in Motion*; and *If I Should Fall from Grace with God*. Only "Young Ned of the Hill" survived from *Peace and Love*.

In 1989 *Peace and Love's* British success suggested that the time might finally be right for the Pogues to break big in the states. The band was very popular on the East Coast, Chicago, and other areas with a significant Irish-American population. But despite their superstar status in the UK, the Pogues were hardly household names in America. The really big money, of course, came with success on both sides of the Atlantic. A September tour opening for Bob Dylan promised the Pogues their best stateside exposure up to that point. It seemed just the vehicle to break things wide open.

Dylan and the Pogues were a good match. The teenage MacGowan was a Bob Dylan fan, and Dylan had become an admirer of MacGowan. Both songwriters have a deep, abiding love of traditional music. Each can take a song hundreds of years old, a song which has been performed by countless artists, and make it their own. Both songwriters were instrumental in revitalizing folk music in their respective countries. Each has the gift of writing new lyrics to familiar folk tunes, transforming timeless melodies into majestic, contemporary art. Dylan was also a Brendan Behan fan. When Behan's play *The Hostage* was staged at Greenwich Village's Sheridan Square Theatre in the early 1960s Behan showed up at a performance. More than a bit drunk, he mounted the stage and delivered an incoherent speech to the cast before staggering out the door and down the street. The young Dylan followed right behind him and into the White Horse Tavern where the future voice of his generation tried to engage the Irish literary giant in conversation before Behan passed out. Dylan also admired Behan's brother Dominic, having appropriated the tune from Dominic's Irish republican classic "The Patriot Game" for his own "With God on Our Side." Dylan apparently used the tune without Behan's knowledge. A few years later when Dylan was touring Britain he asked his entourage if they knew of any poets in town that he could meet. When someone suggested that a meeting might be arranged with Dominic Behan, Dylan quickly changed the subject.

In addition to these connections, the young Dylan had been close to Liam Clancy, another of Shane's heroes, when the Clancy Brothers were Greenwich Village regulars during the early sixties. Dylan has called Clancy the greatest ballad singer he ever heard. In his memoir, *Chronicles: Volume One*, Dylan suggests that Clancy's repertoire of Irish rebel songs was instrumental in inspiring the songwriting that transformed the young folksinger from a Woody Guthrie / Jack Elliot disciple to the American cultural icon he became. "I got to be friends with Liam and began going after-hours to the White Horse Tavern on Hudson Street, which was mainly an Irish bar frequented mostly by guys from the old country," he wrote. "All through the night they would sing drinking songs, country ballads and rousing rebel songs that would lift the roof. The rebellion songs were a really serious thing. The language was flashy and provocative, a lot of action in the words, all sung with gusto. The singer always had a merry light in his eye, had to have it. I loved these songs and could still hear them in my head long after and into the next day. They weren't protest songs, though, they were rebel ballads...even in a simple, melodic wooing ballad there'd be rebellion waiting around the corner. You couldn't escape it. There were songs like that in my repertoire, too, where something lovely was suddenly upturned, but instead of rebellion showing up it would be death itself, the Grim Reaper. Rebellion spoke to me louder. The rebel was alive and well, romantic and honorable. The Grim Reaper wasn't like that. I was beginning to think I might want to change over. The Irish landscape wasn't too much like the American landscape, though, so I'd have to find some cuneiform tablets - some archaic grail to lighten the way. I had grasped the idea of what kind of songs I wanted to write, I just didn't know how to do it yet."

It seemed that having Bob Dylan and Shane MacGowan on the same bill could be very interesting. It was not to be. Shane never made it to America for the Dylan shows. To this day, there is no definitive explanation as to why. The final official word was that Shane was "unable to travel due to nervous exhaustion." Initially, the MacGowan camp claimed that he had hepatitis. Spider Stacy told reporters that Shane had gotten sick at the airport and had stayed in England to have tests run. When the tour was first announced Dylan had recently released an album with the Grateful dead called *Dylan and the Dead*. At the time Shane joked to reporters, "Never mind Dylan and the Dead. This will be Dylan and the nearly dead." Perhaps that was closer to the truth. During the *RockWives* television show Victoria Clarke revealed what she remembered about Shane's no-show. "I spent four days with Shane in a hotel at Heathrow airport, because he was due in America for The Pogues' first-ever major US tour, supporting Bob Dylan. Unfortunately, because of the large quantities of cough mixture and gin that Shane was consuming, British Airways kept refusing to allow him on any of their planes. When he finally got on a plane, it took four people to escort him and he screamed the whole way to Dallas. We didn't quite make it in time for Bob, which was probably a good thing, given the circumstances." Shane's screaming on the plane no doubt had to do with the flight attendant's refusal to serve him alcohol. To compensate, Victoria and Terry O'Neill, the band's publicist, snuck their little bottles of complimentary wine to him. When they got caught and were stopped, Shane went bonkers. His tirade resulted in them all being strip-searched when they landed at the airport in Dallas. By the time they got to their hotel, Shane was in such a state that he set fire to the place and got them all evicted at three in the morning.

John Nelson who worked for Bill Silva, the promoter of the Dylan tour, said they were never notified that MacGowan wouldn't be there. The day of the first show, when he asked about Shane's absence at the sound check he was mislead. Nelson recalled, "When I didn't see him at the sound check, I walked up to the tour manager and said, 'Aren't you missing a band member?' He said, 'Oh, yeah, Shane's been ill; he just got out of the hospital, and we think he'll be rejoining us next week.'" In fact, Shane missed all six Dylan shows, the entire leg of the tour that the Pogues opened for Dylan. Spider Stacy did his best to fill in on Shane's vocals. One fan complained, "Seeing the Pogues without Shane MacGowan was like seeing the Doors without Jim Morrison." An apt comparison since organist Ray Manzarek used to do Morrison's vocals when the Doors' front man was too wasted to perform.

By the time MacGowan joined the band the Dylan gigs were over. The Pogues remaining gigs were in smaller venues, many of them in the South. Reviews of the shows Shane did make ran hot and cold. On some nights he was brilliant, in command of the stage. Other nights it was clear he would rather be back in Silvermines, Ireland, attending the cup presentation to Tipperary's All Ireland Hurling team. During the more ragged performances MacGowan began leaving the stage more. Spider was called in to cover for Shane more frequently. It was evident that increased drugs and alcohol were effecting Shane's ability to lead the band. James Fearnley remembers, "We had to develop strategies for when he didn't show up or didn't show up in a fit state to sing the songs. Spider took a lot of the singing, with help from Darryl, and Terry chipped in." It became pretty common for the press to predict MacGowan's demise. His name began to appear on lists of celebrities to bet on in macabre office "death pools."

Victoria Clarke told Sarah Share, "It wasn't so much that he drank a lot, but that he seemed to be doing it more out of desperation at that point. More as a way of avoiding people than as a way of joining in. Whereas when I first met him he was a very social sort of person. He would drink with people... When it got really bad I could see him put down a bottle of gin before he went onstage just to make himself seem able to get onstage."

The American South made a lasting impression on MacGowan. Nearly 20 years later he told me, "I've been down South. I've been to New Orleans loads of times. Two or three times we've done places like Atlanta, Birmingham, Alabama and places like that. It's still a great crowd and all that, but God it's spooky, man! I've been to Africa and places like that, but I've never seen black people walking around and getting out of my way on the sidewalk because I'm white. It's really weird, because they're always proud. You know what I mean? It wouldn't happen in New York, would it? It wouldn't happen anywhere, except maybe South Africa."

Despite a very shaky autumn, by year's end Shane MacGowan and the Pogues were as popular as they had ever been. In November, *Completely Pogued*, an hour-long documentary film about the band aired on the BBC. Directed by Billy Magra, the film featured interviews with the band's rock star fans and the Pogues themselves. It also used a good bit of footage from the *Live at the Town and Country* video and some from the "Johnny Come Lately" recording session with Steve Earle. There was also an excellent clip of Phillip Chevron performing "Thousands Are Sailing" with an acoustic guitar on a visit back to a record shop that he worked in before joining the Pogues. The documentary further established MacGowan and the Pogues as a significant artistic force rather than a simple pop group. That status was reinforced in December when Faber & Faber published *Poguetry: The Lyrics of Shane MacGowan*. In addition to lyrics the book contained 29 previously unavailable MacGowan poems. It sold well.

CHAPTER 8

"The church bells ring, an old drunk sings. God can't help the shape I'm i.

Shane MacGowan, "Rain Street"

While *Peace and Love* might have been a low point in the Pogues' recorded output, it did nothing to slow down their economic engine and expanding fan base. The band toured Australia and New Zealand for the second time in early 1990. In February they released a cover version of the old Elvis Presley number "Got a lot of Livin' to Do" on a charity compilation album. By March they were playing in the Unites States again, including a memorable nation-wide St. Patrick's Day television appearance on *Saturday Night Live*. That spring and summer there were lucrative European tours.

Eventually, the Pogues left the road to work on their fifth album, *Hell's Ditch*. By this time it was clear that all was not well. The money was coming in, but there were cracks in the foundation. MacGowan seemed increasingly alienated from the band and increasingly reluctant to perform. He would have been happy to spend most of his time in Thailand living off his songwriting royalties. The rest of the band still needed the money concerts brought in and still coveted a larger portion of the income songwriting generated. Making matters worse, heroin had entered the picture.

Frank Murray thought that Joe Strummer, an old friend of the Pogues, would be the perfect producer to bring the band back together as a cohesive unit. He chose Rockfield Studios in rural Wales in hopes that the remote country atmosphere would be conducive to healing and camaraderie. He was also keen to get MacGowan away from London's temptations and distractions so that he could better focus on the record-ing sessions.

In regard to MacGowan, at least, Murray's plan didn't work. Shane frequently missed sessions, preferring to spend his time with Victoria than in the studio. He showed up to do his vocals, usually late, and then left. With the exception of what some call his Thailand trilogy ("Summer in Siam," "Sayonara," and "House of Gods") Shane appeared more than distracted. He seemed disinterested.

Under these circumstances the results were surprising. While most Pogues and MacGowan fans with a taste for things Irish roundly condemn *Hell's Ditch* (and depend-ing on the interview they are often joined by MacGowan himself), it is a good record. Certainly it is far superior to *Peace and Love*. When *Peace and Love* was released MacGowan told anyone who would listen that the band had abandoned its Irish roots. "They were trying to divorce themselves from the Irish thing," he complained. With *Hell's Ditch* the divorce was finalized and MacGowan had lost custody of the leprechauns. Panning a record because it has no Irish flavor, however, is shortsighted at best. By that standard, *Rubber Soul* and *Highway 61* are dismal. If *Hell's Ditch* had been released by another band

and therefore not compared to the Pogues' first three LPs, more listeners would rec-ognize it for the wonderful rock album it is. MacGowan's heart may not have been in it, but his presence was. His voice is more ragged, but it drips with attitude and oozes anger. Perhaps Joe Strummer's punk sensibilities made the difference. Perhaps the fact that Finer and MacGowan collaborated more than they had done on *Peace and Love* made the difference. Whatever the reason, it's a damn fine post-Irish Pogues LP.

MacGowan's complaint concerning *Hell's Ditch's* lack of Irishness is hard to rec-oncile with the fact that he wrote or co-wrote nine of the album's thirteen songs. Although he complained that the band's democratic nature once again deprived him of creative input and took the music in a direction he didn't want to go, the other Pogues don't agree. It's hard not to appreciate their point of view. The Thailand trilogy that MacGowan was so enthused about is a far cry from "Whiskey in the Jar." Moreover, Shane's "Pinned Down," a decidedly non-Irish dub track, was a cut Shane was particu-larly pissed off about not making the disc. Also, Jem Finer contends that he was more than willing to do Irish tunes, pointing out that he had written "The Last of McGee" for *Hell's Ditch*, a song he called an "archetypal Pogues Irishy song," but it was left off the album. On the other hand, so was MacGowan's incredibly beautiful "Aisling," a song as steeped in Irish tradition as anything he has ever written. The argument is superfluous. *Hell's Ditch* may not sound like a Pogues' album, but it sounds very good.

To be sure, the record continued down the fusion path. "Maidrin Rua," a traditional instrumental, is the only straight up Irish number on the disc. Most of the album, despite typical Pogues' acoustic instrumentation, rocks hard. Only three cuts use an electric guitar. While there are some other instruments that the band didn't normally use in the past, they're not those typically found in a rock band. For instance, Finer played a hurdy-gurdy he built himself, and Fearnley used a sitar on one track. Under Joe Strummer's production, however, the overall sound is not what you'd expect from mandolins, mandolas, citterns, auto harps, accordions, concertinas, tin whistles, banjos and the like.

"Sunny Side of the Street," "The Ghost of a Smile," and "Rain Street" rock the best. None of the three reach the lyrical heights MacGowan had attained in the past, but two of the tracks boast lines any rock and roller would be proud to have penned. "Sunny Side of the Street" was co-written with Jem Finer. Lyrically, his contribution was the title, which was used in the refrain. "I wrote this in New Zealand," he remembered, "walk-ing down the street in the shadows I thought 'sod this' and crossed over to the sunny side. The only words I wrote were 'sunny side of the street.' Later, back in England, Shane wrote the rest." The best of what Shane contributed came in the opening verse: "Seen the carnival at Rome. Had the women, had the booze. All I can remember now is little kids without no shoes." "Rain Street" is one of the album's strongest tracks. Its focus on a particular street brings to mind Dylan's "Desolation Row." The depiction of MacGowan's street is far more stripped down than Dylan's classic, but no less compel-ling. Crammed with Christian imagery, it is peopled with priests in a bar (one with a venereal disease), St. Anthony, Judas, and Jesus himself. For good measure a singing drunk and a young girl hocking her wedding ring are thrown into the mix. My favorite verse is the second: "Down the alley the ice wagon flew, picked up a stiff that was turning blue. The local kids were sniffing glue. Not much else for a kid to do on Rain Street."

The musical fusion MacGowan lamented is blatant in three of his own songs: "Lorca's Novena," "Hell's Ditch," and "Five Green Queens and Jean" (the last two co-written with Finer). "Lorca's Novena" is about the execution of Spanish poet Federico Garcia Lorca, a Spanish folk hero killed by pro-Franco forces during the Spanish Civil War. The music is unusual, even by Pogues' standards. It builds gradually and dramatically with a distinctive Spanish feel. The album's title cut, "Hell's Ditch" centers on Jean Genet, a homosexual French writer who spent a great deal of his life in prison, some of it in Spain. Musically, the track feels Spanish and Mideastern at the same time, acknowledging, as so much Spanish music does, Muslim influences dating back to the middle ages. "Five Green Queens and Jean" is the best of these three cuts. Lyrically sparse, the song defies interpretation. MacGowan has said the five green queens refer to a dice game where one surface of each die depicts a queen colored green. MacGowan intended the track to be recorded with just an acoustic guitar but was overruled. The final arrangement was probably intended to sound Spanish as well, but to an American ear it brings Mexico to mind. Terry Woods' mandolin playing is perfect, and James Fearnley's accordion work would make Flaco Jimenez proud.

"Sayonara," "House of Gods," and "Summer in Siam" have been called MacGowan's Thailand trilogy. All three are set in the Far-eastern nation where Shane has so often retreated for R & R. As one would expect, there's little of the Dubliners' influence evident on these cuts. The songs are loaded with references to Thailand's beaches, whiskey, beer, and women. All three work quite nicely, especially "Summer in Siam." Lyrically the song is spare, more so than anything else MacGowan has written. Apart from repetition, there are just six lines and 27 words. It is none the less beautiful. Shane calls it a musical haiku. The music, complete with a kalimba, harp, and congas, is slow, soft, and elegant.

By August, having completed recording his vocals, Shane MacGowan was back in Thailand. In September he called Frank Murray to say that he wouldn't be coming back home to London for the UK tour scheduled to begin in just two weeks. Whether it was the money, a sense of duty, or the effects of extended R&R, he did return in time to take the concert stage with his band mates that autumn to support the *Hell's Ditch* October release. It stayed on the UK charts for five weeks, debuting at #12.

The tour got off to a shaky start. From the outset the press focused on MacGowan's shambolic state. He was generally wasted and made no attempt to hide it. In late October at Wembley Arena for instance, reviewers remarked that Shane wasn't holding up the mike stand as much as it was holding up him. He left the stage to get a fresh drink every time another Pogue did a vocal. He slurred his way through most of the lyrics. It didn't matter. The crowd loved every minute of it. They knew the words anyway and sang along enthusiastically. Things continued along those lines for the remainder of the year and the beginning of the next.

In the spring of 1991 the Pogues fired a surprised Frank Murray. His contract had run out, and they decided not to sign a new one. Joey Cashman, who had long worked with Murray as part of the Pogues' team, moved up from road manager into Murray's position. MacGowan always contended that things would have gone better for him and the Pogues without Frank Murray. That turned out not to be the case. Throughout the rest of that spring and into the summer, little else changed. The Pogues kept touring, MacGowan kept mailing it in, and the crowds kept growing.

Although *Melody Maker* called a festival gig in Paris "utter shite" and ripped MacGowan apart for "shuffling into the wings after every other song," the audience thought the show was wonderful. While it's true that his good nights were becoming less and less frequent, when Shane found a reason to be inspired he still delivered. That St. Patrick's Day at Glasgow's Barrowlands, a venue known for particularly loyal and exuberant Pogues fans, the band was joined onstage by Gerry Conlon and Paddy Armstrong, two of the Guilford Four who just three days earlier had been released from prison after 15 years incarceration. Clearly inspired, MacGowan gave an outstanding performance. He was just as good six months later at London's Brixton Academy when he was excited to be sharing the stage with traditional Irish folk music legends, the Chieftains.

By August, however, not even sharing a bill with Van Morrison, one of his childhood heroes, at a show in Thurles, in Shane's beloved County Tipperary, was enough to elicit a decent MacGowan effort. He was so out of it he apparently forgot to put a stamp on his performance before mailing it in. The rest of the Pogues were visibly concerned. Reviewers cited Steve Earle's guest appearance on "Johnny Come Lately," "Ned of the Hill," and anything else Shane took a back seat on as set highlights. In retrospect it is easy to see that things were coming to a head, but there were probably few in the boisterous crowd at Feile '91 in Thurles, County Tipperary that night who suspected they had witnessed one of Shane MacGowan's last concerts with the Pogues.

The feces hit the fan in Japan. MacGowan and the Pogues flew there for a September concert tour. In two weeks the band did just four shows, and Shane missed two of them. It's not far from the truth to say he also missed the shows he did make. He spent a good bit of time sitting on the drum riser. His vocals were nearly incomprehensible. The debacle that was Shane MacGowan's last performance with the Pogues during their first incarnation took place at the Womad Festival in Yokohama. The show was broadcast on Japanese television. The band opened with "Streams of Whiskey." Shane joined in several beats late and struggled to keep up throughout the number. His vocal was so garbled he may as well have been humming. Only when the other Pogues joined in and drowned him out on the chorus did the song come together. On "Rain Street" when

Shane sang "The church bells ring, an old drunk sings. God can't help the shape I'm in," there was no arguing with him. He blew most of the lyrics. When the song ended Spider told the audience, "We all make mistakes."

On the slower numbers like "Dirty Old Town" MacGowan fared slightly better. He was still awful, but at least he managed to keep up with the band. Unfortunately, the set list was comprised primarily of full speed ahead rave ups like "Greenland Whale Fisheries," "If I Should Fall from Grace with God," and "Sally MacLennane." Had they included more slower songs it might have helped; but inexplicably, masterworks like "The Broad Majestic Shannon," "A Pair of Brown Eyes," "A Rainy Night in Soho," and "Dirty old Town" had been exorcised from the set. On "Sick Bed of Cuchulainn" MacGowan made it through the slow introduction reasonably well, but was left in the dust when the band kicked the song into high gear. Despite Shane's sheer ineptitude, the show went over very well with the Japanese crowd. After all, the band played well, and MacGowan's up-tempo vocals can be difficult to follow even for native English speakers. On top of that, Terry Woods and Phil Chevron were fine on "Young Ned of the Hill" and "Thousands Are Sailing."

"Touring was getting to me," Shane later recalled. "In Japan we went on a train from Tokyo to Osaka and I drank Saki all the way and when I got off the train I fell and broke my head open and was unable to do the gig that night. Two days later they said to me it would be better if we didn't play together anymore and I agreed with them." Phillip Chevron remembers the fateful night in Japan. "We sat down with him and said, 'You don't look like you're having much fun with this anymore. It seems obvious you don't want to continue, but as it turns out we do.' He said that was pretty much the story, and we all went out and had dinner... It was painful for everybody at the time. We were all in a spiral of too much touring and drinking. And Shane was suffering the most, so when he left it was like putting somebody out of his misery."

Chevron's recollection squares up pretty well with what MacGowan says he was feeling at the time. "The Pogues was originally a lot of fun," he told one journalist, "but it soon turned into a job. Quite honestly, I was glad to leave it behind. If I hadn't left when I did I'd be dead or in an institution." But in subsequent interviews MacGowan downplayed the idea that he left the Pogues by mutual consent, insisting that he was fired. Phil Chevron disagrees. "Did we sack Shane MacGowan? There is the question. No. It's just never as simple as that." Chevron says Shane wanted to leave the band in order to spend more time at home, and that MacGowan "is not the sort of person who can tell you in a straight way, 'Look, I'm not digging this.'" Chevron thinks that rather than directly telling the other Pogues that he wanted out, Shane let them know "by the inconsistency of his behavior... Shane is magnificent at twisting everything around... He probably thinks we sacked him, yes, but he knows in his heart that it's not true." Others have said that MacGowan wanted to leave the Pogues but stayed on out of a sense of loyalty, unwilling to abandon the others. Joey Cashman concurred with MacGowan. "They fired him," he said. "I was at the meeting. They fired him."

Exactly what happened in Japan may be open to debate, but two things are certain: Shane MacGowan was no longer in the phenomenally successful band he had founded, and substance abuse played a major role in his departure. To those unused to the clear Japanese rice wine, Saki can be problematic. Good quality Saki, in addition to being clear and having little alcohol smell, really does go down like water. It is not unusual for the uninitiated to seriously over indulge before realizing it. For someone who has already ingested various other nefarious substances, swilling Saki all day is never a good idea.

More than two decades later Shane admitted to television talk show host Frank Skinner that there was more to it than the Saki incident:

FS: *After they threw you out, that must have made things a bit difficult.*

SM: *I think they all hated my guts by the time they threw me out. But I'd been screaming to get out of the bloody thing for awhile, it had run its course.*

FS: *It ended in Japan didn't it, I heard you fell out of a …*

SM: *I fell out of the train. It was three hours after them bringing you around Saki after Saki after Saki. But anyhow I fell from the top step of the train. They're very safety conscious and everything, but somehow I managed to break my head open on the platform. It just brought matters to a head.*

FS: *It wasn't moving, the train?*

SM: *I haven't got a clue. I couldn't tell you if it was moving or not.*

FS: *It's a bit harsh sacking a man for falling off of a train.*

SM: *Well, it wasn't the first incident of that nature.*

Spider Stacy, MacGowan's oldest friend in the band, affirms that the problem was more complicated than Shane drinking too much. "To say Shane couldn't control the drinking is only half right. By the time we made *Hell's Ditch*, he'd become unhappy with the direction he saw the band going. He felt his influence declining and that led to the heavy drinking." The Pogues' publicist released an official but short statement saying that MacGowan would not be completing the Japanese tour "due to Shane's ill health." Joe Strummer was recruited to replace him for the remaining gigs. Strummer seemed like the perfect replacement. His angry, sometimes snarling vocal style with the Clash seemed suited to MacGowan's material. He had been affiliated with the band for a long time. Moreover, having just produced *Hell's Ditch*, he was very familiar with the new material in the set. In the end, Strummer was not up to the task.

That many of Shane MacGowan's lyrics are stamped with genius is indisputable. Many, however, are oblivious to the remarkable quality of his singing. Like most great artists, he makes what he does appear artless. The fact that Joe Strummer, seemingly the perfect replacement, never came close to filling MacGowan's shoes is ample testament to Shane's vocal prowess. It's undeniable that Christy Moore and Ronnie Drew have recorded magnificent covers of MacGowan's songs, but their versions are *their* versions and are quite different. Strummer, despite a valiant effort, proved that nobody can sing a Shane MacGowan song like Shane MacGowan.

Strummer toured with the Pogues for the next three months. To his credit, he never lost sight of his replacement status. At the Orpheum in Boston, before starting "Turkish Song of the Damned" he said, "I'm deep inside the mind of Shane MacGowan right now." When Strummer took the stage of San Francisco's Warfield Theatre for two sold out shows in October he told the crowd, "You mighta heard that your man is ill. I'm just keeping his seat warm." That night there was a note taped to the Warfield's box office window offering a refund to anyone who didn't want to see a MacGowanless Pogues' concert. There were few takers.

To be fair, it should be noted that not everyone agreed that Strummer was unable to handle MacGowan's role as the Pogues' front man. One reviewer of the Warfield shows called the crowd "ecstatic" and said the show was "one of the most invigorating and deeply satisfying concerts of the year," adding that Strummer's vocals were "every bit as commanding as MacGowan's." He concluded that while Shane could never be replaced the Pogues would get along just fine without MacGowan. Of course the next year or two would prove the critic wrong.

Bootleg recordings of several Strummer/Pogues' shows are in circulation. These recordings bring into question the San Francisco reviewer's critical faculties. The recorded evidence supports the *Globe's* review of the Boston show. Appropriately, as Strummer and the Pogues took the Orpheum stage the theme from *Mission Impossible* played. As it faded the band broke into "If I Should Fall from Grace with God." The reviewer quipped, "If God's a music lover, they did." He went on to pan the show, reporting that Strummer did most of MacGowan's vocals, adding "That was a mistake; he went at them like a rapist, with wild and unfeeling energy." The review was especially hard on Strummer's failure to pull off "Sick Bed of Cuchulainn."

For their part, the rest of the Pogues must have realized that Strummer needed help with some of Shane's vocals. Stacy was experienced in this regard. Naturally, Chevron sang lead on his own composition, "Thousands Are Sailing." Rankin took a stab at "The Broad Majestic Shannon." Strummer did pretty well on the recent songs he had produced for *Hell's Ditch*. He was best on the few Clash tunes the Pogues had added to their set. One reviewer thought that the Pogues "spooky, ethereal instrumentation" improved the Clash's "Straight to Hell."

When all was said and done, the Pogues were still pleasing audiences. The crowds continued to get caught up in the fun of a wild show. After all, by this point the Pogues were a damn good band, and they still did some of the music from the time when they were MacGowan's vision of an Irish dance band. Still, by the end of the year it was evident that it wasn't the same. The December shows in the UK got luke warm reviews. In a review of a Brixton Academy show, the *Times* said Shane was sorely missed. "Nearly everyone had a stab at the singing, with uniformly dreadful results," their reviewer wrote. He added that Strummer "mangled 'Dirty Old Town' and 'Sickbed of Cuchulainn.'"

None the less, according to Phillip Chevron, Strummer was offered a permanent spot in the Pogues. He declined. "Joe felt that it was great while it lasted, but it wouldn't have worked out in the long run, because we never wrote any music together," Chevron said. "I don't think that Joe wanted to spend his life touring the world, which is what you have to do if you're in the Pogues."

In October Stacy said that Shane's relationship with the band was "somewhat ambiguous at the moment" and suggested that Shane might continue to write for the Pogues. He told a Canadian reporter, "He is just generally run down from being on the road where he spends a lot of time sitting around brooding. He doesn't eat, he doesn't sleep, and obviously his body sustained a certain amount of damage when he was drinking heavily."

To take advantage of the Christmas market, or perhaps to cash in while the Pogues were still a viable commodity, WEA released *Best of the Pogues*. It was clear that the record company knew what made the Pogues great. The compilation album leaned very heavily on MacGowan compositions. Every track featured Shane MacGowan on lead vocal. Only three of the album's fourteen songs were taken from *Peace and Love* and *Hell's Ditch*. It sold well.

When the New Year started, Spider Stacy was the new lead singer of the Pogues.

MacGowan's cottage in Tipperary
(Robert Mamrak)

Cloughprior cemetery in Carney Commons
(Robert Mamrak)

The old hearth in Ryan's pub, Carney Commons
(Robert Mamrak)

The backroom of the Yank's in Borrisokane
(Robert Mamrak)

Burton Street, London, where the Pogues were born
(Robert Mamrak)

"Fairytale of New York" with Kirsty McColl (1994)
(David Major)

MacGowan with Anna Mamrak in his Dublin home (1/2/08)
(Robert Mamrak)

In concert with Sharon Shannon (12/27/08)
(Hauke Steinberg) www.HaukeSteinberg.com

Looking good onstage (7/24/09)
(Imelda Michalczyk) www.rebeladelica.com

MacGowan with his new band (9/17/10)

(Suzi Sue Kelly)

CHAPTER 9

"I've read all the cliches. Apparently I'm a hopeless drunk, I'm gonna die, I'm fat and I stumble and stagger all over the stage like an idiot. It gets a bit boring after a while."

Shane MacGowan

MacGowan spent most of 1992 keeping out of the public eye, regaining, what was for MacGowan, a semblance of normalcy in his life. Victoria Clarke was instrumental in leading him back from the brink. She had left her day job as a shop assistant a few years earlier to be with Shane on the road. Now she became much more than a significant other. She picked up his pieces and held him together. "I owe her my health, sanity, and happiness," he has said. "My blood still boils when I think about her, which is most of the time."

Serving as Shane MacGowan's keeper was nothing new for Clarke. "I saw rescuing Shane from the brink of madness and death much in the same way other people might view becoming a social worker: as a kind of vocation," she said on *Rock Wives*, the BBC television special. "As the task became more insurmountable and the prospect of finding happiness less likely, I comforted myself with thoughts of other brave women who had sacrificed themselves for famous alcoholic poets: women like Mrs. Brendan Behan and Mrs. Dylan Thomas. People kept telling me that Shane was a living legend, a kind of Irish National Monument, and I should consider it a privilege to preserve him. This is a classic syndrome... I was useful as a kind of nurse/therapist/minder, who could be relied on to feel guilty if I didn't manage to get Shane on the tour-bus, off the tour-bus, on the plane, out of the bar, on the stage or whatever. This despite the fact that other people were employed to do that job and I was not being paid to do anything. It was many years before I realized that my life would not be significantly affected if Shane fell off the stage every night and I abdicated responsibility."

Victoria Mary Clarke, the daughter of what she describes as Irish "hippies," grew up in West Cork. "I was born into a family who already had the *Tibetan Book of the Dead* on the bookshelf, and a genuine Indian guru (Bhagwan Shree Rajneesh), plus the obligatory natural, organic, communal, eco-friendly lifestyle. I was meditating, chanting, and seeing a homeopath before I could walk." When she was eleven years old she saw MacGowan's picture in a music magazine while he was still calling himself Shane O'Hooligan. Five years later she moved to London and met him in the Royal Oak pub. It was 1982, and the Pogues were just getting off the ground. She was only 16, eight years his junior. They got to know each other through a mutual friend, Spider Stacy. It was Spider's birthday and Shane ordered Victoria to buy Stacey a drink. Shane recalled, "I was gobsmacked. She was the most beautiful thing I had ever seen." Initially she was unimpressed with the man with which she would spend most of the next 28 years (and counting). She found him less than attractive physically, arrogant, aggressive, and "stuck up." On top of everything else, she didn't like Irish music. "He was just a bloke with a band who played old Irish songs very badly," Clarke said years later. "Nobody could have known he was going to be big." Slowly but surely her mind changed. On her twentieth birthday they shared their first kiss. Soon after, she fell in love with him in the back of a taxicab after an argument about, of all things, Irish *Sean Nos* singing. By the following year Clarke had quit her job as a shop assistant and joined MacGowan on the road where he and the Pogues were then spending up to 300 days a year.

"For the next ten years life was never boring," she wrote in her column in *The Independent*. "We traveled all over the world and met our favorite rock stars, all our favorite movie stars, all kinds of amazing people. And we drank and took drugs with them, all night long. Shane's picture was on the cover of magazines and newspapers, he was on *Top of the Pops*, we were rolling in money. We lived life exactly the way we felt like living it and we didn't have to do boring jobs. If we weren't hanging out with Keith Richards or Johnny Depp, we sat up all night doing coke and watching crap on television, playing our guitars, writing, generally amusing ourselves. We were the luckiest people in the world; we were soulmates, we adored each other and we were blissfully in love. For hours and hours, we could sit and gaze into each other's eyes and we didn't need anybody else to complete our happiness. We were each other's world."

Clarke and MacGowan give credence to the old adage about opposites attracting. Friends say that one of the wonderful things about MacGowan is his complete lack of pretension. While he is not shy in acknowledging his contribution to Irish culture, he is far more concerned about what he has achieved musically than with the celebrity that comes with his accomplishments. He is totally unimpressed with the mega-stars of the music and film industry he meets through his music. The rich and famous hold no more interest for him than the beggar in the street does. Although he can be obsessive about a top hat or full length leather coat, he thinks nothing of wearing the same wrinkled, cigarette burned, multi-stained suit for days on end. Clarke, on the other hand, is open about being obsessed with fashion and celebrity. In *The Independent* she admitted to having "a compulsion to be perceived as special and important by people I don't even know...My addiction to feeling important by association could be a painful and potentially destructive one, if left unchecked...When I get my picture taken at premiers, or at fabulous balls, I like to think it is because I have a newspaper column, or of having written books, or because I am extraordinarily gorgeous, but in truth it is because I am generally accompanied by my rather outrageous fiancée Shane, who has been having his picture in the papers since he was a teenager."

Over the years Clarke developed her own career as a writer. In addition to her weekly column in Ireland's biggest Sunday newspaper, she has written five books. Her first book, *Astral Weekends*, remains unpublished, as does a biography of Seattle grunge rockers Nirvana. While researching that book in 1992, Courtney Love beat up Clarke in Reggie's, a Los Angeles nightclub. Victoria had interviewed some people who had bad things to say about Love, an ex-stripper who had made herself very unpopular with the Pogues during the filming of *Straight to Hell* a few years earlier in Spain. Her husband, Curt Cobain, left threatening messages on Clarke's answering machine. (Years later MacGowan considered releasing the taped threats mixed to a dance beat.) Victoria pressed charges against Love, but the judge dismissed the case as frivolous. Clarke told me in 2008 that she believed Love's continued threats frightened publishers away from the book. A third book, *Crash Course to Oblivion*, is about MacGowan. Year after year Amazon.com lists it as out of print and unavailable. Clarke's fourth book, *A Drink with Shane MacGowan*, sold well enough to be reprinted in a paperback edition.

Her most recent work, *Angel in Disguise?*, was published in 2007. It made it to the number four spot on the British best seller list. It deals with the period that she and MacGowan were separated, a painful time when she was depressed and suicidal. In the book she claims to have gotten through it all with the help of an angel she calls Gabriela. No, it's not a work of fiction. Clarke maintains that she continues to communicate with Gabriela and has even given seminars to help people channel their own angels. Clarke has long been interested in New Age type self-help spirituality. MacGowan once referred to her collection of spiritual and self-help books as her "library of bullshit." He told the press, however, that he liked *Angel in Disguise?* and helped promote it with a series of appearances at book signings. At one such event in Wexford he jammed with a local band on Elvis Presley's song, "She's an Angel in Disguise." In Dublin, a few celebrities showed up, including author J.P. Donleavy, who wrote a blurb for the book's cover.

A Drink with Shane MacGowan, published in early 2001, is a must read for anyone interested in MacGowan. Shane is credited with co-writing the book, but is less than comfortable with that. "I don't see the point of it being called 'by Victoria Clarke and Shane MacGowan,' when it was already called *A Drink with Shane MacGowan*. I didn't have anything to do with the writing of the book, I didn't have anything to do with the editing of the book, and, in the end, I couldn't fucking stop them putting in the stuff I didn't want to have fucking put in... all I did was shout into a fucking tape recorder when I was in full flight about this, that or the other." Shortly after its publication MacGowan began to distance himself from the book. He made it clear he wasn't pleased with it.

Some of Shane's family and friends and most of the Pogues were rankled by its publication. Spider Stacy's reaction was not untypical. "The book? We had a look at it in a book shop. I think it is a pile of rubbish and by all accounts so does Shane. He tried to get an injunction taken out to stop it being published but Victoria was so upset that he relented. It's just the latest in a long line of Victoria's attempts to be somebody. What it has achieved, however, is the complete scuppering of any sort of Pogues reunion however much he might want it."

A Drink with Shane MacGowan managed to stir up controversy even before it came out. The publisher, Sidgwick and Jackson (an affiliate of Macmillan) had what seemed like a great idea to publicize the release. In January they sent a sample chapter to newspaper and magazine literary editors along with an invitation to "Come and have a drink with Shane MacGowan." Their intention was to put Shane up in Bloom's Hotel in Dublin for a few days at their expense while journalists poured in to interview the ex-Pogue. Two months later Shane was still residing at Bloom's, having run up a $3,000.00 bar tab that Sidgwick and Jackson did not feel obligated to pay.

The publicity ploy generated more press than the publisher could have hoped for. It's unlikely they were pleased with all of it. Apparently they were unfamiliar with MacGowan's reputation for candor. He called the book "garbled, dodgy, and well-suspect," adding that if he had his way he'd "burn every fucking copy." According to John Moore of the *Denver Post* Shane considered the book a "betrayal" by Victoria. "I wish I hadn't done it," he said. "They really stitched me up. I rambled drunk into a recorder on and off for five years to my girlfriend, well, my missus, really. It was meant to be like *The Way We Were*, and she made it all Frank McCourt-like sad."

The problem was that MacGowan had said some pretty offensive things about his fellow Pogues, and especially about their manager, Frank Murray. Moreover, he was not reluctant to take credit for the Pogues' success. Among other things he said, "There were a lot of bad musicians in the band." He was very critical of James Fearnley's accordion playing, saying he tried to teach James to play in a proper Irish way, "but he never learned." MacGowan said his Auntie Ellen "could show Terry Woods a thing or two" on concertina. He also said that bringing Phil Chevron into the band was a bad idea. He was particularly hard on Frank Murray, implying that the Pogues' manager didn't care if excessive touring killed him as long as Murray got his 20%. He insinuated that the Pogues were successful more in spite of Murray than because of him, adding that the publicist at Stiff Records had "100 times" more to do with the Pogues' success than Murray did. One would assume the other Pogues were particularly embittered that Shane attributed the Pogues' demise more to his bandmates' "egomania" than to his substance abuse. He asserts that by the end of his stint with the Pogues the others in the band hated him and were "using" him. There's little doubt that MacGowan knew *A Drink with Shane MacGowan* would ruffle feathers. The last page of the book is a handwritten "uncoditional apology" (sic) from Shane to the Pogues and Frank Murray. In it he wrote, "I was speaking from the heart when I spewed this stuff. I was a stranger in my own soul."

MacGowan never denied having said any of the things in the book; he just contends he should have been more circumspect in comments destined for publication. He explained to one of the journalists who descended on Bloom's Hotel, "If it had been somebody other than Victoria, then I woulda watched what I said a lot more. There'd be a lot less trouble now. So she would get everything with a tape recorder. When I was drunk. When I was just sitting at home with my missus. Ranting your way about this and that and telling her stories I certainly wouldn't tell you." When the interviewer asked Shane if Victoria had ever recorded their conversations without his knowledge he quickly came to the defense of her journalistic integrity. "Oh, no, no, no, no. She didn't have to tell me because I was so out of it that I kept forgetting everything. She kept reminding me, she kept saying, 'Are you sure you want to say that?' and at the time I'd say, 'Yes I want to say that. It's true.' And now I look at it in cold print, and think, 'Oh God.'"

Shane and Victoria separated shortly after *A Drink with Shane MacGowan* was published. When he checked out of Bloom's Hotel MacGowan moved into the 350 year-old stone cottage in Carney Commons. It would be tempting to surmise that the book was the reason the couple split up. Tempting but wrong. There was much more to it. In addition to his drinking, Shane had developed a problem with heroin. "I separated from Shane because I could no longer be happy with his lifestyle," Victoria has said. "It was having a destructive effect on my own, and even though I tried very hard to reconcile myself to this, because he was so very special to me, I eventually found my own sanity suffering." In December of 2004 she wrote in her newspaper column, "Shane had been in intensive care and had been very sick; I was seeing a counselor because I no longer saw the point in living and I was begging to be locked up. Nature was taking its inevitable revenge and our life together was unraveling into a very, very sticky mess indeed. With bailiffs hammering at the door and dead friends on the living room floor. In the end, I chose another kind of life. I had had a wild and wonderful adventure and I had met my soulmate and spent 15 years with him, but I don't think I would be alive today if I had carried on living that way."

Victoria moved in with her sister Vanessa, who lived in Dublin. She gave up drugs completely and drank only moderately. It was around this time that she began communicating with her angel, and with the encouragement of Ann Kelly, a life coach, began work on *Angel in Disguise?* She eventually began dating other men, did a workshop in Dublin on "Getting Dumped," wrote her Sunday column, and saw Shane occasionally. Their relationship began to rekindle when he finally kicked his heroin habit. "I genuinely got incredible enjoyment out of it for years, but towards the end it really fucked me up," he told a reporter. "Giving it up was the closest thing I've been to hell on earth. It was like my own personal Iraq. I didn't give a fuck about wasting any talent I had. It broke up my relationship with the only woman I ever loved and that's all I give a fuck about."

In Early 2005 MacGowan and Clarke vacationed together again in Thailand. The following year, at Spider Stacy's Las Vegas wedding during a Pogues' reunion tour, Victoria realized that she wanted to marry Shane. "We started meeting again," she said, and "realized that we were probably going to spend the rest of our lives together." She announced their wedding plans in *The Independent*. "Just the other day, I decided to take the plunge and get married... Shane and I have known each other for nearly 25 years, and over that time we have definitely seen each other behave badly. In fact we have both disgraced ourselves, repeatedly. We have already got the infidelity out of the way, as well as the dirty washing left on the floor, the arguments about who will wash the dishes and hoover, the odd bit of domestic violence and abandonment, alcoholism, drug abuse and what have you, so there can be no unpleasant surprises." They set the date for September 8, 2007.

Over the years Shane had proposed marriage to Victoria on several occasions, but she had always turned him down. She said that she had wanted him to stop drinking first, and any discussions along those lines led to arguments. When she finally accepted she explained, "I've given up trying to change him. I'm much happier for it. I've accepted that he's never going to leap out of bed at dawn and jog to the yoga studio... Most mornings I would just be getting up as he was staggering home."

Plans for the big day got under way. Engagement rings were exchanged. They hoped to have Sinead O'Conner (or is that Mother O'Conner?) perform the ceremony. A mini-festival atmosphere in a field with several bands performing was discussed. Victoria bought a vintage wedding dress for $75.00. When September 8th finally arrived there was no wedding and no explanation. As of this writing they remain together, single but happy, spending most of their time in Dublin, Tipperary, London, or on the road with the Pogues; and of course, on holidays abroad.

Back in 1991, when MacGowan left the Pogues, he and Victoria initially stayed as Bono's guests in his luxurious Martello tower in Dublin, but they eventually got their own flat. MacGowan watched a lot of television. *Frasier*, *French & Saunders*, and *King of the Hill* were some of his favorite shows. There were many trips to Shane's old home place in Carney Commons. When the press did spot him he told them, "I wish people would just leave me alone so I could drink in peace."

And drink he did. MacGowan made progress from the nadir that was Japan, but substance abuse continued to plague him. He stopped drinking whiskey and brandy, but made up for their absence with wine and Guinness. Worse yet, he spent a great deal of time in a North London apartment doing harder drugs, especially heroin. "After the Pogues broke up," he remembers, "that's when I had the most fun. Probably because it's the lowest I've ever sunk... I was having a great time." He sold his gold Pogues discs for drug money, boasting that he had gotten a better price for his than Spider did when Stacy sold his.

"After leaving the group I wasn't interested in carrying on. I was interested in carrying on playing music, but I had a lot of things to sort out before I got embroiled in this rock business shit again," he recalls. "I was playing with various friends and we could just relax 'cos after being on tour for about eight solid years and all the recording, it was relaxing." Eventually his muse began pulling harder at MacGowan's addictions. The need to make music was still there. In September he showed up in New York at the city's short-lived Bang On club. He took the stage with Rogues March, Joe Hurley's New York-based Irish band. Rogues March began the night with their own set before Shane joined them onstage. He did eleven songs in all, mostly from the first three Pogues albums. Three of his *Peace and Love* compositions were included, but nothing from *Hell's Ditch* made the set list. MacGowan relied heavily on the traditional Irish sound that night. He included the Irish rebel standard "The Rising of the Moon," a song he'd later record on *The Snake,* his first album with the Popes.

John Sullivan, a long time New York Pogues fan, was there. "Shane was in very bad form when I saw him there," he said. "At one point he blew his nose onto the audience and said 'If you want me to play then somebody get me some smack,' then stumbled off the small stage and into the ladies bathroom. He was essentially dragged back onto the stage by the show's promoters and forced to finish the show. I was convinced that this would be the last time I would ever see Shane, and he was going to turn up dead somewhere. It was really very upsetting." Bootleg recordings exist of both MacGowan's last show in Japan with the Pogues and his show in New York with Rogues March. The comparison is telling. Despite his condition in New York, MacGowan's Bang On performance was a vast improvement.

Apparently, MacGowan's period of seclusion was coming to an end. In November he recorded "What a Wonderful World" with Nick Cave. "Lucy," a MacGowan composition, was the B-side. A less than stellar effort, the single tanked, but at least he was making records again. By the time the New Year began he had signed a new recording contract with the ZTT label. In February he made a few guest appearances with the Dubliners. Shane spent the next several months putting together a new band. This time it would be a back-up band. There would be no democracy.

As 1993 began things were looking up for MacGowan. He was spotted in public a great deal more, mostly in London at Jerry O'Boyle's new pub, Filthy McNasty's Whiskey Café on Amwell Street in Islington. He became a fixture at the pub, regularly chatting with fans and journalists. Looking as healthy as he had in a long time, he told the press he was "practicing moderation in all things...I know that I'm going to live to be eighty-eight, at least, and I'm still going to feel cheated... but you can't argue with death." Beyond looking healthier than he had in many years, MacGowan seemed happier. He attributed that happiness to writing and rehearsing with his new band, the Popes. "I'm doing what I want, and I've got a great band, that plays what I ask them to play," he said, "and I'm doing what I want, within the confines of this shitty, stinking, music business."

The Popes, Pogues fans to a man, began as a six piece band: Paul McGuiness (guitar), Bernie France (bass), Kieran O'Hagan (rhythm guitar), Colm O'Maonlai (whistle), Danny Heatley, AKA Pope (drums), and Tom MacManamon, AKA MacAnimal (banjo). Apart from one traditional Irish sounding instrumental, the Popes were clearly Shane MacGowan's back-up band. He did all the lead vocals. There was no more taking turns in the spotlight. The sound was decidedly Irish, but more electric and much louder than the Pogues. Most importantly, the original punk spirit returned. "The Popes are doing just what the Pogues were doing before it went wrong," MacGowan said. "We're doing it a lot better than the Pogues were doing it in the last few years. I'm not into progression. I'm not into fusion. I'm not into any of this shit."

In addition to the punk spirit, a spirit of camaraderie returned. Bernie France had gone to school with MacGowan some 20 years earlier at the College for Further Education in Hammersmith. He remembers he and Shane "smoking dope in the common room before sneaking off to get pissed in the pubs." Danny Pope, whose father Spike Heatley played bass on early Small Faces records, had been drumming in bands since he was 16. He has said, "We've grown up together. It's kicking. It's going really, really well, because we know what Shane wants, plus we're really good friends. We hang out together." Kieran O'Hagan, from County Armagh, in Northern Ireland, came to the Popes with a broad knowledge of traditional Irish folk music. He and MacGowan had known each other for more than a decade. They'd worked together on several musical projects over the years. Paul McGuinness cut his teeth in various Dublin punk bands in the seventies. Dublin born Colm O'Maonlai, the brother of Hothouse Flowers lead singer Liam O'Maonlai, played drums and some guitar in addition to the whistle. He was also fluent in Gaelic. After his stint with the Popes, O'Maonlai did quite well acting in films and television. Tom MacManamon began playing publicly as a teenager at traditional sessions in The Favourite, his father's North London Irish bar. At just fifteen he was featured on *Paddy in the Smoke*, an album recorded in the pub. Later he played with Dinglespike and Irish Mist, two bands that recorded on traditional Irish labels. Eventually, when the Popes trimmed down the lineup, his banjo style was essential in maintaining the band's Irish flavor.

MacGowan's star was about to rise again. The Pogues' star, however, was about to begin its descent. In September they released their first post-MacGowan album, *Waiting for Herb*. Highly anticipated by Pogues fans, the album sold well upon release but tanked rather quickly. The album's first single, "Tuesday Morning," fared better, charting in the top twenty. Written and sung by Spider Stacy, it was a pleasant enough pop song but as far from MacGowan's concept of the Pogues as the East is from the West. It was not the stuff legends are made of. Before long Terry Woods and James Fearnley saw the writing on the wall and quit the Pogues. Philip Chevron left soon thereafter. MacGowan, who undoubtedly knew he'd been right all along, felt vindicated. He laughingly told a journalist, "I'd be quite prepared to write their next album for them if they feel like playing some good music for a change. Seriously, though, I still love them. I love them all. What's left of them."

Pogues fans, however, kept the faith. Tickets for the tour in support of *Waiting for Herb* sold well. Crowd reaction was generally very good. After all, even without MacGowan, the Pogues could play. The fast numbers still cooked. The dancing and drinking went on unabated. MacGowan himself went to see the Pogues when they were in town. Spider Stacy commented, "I hate playing London. Shane always comes to the shows and sits in the wings. You can imagine the pressure, what with him looking over us like Banquo's ghost come to dinner." You could still have a good time at a Pogues show. The general consensus, however, was that it just wasn't the same. It wasn't special anymore. At some point the official Pogues fan club changed its name to Friends of Shane (FOS).

In December MacGowan joined the remaining Pogues onstage at Kentish Town's Forum to sing "The Irish Rover" and "Streams of Whiskey." It was not an impromptu guest appearance. Everything was arranged in advance, right down to the songs Shane would do. Rumors flew that MacGowan was rejoining the band. Even though the rumors were untrue, they reportedly caused tensions in the band. *NME* ran a story contending that Shane was invited back and that the invitation was part of the reason Fearnley and Woods quit. Stacy said the press had gotten it all wrong. It was never intended to be more than a one-night stand.

The same month British Prime Minister John Major and Albert Reynolds, Prime Minister of the Irish Republic, issued the Downing Street Declaration. In a nutshell, it affirmed the right of the people of Ireland, both North and South, to democratically determine if and when the 32 counties would unite as one. This position was, in effect, the same one the British had taken in the Sunningdale Agreement of 1973. That agreement pleased few and dissolved within a year. Avid Republicans rejected it because it affirmed the right of the six northern counties to remain under British rule. Unionists rejected it because it was seen as a stepping stone to Irish unification and because it gave the Republic a voice in Northern Ireland's affairs. Unionist opposition, in addition to violence, took the form of a general strike bringing two weeks of shortages, rioting and intimidation, causing the agreement to collapse. The British put the same position forward again in 1985's Anglo-Irish Agreement. It too affirmed that the people of Northern Ireland would democratically decide if and when they would unite with the Republic, and it also gave the Irish Republic a role in Northern Ireland's government. Both sides rejected this agreement for the same reasons the Sunningdale Agreement was rejected. The Anglo-Irish Agreement did little to stem the violence. The Provos continued their terrorist campaign. Gerry Adams, the president of the IRA's political wing, Sinn Fein, called the agreement "a disaster for the nationalist cause." If nothing else, the Anglo-Irish Agreement did, however, improve co-operation between the Irish and British governments.

MacGowan is a huge Adams supporter. "The thing about Gerry Adams," Shane says, "is that when he talks, right, he means what he says. He's actually saying something, he's telling you something, he's answering the question. Every other politician, they sidestep, they talk for three minutes and say fucking nothing." Adams has an impressive Republican pedigree. His father joined the IRA in 1942, was shot and captured in a raid, and spent eight years in prison. His grandfather was in the Irish Republican Brotherhood during the Irish Revolution. His great-grandfather was a Fenian during their English dynamiting campaign in the late 1800s. Adams joined the Northern Ireland Civil Rights Association in 1967. In 1972 he was arrested under Britain's internment policy. He was arrested again the following year and served time in Long Kesh prison. Elected president of Sinn Fein in 1983, Adams was instrumental in convincing Republican militants to consider political solutions to unite Ireland. He led Sinn Fein to change its policy of abstentionism. Just as the Republican movement had refused to recognize the Parliaments in London and Belfast, it refused to recognize the Parliament in Dublin when it ratified the treaty partitioning Ireland at the end of the Irish Revolution. Since the Irish Civil War, Sinn Fein had abstained from participation in parliament, refusing to take the seats it won in elections. In 1986 Adams convinced Sinn Fein to take its seats in Dublin's government and later in Belfast's. Sinn Fein continues to boycott London's Parliament. In 1983 Adams himself was elected a member of the English Parliament representing West Belfast in the House of Commons. He has been re-elected several times but continues to refuse to take his seat in London.

The Downing Street Declaration, while offering nothing very new in the British position, was met with great optimism. The position may not have changed, but the times had. Ever since the Enniskillen bombing in 1986, the IRA's military campaign was getting increasingly unpopular with Catholics in both the North and the South of Ireland. They had exploded 258 bombs in 1987, 304 bombs in 1988, and 269 bombs in 1989. By 1990 the Provos had killed 1,593 people and wounded more than 15,000. In early 1992 a bomb killed eight Protestant workmen in the Tyrone countryside, sparking a public outcry not heard since Enniskillen. In addition to the decline in IRA support, the nationalist cause lost some of its intensity when the much-hated Republican nemesis, British Prime Minister Margaret Thatcher, resigned in late 1990. Her successor, John Major, quickly committed to an Irish peace initiative. Moreover, there was a growing consensus that the development of the European Union would change the context of British-Irish relationships, helping to mitigate the basis of the conflict in Northern Ireland.

Perhaps the greatest cause for optimism, however, was the revelation that Gerry Adams had been secretly involved in the Downing Street negotiations and was authorized to negotiate on behalf of the Provisional Irish Republican Army. For the first time the IRA was wavering on it's bedrock "Brits out" position and considering a peaceful, political resolution to the conflict, and the British government was willing to hear what their new position might be. None the less, while the negotiations were going on, the IRA kept up its military campaign nearly derailing the project with a bomb just two months before the talks were completed. An explosion in a fish shop on Shankill Road, in the heart of Protestant Belfast, killed 10 civilians and injured 58 more. The Unionist retaliation took 10 Catholic lives in a bar in Greysteel, County Derry. It would take eight more months after the Downing Street Declaration was presented on December 15th before a cease-fire was declared. The IRA continued bombing and shooting. There were 37 separate incidents before February was out. The Unionists had not been idol either. By the summer the casualties were adding up. July's numbers were in. Fifteen Catholics dead, four Protestants dead. Fifteen Republicans, four Unionists. Fifteen Nationalists, four Loyalists. Surely, it had to stop. Finally, on Wednesday, August 31, 1994 the IRA released this announcement.

Recognizing the potential of the current situation and in order to enhance the democratic process and underlying our definitive commitment to its success, the leadership of the IRA have decided that as of midnight, August 31, there will be complete cessation of military operations.

The leaders of the IRA no doubt also recognized that the inflexible "Brits out" policy had never been successful, and that in the last two decades their military campaign's terrorist actions had lost the IRA much of the people's support. Moreover, they saw some advantage in negotiating with the British. It gave them more credibility. Bill Clinton, recently elected to the American presidency, had committed himself to aiding the Irish peace process. He broke a long-standing policy of refusing to admit Gerry Adams into the States because of his ties to the IRA. Adams, whose visa request had been turned down seven times over a 20-year period, was given a 48-hour visa to address the National Committee on Foreign Policy's conference on Northern Ireland. In the Republic of Ireland, a decades old broadcasting ban on paramilitary groups was eased, permitting Sinn Fein's message on the airways.

The Downing Street Declaration had assured the world that the Irish people could "bring about a united Ireland, if that is their wish." Given a place at the table, Sinn Fein sensed they had a better chance achieving a 32-county nation with ballots than with bombs. After all, the Declaration also promised that the decision would be made by "…the people of the island of Ireland alone." The killing had stopped. The IRA's representatives were at the peace table. Things were looking very good in Ireland.

Things were also looking good for Ireland's favorite son. As John Major and Albert Reynolds were issuing the Downing Street Declaration, MacGowan was preparing to resurrect his career. He was off and running when 1994 began. He regained national attention when Van Morrison asked him to do a duet with him at the prestigious annual Brit Awards. It was MacGowan's first appearance on prime time UK television in awhile. He took it in stride, joining Morrison on a memorable version of "Gloria," and later telling a journalist, "The Brit Awards? A pile of fat greasy wankers in tuxedos, with a load of scum up the front, who I couldn't identify with, who were there to dance for the cameras, because the guys in the tuxedos were too busy stuffing their faces and drinking… Elton John was really nice to me and my girlfriend, Victoria, though, and the whole thing was a really good laugh."

The following month Shane MacGowan and the Popes played what has been called their debut performance at the Grand in Clapham on St. Patrick's Day. In fact, they had played several lower profile gigs by then, including a couple of well-received shows at Fleadh Mor in Tramore, Ireland, and the Mean Fiddler in Halesden, London. For the more heavily promoted St. Patrick's Day concert MacGowan was careful to be sure the Popes were ready. He and his new band polished 26 songs. The *NME* reported that the Pogues were initially intended to be on that same St. Patrick's Day bill but wisely took a pass, opting for another North American tour. They played Toronto that night.

MacGowan and the Popes continued to rehearse and play live, and between dates they worked on MacGowan's first solo album. They also managed to find time to appear in *A Man You Don't Meet Everyday*, a movie about an Irishman who gets caught up in terrorist activity in London. Shane and Popes appear as themselves performing "The Old Main Drag" in a pub. Touring was different this time around. For one thing, the schedule was not nearly as relentless. For another, the gigs were not as lucrative. Shane MacGowan and the Popes were not the headliners the Pogues had been. At London's Finsbury Fleadh in June, for instance, they played at 2:30 in the afternoon, hardly a prime spot. Still, MacGowan remained happy and optimistic. Leaving the stage that day he shouted to the crowd, "*Tichaid ar la*," Gaelic for "Our day will come." That night he did two guest vocals with the Dubliners during their 10:00 PM set.

In the studio things were going very well. While the world's eyes turned to the Irish peace process, MacGowan turned to making a very Irish album. Several guest musicians including some steeped in traditional Irish folk styles and two Pogues (Spider Stacy and Jem Finer) augmented the Popes. Sinead O'Conner dueted with MacGowan on "Haunted," a song MacGowan had written for *Sid and Nancy*, Alex Cox's film about the Sex Pistols' Sid Vicious. Originally Cait O'Riordan did the vocal. Most surprisingly, Hollywood heartthrob Johnny Depp added some guitar. A huge Pogues fan, Depp had once been in a Florida band called the Kids. They had managed to open for Iggy Pop once before Depp packed it in to take a shot at acting. Depp had been spending a lot of time in London pursuing another interest, Kate Moss. The Depp/Moss connection generated some extra press interest, especially when Johnny appeared in a video and on the BBC's *Top of the Pops* on "That Woman's Got Me Drinking," a subsequent single. Shane said he wanted to get Jerry Lee Lewis to sit in on "King of the Bop." Lewis didn't, and the old Nips' rock-a-billy number never made the album.

**"I'm looking after myself these days. I'm eating regularly
and cutting back on booze. I feel pretty good."**

Shane MacGowan

By 1994 it was clear that MacGowan was still a musical force to be reckoned with. His show with the Popes at the Clapham Grand on St. Patrick's Day left no doubt of that. The Grand is an ornate Victorian theater. Built in 1900, its sweeping balconies and ornate ceilings overlook the largest flashing dance floor in Europe. Its three bars made it an ideal venue for a Shane MacGowan concert.

Shane must have felt some anxiety as show time approached. There was anticipation in the audience as well. They seemed to sense that they were about to witness something important. A Phoenix was about to rise. MacGowan took the stage dressed entirely in black. In a strange show of affection, some in the crowd pelted him with empty drink cups. He responded with, "I'm trying to give you a bit of culture and what do you do? You're throwing fucking glasses at me. Jesus Christ!" He then launched into "Streams of Whiskey," from the first Pogues album. MacGowan and the Popes went on to deliver a torrid set mixing Pogues classics, Irish traditional tunes, and several new numbers. For good measure he threw in the old Nips rocker "King of the Bop." The sound was Irish, but the Popes were more electrified and rocked harder than the Pogues had. There was nothing from either *Peace and Love* or *Hell's Ditch*.

The set initially ended on a low point. The last song was the traditional "Irish Rover," a number which had long been a favorite at Pogues gigs. Something went horribly wrong. Shane and the Popes seemed to have had little regard for what the other was doing. At points it sounded as if they were doing two different songs. If ever MacGowan's fans were going to sacrifice the Popes on the Pogues' alter, this performance of "Irish Rover" would be the time to do it. They didn't. The crowd was jubilant, bringing MacGowan and his new band out for several encores.

One of the encores had been conspicuously missing from the set, "Fairytale of New York." Siobhan MacGowan sang the duet with her brother, doing a credible job on Kirsty MacColl's part. Nick Cave came onstage to duet on "Love's Been Good to Me," an old Frank Sinatra number, which Shane called "I've Been a Rover." That was less than successful, but the lapse was more than made up for with "The Boys of Kilmichael," the old IRA rebel song Shane had learned as a child. MacGowan's arrangement had a marching cadence similar to the Clancy Brothers' "Boys of the West." He spat out the violent lyrics with a passion that would have made Margaret Thatcher a fan of Tom Barry's West Cork flying column.

By all accounts, Shane MacGowan was back. The concert crowd was ecstatic. To make his redemption complete, he closed the evening with a reprise of "The Irish Rover." Shane told the crowd, "We're gonna try 'The Irish Rover' again." Someone on the stage added, "We'll get it right this time." That they did. The reviews in the next day's press raved.

The Snake, Shane MacGowan's first solo album, was released on October 29, 1994 on the Warner, Electra, Asylum label. It was preceded by a single, "Church of the Holy Spook," which stalled at number 72 on the UK charts. In the liner notes MacGowan credits "The Holy Spook" for spiritual guidance. Clearly, he was not trying to endear himself to the Catholic Church. In Catholic doctrine the Holy Ghost is one of the three-person Godhead along with Jesus and God the Father. Moreover, as if naming his band the Popes was not enough, he told the press before the release that the album would be called *Kiss Me Ring*, referencing the Catholic indulgence ritual of kissing the Pope's ring to take time off one's sentence in purgatory. Someone at the record company did change the original album cover, which depicted Shane crucified, perhaps a reference to being sacked by the Pogues.

MacGowan's work has always drawn heavily from his religious upbringing and spirituality. "I am a religious writer," he says. "I believe the Holy Ghost, or God or the Tao or whatever, is in everything and we're all part of it." Christian imagery and symbolism inform much of what he does artistically and personally. He is seldom seen without a collection of Catholic paraphernalia: rosary beads, scapulars, holy medals, and the like. Most of it he wears around his neck. When he first heard of New York Doll Arthur Kane's death, he instinctively crossed himself as a Catholic does in church. MacGowan's knowledge of church history is as impressive as his knowledge of Irish history. In truth, these histories are inexorably intertwined.

Irish secular history was consolidated in Catholic monasteries. Reading and writing arrived in Ireland with the church. The island's monasteries became islands of literacy. Monks worked daily in scriptoriums laboriously copying parchment manuscripts. Slowly, libraries of scripture, law, and history grew within the monastery walls. The only schools in Ireland were within those walls as well. Important families sent their sons to the monks to be educated, and the church gradually became extremely powerful, wielding an influence that has only begun to wane in recent years.

St. Patrick is popularly credited with bringing Christianity to the Irish in the fifth century. At the time Celtic Ireland's religion was centered on a priestly caste of poet/seers called Druids. They were believed to be in communion with natural forces, to the extent that they exercised some control over the sun, wind, and rain. The people looked to the Druids to mediate between them and the spirit world. Patrick, the son of a government official and the grandson of a Catholic priest, was born in England. When he was 16 years old an Irish raiding party captured Patrick and took him as a slave to Ireland, most likely to what is now County Mayo. When he managed to escape and return to England some seven years later, he regarded his deliverance as a miracle. Feeling a new sense of obligation to God, he became a Catholic priest.

Not one to hold a grudge, Patrick returned to Ireland hoping to convert his pagan captors to Christianity. He was not the first Christian missionary to the Irish, but he was either the first to chronicle his efforts in writing or the first whose writings survived. Most of the little we know about Patrick comes from two of his manuscripts. Patrick founded churches throughout the north and west of Ireland. He hoped to build a centralized church structure on the island, like the Roman churches in Europe. In this he failed. The independent Irish spirit made local, autonomous churches the rule. The church in Armagh, which Patrick founded, became important after his death in large part because it claimed to possess the saint's bones. An important pilgrimage site by the 7th century, it helped to develop the cult of St. Patrick that came to dominate the Irish church.

When Patrick died Ireland was still largely pagan with pockets of Christianity. By the 7th century that had changed. Christianity had become very well established. Unlike in other countries, the conversion of Ireland to the faith was non-violent. There are no early, Irish Christian martyrs. The church accomplished the peaceful transition in large part by embracing and adapting pagan religious practices and customs rather than replacing them. Of course, this had been going on since the Roman Emperor Constantine made Christianity his empire's religion. Every theologian knows that Jesus was not born in December. The date was picked hundreds of years after the fact to coincide with the ancient pagan feast of Saturnalia. Bunny rabbits and eggs have little to do with Christ's resurrection, but they were natural symbols for fertility goddess Eoster's feast, also held in the spring. The assimilation of pagan symbolism in Ireland was wholesale. The distinctive Celtic cross is a mix of Christian and pre-Christian imagery. "People say that the Christian church in Ireland was overlaid on a pagan culture, using the word 'pagan' as a slur," MacGowan once told a reporter. "But all the ancient religions of the world have the same basic idea of an all-enveloping creative being or force, which the old Irish religion represented by a circle, because they worshipped the sun... Patrick inscribed a cross over the circle, although the cross is a mandala anyway. The mandala of Christ, the crucifix, is a strong protective thing and guide. I feel a lot better with a Gaelic cross around my neck..."

During the Middle Ages the Irish church was quite laid back and relaxed. The early Christian settlers had adapted comfortably to Celtic spirituality, incorporating many of their feast days and celebrations into their own tradition. Later, the Norman invaders were Christians as well, and they easily integrated into Irish society. In the 1500s when the Protestant Reformation unleashed Lutheranism, it had little impact on this remote corner of Europe. Ultimately, it took a fat, horny, English king to shake things up. When Henry VIII broke with the Catholic Church in Rome, the repercussions shook the Emerald Isle. In 1536 the English Parliament passed the Act of Supremacy, making Henry head of the Church. The suppression of monasteries followed, entailing the loss of vast tracks of church land, not to mention lives. In 1539 Parliament prohibited the Catholic Mass and the use of sacred images, candles, and rosary beads, all of which were part and parcel in Catholic worship. Moreover, the public use of the Protestant *Book of Common Prayer* was commanded, and anyone who refused to attend Protestant worship services was fined 12 pence for each offence.

The Irish refused to abandon their faith or the religious rituals that went with it. Over time the British grew lax in enforcing the laws designed to wipe out Irish Catholicism. That changed when the Puritan, Oliver Cromwell, came to power. He was called to Ireland to extinguish the Rebellion of 1641, which began in Ulster. Having done so, he stayed on to punish the Irish with crippling policies that plagued the island for generations to come. Under Cromwellian rule Irish farms were confiscated at an unprecedented level. Catholicism was outlawed. No mercy was shown to the clergy. Ordered to leave Ireland, those that dared return were put to death. Churches soon fell into ruin. At the end of the 17th century Penal Laws were enacted comprising the most repressive religious and social legislation the modern world had ever seen. The right to worship, the right to congregate, the right to own property, even the right to speak their native tongue was taken from the Irish. Catholics who refused to work on Sunday were whipped. Every vestige of dignity was stripped away by the British occupiers. History has proven the maxim, "The blood of the martyr is the seed of the church." The saying held true in Cromwellian Ireland. The Irish, having been ripped from their land, banished from their homes, robbed of their freedom, and deprived of their dignity; found in Catholicism a rallying point for their nationalism and distress. The struggle between the Irish and the British had evolved into what many saw as a conflict between the Catholic and the Protestant.

By the time of the Irish Rebellion of 1798 it was obvious to all that Irish Catholics would never embrace Protestantism, and enforcement of the Penal Laws was futile. Despite the rebellion having been supported by many Protestants (Wolfe Tone, the primary leader, was Protestant), British propaganda painted the insurrection with a Catholic brush in order to divide the rebels. A Catholic priest became an Irish folk hero when he led his parishioners against the British during the ill-fated uprising. Father John Murphy was the parish priest of Boolavogue, a small village in County Wexford. Over a period of about 30 days he led his county in several successful ambushes against British troops, encouraging and swelling the rebel forces. Once he was captured, Father Murphy was convicted of treason and tortured before being hanged and beheaded. As if that were insufficient, his corpse was burnt in a barrel of tar and his head was impaled on a spike. He became more than a martyr to the cause of Irish freedom, he became a martyr to the cause of Irish Catholics. Murphy was immortalized in the popular Irish rebel ballad "Boolavogue" written in 1898 to commemorate the rebellion's 100th anniversary.

When the famine struck Ireland in 1845, Catholicism had become so integral to Irish life, many chose to starve to death rather than renounce their religion for a bowl of soup. The British opened soup kitchens offering famine relief on the condition that the recipients convert to the Protestant faith. Most families refused. Those that didn't were called "soupers" by the faithful majority and were ostracized in their communities.

By the 20th century, Ireland was recognized as one of the world's most prominent Catholic countries. Long after its influence had dissipated throughout most of Europe, the Catholic Church maintained a strong grip in the Irish Republic. Homosexual acts remained illegal in Ireland up until the summer of 1993. Irish law required married couples to remain married for life until the Fifteenth Amendment repealed the constitutional prohibition on divorce in 1996. Even then, the referendum that approved the change passed very narrowly, 50.28% to 49.72%.

"I'm a lapsed Catholic, but I'm still a Catholic," MacGowan told the *Sunday Tribune* in 1987. "I wouldn't say I'm a bad Catholic. What my Catholic upbringing means to me now is, I have an idea of the connection between the physical world and the supernatural world, or whatever, and a lot of things still really move me. I occasionally go to Mass and that still moves me. Things like the rosary still move me. There's a lot of different ways of appreciating life: through music, or nature, or through people whether it's conversationally or sexually or just looking at them. A very deep, heavy, powerful, symbolic religion like Catholicism is another way of appreciating that. I know it's been corrupted over the years, and abused. I think the church's position on things like divorce in Ireland is wrong, in terms that it causes a lot of suffering. I don't think these should be crucial issues in the church. But I think most religions have got heavy attitudes about things like that. Catholicism is not an isolated religion."

"I remember the day I lapsed like it was yesterday," he said on another occasion. "'I was walking up a country lane, and it just hit me. Hang on. Just supposing it isn't true. Suppose there's no heaven or hell? Suppose there's nothing after death? And I just couldn't get that out of my head. It was my Auntie Nora. She used to indoctrinate me with loads of Catholic magazines and make me do the Rosary. When I got to about ten, I'd go back to Tipperary in my holidays and stay with her. Auntie Nora used to smoke and gamble. Those were the vices she passed on to me. We used to do the horses and she'd give me cigarettes and port."

MacGowan says that his religious feelings and his music are "…inseparable. Music makes you more God-like. Music is my God in a way. I go with the flow. I'm not preaching any kind of answer. I've had a fair amount of heaven on earth, a fair amount of hell. If I can just minimize my suffering and maximize my joy… and other people's. I want to stay close to God and close to everything I love: drugs and booze and casual violence and my girlfriend and my parents and Ireland. The things that make being human worthwhile." Going with the flow, a concept intrinsic to Taoist philosophy and religion, is a notion MacGowan has come to embrace strongly.

"I'm Taoist Catholic," he says. "I believe in yin and yang, too. I like to go with the flow." At first glance MacGowan's assertion that he is a "Taoist Catholic" seems to be at odds with itself. Christians, and Catholics in particular, breech little compromise on their claim to be the one true religion. Until *Vatican II* in 1962, Catholics wouldn't even concede that non-Catholic Christians had any chance of escaping hell's fires. However, Taoism is both an East Asian religion and a philosophy. Many in Eastern religions include Taoist philosophy in their tradition. It is perfectly logical for adherents to Confucianism or Buddhism to be Taoists as well. The word Tao is literally translated "path" or "way." It's notable that Christianity was called "The Way" before its adherents were called Christians.

Those who embrace Taoism as a religion generally observe some of the traditional rituals and practices handed down over the centuries: burning Joss paper to benefit ancestors and departed loved ones in the spirit world, slaughtering animals as sacrifices to the gods, participating in elaborate ceremonial street parades on religious holidays, etc. MacGowan, to my knowledge, does none of these things. Neither am I aware of Shane worshiping one of the many gods in the Taoist pantheon, worship that in and of itself would just about by definition eliminate one from the ranks of Christianity. MacGowan believes that any freethinking Catholic can be a Taoist. He says he has no doubt that St. Francis of Assisi was a Taoist because the medieval Italian monk believed that God was in everything.

The philosophy of Taoism grew out of Chinese prehistoric folk religions that were systemized about 200 years before Christ, gaining official status during the Tang Dynasty. The philosophy centers on the themes of compassion, moderation, and humility. Taoists believe that nature works in harmony according to its own ways. When a person exerts his own will against natural harmony, he disrupts it. MacGowan sums up the basic principle of Taoism as trying "to go with the flow because we are all a part of each other." Non-action, detachment, and flexibility are character traits a Taoist strives to cultivate. To that extent, Shane's life would seem to be in the way of the Tao. In regard to moderation, not so much.

Taoist philosophy has not caused MacGowan to abandon the faith in which he was indoctrinated from early childhood. The family that surrounded him in Carney Commons were all devout Catholics. Along with Dan Breen's *My Fight for Irish Freedom* he includes the Catholic *Catechism* as "The two most important books I read" in childhood. Shane's rearing was liberal ("anti- Puritan" in his words) in many regards; from a young age he was permitted to drink, smoke, and gamble. What he was not allowed to do was blaspheme or miss Mass on Sunday. He attended Mass in the little village church in nearby Kilbarron. To this day he calls the traditional Roman Catholic Mass "one of the most beautiful things" a person can experience: "The priest chants beautiful Gregorian chants in Latin. It's a beautiful Mass and it's a situation I love to write songs about. The drunk at midnight Mass, the sublime and ridiculous at the same time, the debased and the divine, beautiful experience." Up until the age of eleven he considered becoming a priest.

MacGowan's estrangement from the Catholic Church has far less to do with Catholic beliefs than with the church itself. "I'm a Catholic," he insists. "I always believed in

Jesus, but I believe His words have been corrupted by the Catholic institutions, by the Vatican. And it has filtered right down. I think that it's a good thing that the church has lost its grip… I believe in the teachings of Christ, but not in the way that it's practiced by the priests. I believe that guilt is useless. Awful fucking emotion. I really blame and hate Catholic priests and popes and cardinals for using and abusing children. I think it's something that eats me up inside. Self-hate and the hate for the people that made you feel that way in the first place."

MacGowan says he is convinced that he is bound for "…either heaven or purgatory. Definitely not hell." He says he prays every day and goes to church occasionally. When I spoke to him a few days after his 50th birthday, I asked him if he had been to Mass on Christmas. "What, this last Christmas?" he asked. "No, but I usually do. And I go to church whenever I feel like going to church. There isn't so much of it." When I asked if he felt the church was still relevant he said, "I don't know if – yes, the church is relevant. It's like any thing else. It's like any kind of organization. The point is that the message, the belief, the fucking – the faith, and the fact that it doesn't do anybody good to go around killing each other, and stealing off each other, and fucking up the planet – fucking up, without any regard. Over the years, I'd say, in Ireland the church – until independence – the church was a massive load of contradictions, and people went to church because – there are a 100 different reasons to go to church. You know what I mean? But the main reason to go to church is because whatever human beings do – you know, priests or – you take any section of human beings – you take journalists – you take, well politicians – there's gonna be a certain percentage of shit that rises to the top. The hierarchy. And then it spreads down again. But these institutions can't survive without the support of the people, or not in Ireland anyway."

Earlier that week Irish television had aired a year-end special documentary based on a survey done in 1977 and repeated in 2007. In 1977, 90% of Irish Catholics said they went to church every week. In 2007 the figure was down to a little under 50%. Everybody I spoke to that week thought that 50% was too high an estimate. The Sunday after Christmas I attended Mass at Shane's childhood parish church in Kilbarron. There were about 80 people there, about half the building's capacity. The entire service lasted 25 minutes. Parishioners didn't arrive early or linger afterwards to socialize and speak with one another. There was a real sense of the event being an obligation to get over with rather than something that had been looked forward to.

When I told Shane about my experience, he was quick to put a positive spin on it, rightly pointing out that 80 people attending Mass in the sparsely populated area that encompasses Carney Commons and Kilbarron was not half bad. "We could talk about this for weeks, months, years. People have," he said, before he went on passionately engaging in the Irish penchant for mixing religion and politics. "The main thing is do you believe in love or do you believe in hate? Do you want to hate people or do you want to love people? Or at least tolerate people. Intolerance, is – it's impossible to fucking forget what the Brits did in Ireland and what they did all over the bloody place, and what the yanks have done – I mean what their governments have done all over the bloody place. But it has to be forgiven because we're all part of the same soul." In the end, MacGowan's religious beliefs are much like his songs: complex yet simple. "All I can do is go by the words of Christ, who was the only talker we had, for fuck's sake," he says. "Buddha didn't speak. The Holy Ghost didn't speak. But I think it all boils down to the same thing - it's all about unity, love, compassion."

While the Catholic Church had little love or compassion for MacGowan's new album, Shane was clearly excited about *The Snake*. "It's the first album I've been so heavily involved in," he told a reporter from *Rock and Reel*. "We laid it down in a month 'cos the songs were ready from the live shows. I decided what went on it. In the past there had always been the producer to come up against, but I co-produced the album with Dave Jordan, who was the soundman with the Pogues. I have a good working relationship with him. We produced things like 'Rainy Night in Soho.' Dave produced 'The Irish Rover,' but because of managerial policy and time he didn't get his name on the record. I'm in control of what I do now. This is the situation I was in before the Pogues and during most of the Pogues, but then I felt that people could make me do some things – so I got out in the end."

As with so many things, MacGowan's true feelings about *The Snake* can be hard to pin down. He has said that when it first came out he was "ashamed of it" but that he's not ashamed of it anymore. While promoting *The Crock of Gold*, his second solo album, he dismissed *The Snake* offhand. "Well *The Snake* was a mess. It was basically a rock album. It was an atrocity, two or three good tracks and the rest of it was rubbish." The dismissal is ironic given that MacGowan had complete control of the project. Just before *The Snake* was released Shane enthusiastically described the new music in an interview for the Friends of Shane fan club website. "...two thirds like the early Pogues, what we used to call 'Paddybeat' and the rest is R'n'B and Rock'n'Roll and Hard Rock... and there's even one track with a Reggae beat, a toasting number... and there's Thai-beat and a coupla Jazz-Soul type numbers, like Sly meets Coltrane downtown. But the greater part is paddybeat, early Pogues style. Nothing to do with what the Pogues are doing now.... We follow a tradition, the Irish tradition, and it's an aural/oral tradition, not written down, which has lasted for thousands of years and we're part of it. The English folk tradition - and I've seen it in Kent, proper Morris dancers having a ceili, with bodhrans, the lot - is rare, but it exists... Industry has wiped out the folk tradition in England. The folk tradition will die if it isn't followed."

The bottom line is that *The Snake* sounds like Shane MacGowan wanted it to sound like at that point in time. Post Pogues MacGowan was older, perhaps mellowed, and in charge of the recording studio. The eight years spent touring with the Pogues had taken some toll on MacGowan's voice, but the wear and tear accented the spirit of the songs. Co-producer Dave Jordan, a long time Pogues technician and friend, knew first hand what the early Pogues, Irish dance music, and Shane MacGowan were all about. Not only does it sound the way MacGowan wanted it to sound, it sounds very good.

Significantly, Irish rebel songs are back. It's true there is country, rock, and punk in the mix, but the spirit and overall sound is Irish dance music as only Shane MacGowan can deliver it. Two of the Dubliners, John Sheahan (fiddle and whistles) and Barney McKenna (banjo), played on the record. Siobahn Sheahan contributed Irish harp and Tomas Lynch added uillean pipes. Apart from a few traditional numbers, MacGowan wrote all but one of the songs. The themes are Irish to the core. There are drinking songs, songs steeped in Irish history, songs touched by Catholicism, an Irish instrumental dance number, and above all love songs.

MacGowan wrote the instrumental, a galloping tune called "Bring Down the Lamp." "A Mexican Funeral in Paris" is the album's only track to abandon Ireland, and even it references Catholicism, albeit the Hispanic strain. "Church of the Holy Spook" and "Donegal Express," however, are Irish Catholic to the core. During the album's recording, the studio was littered with MacGowan's holy hardware. A crucifix hung directly in front of Shane's mike. Another larger crucifix sat on top of a speaker. A picture of a nun, with the caption, "Sister Margaret leads a life of chastity, poverty and obedience" was pinned to an amplifier. An even larger display of religious paraphernalia, however, would have done little to endear "Church of the Holy Spook" to the Pope. In Christian theology the Holy Ghost is an equal part of the Trinity, a three person Godhead made up of Jehovah (God the Father), Jesus (God the Son), and the Holy Spirit (God the Spirit). Referring to the deity as the "Holy Spook" is right out. MacGowan, however, says the song is an affirmation of his parents' religion. "'Church of the Holy Spook' is straight down the line what it says," he maintains, "ol' Irish Catholicism was good enough for my dear old dad or mum or granny, if people died for it, then it's good enough for me. I don't believe in the Holy Trinity, but I do believe in the Holy Ghost. The Holy Spook is just a friendly way of saying Holy Ghost." The sentiment in one verse in the song, "When the sacred blood of the Holy Ghost is boiling in my veins, I think of Jesus on the cross and I scream out for his pain" would not be out of place in any mainline Christian denomination's hymnal.

"Donegal Express," a song Shane had already begun performing in his last days with the Pogues, is another story. About a randy Irish priest, the song features the couplet, "I might have fucked your Missus, but I never fucked your daughter." I asked Shane if he considered the randy priest an important traditional theme in Irish folklore. "Yes," he said. "The first guy that had the guts to go out and say that he wasn't celibate -and he wasn't any kind of bloody fucking - was Bishop Eamonn Casey, or ex-Bishop Eamonn Casey. All he was doing was – all he had was a mistress. He drank a bit and did a bit of coke. You can't impose celibacy on people – that wasn't anything to do with Christ, it's all to do with Paul and all that." Casey, the politically active ex-Bishop once known for his work with Irish emigrants in Britain, resigned and left Ireland in 1992 when it became known that he had fathered a son by a distant American cousin half his age. The situation got even worse when it was revealed that Casey supported his family with funds he siphoned from the Galway diocese. Many in Ireland cite the crisis precipitated by the scandal as the beginning of the Catholic church's declining influence over Irish society.

MacGowan reached deep into the bag of Irish tradition for the album's two rebel songs, "Roddy McCorley" and "The Rising of the Moon." McCorley, a young Irish rebel captured at the battle of Antrim during the 1798 uprising against the British, was executed on a bridge in the tiny village of Toome in County Antrim on Good Friday, 1799. The British dissected his body and buried it under the road that went from Belfast to Derry. In the mid 1800s he was dug up and given a proper burial in an unmarked grave. Today a memorial honoring McCorley greets visitors entering the village. "The Rising of the Moon," perhaps the most ubiquitous song about the 1798 rebellion, has been recorded by nearly every folksinger to come out of Ireland. Bobby Sands referenced the song in the final line of his hunger strike diary. Shane's retelling of Irish farmers optimistically gathering by the river in the moonlight, primitive weapons called pikes in hand, is as stirring as any I've heard. MacGowan's pursuit of Irish history continued in what came closest to the album's title song, "The Snake with Eyes of Garnet."

The song deals with James Mangan, a Dublin born Republican Catholic who some critics consider the first modern Irish poet. It's a fine, if cryptic, MacGowan composition of which he has said, "It's one of those ones that I don't know if I was asleep or awake when I wrote it." In it the dead Republican poet takes the songwriter on an alcohol and drug fueled trip into Irish history. They witness an execution, presumably of a Republican, on Stephen's Green in Dublin. Mangan gives MacGowan a ring in the shape of a snake with eyes of garnet. The ring seems to symbolize perseverance in Ireland's longing for a 32-county republic. MacGowan criticized the documentary *The Great Hunger* for making too much of a MacGowan-Mangan connection. In fairness to the filmmakers, MacGowan himself has made much of the connection. According to Victoria Clarke, Shane has been communicating with Mangan (who died in 1849) for years. She says she once found him locked in the bathroom, refusing to come out, because he was deep in conversation with the dead poet. It's not difficult to see why MacGowan would relate to Mangan. Both men are associated with flamboyant eccentricities. Mangan, generally described as unkempt, pale, and in bad health, always carried an umbrella. He usually wore a tight, blue cloak and a witch's hat. Like Shane, he had a fondness for drink that got him sacked from writing gigs despite his formidable talent. One magazine said they fired him because "his habits rendered him incapable of regular application." Much of Mangan's poetry was patriotic. One of his most famous pieces is an aisling called "Roisin Doebh."

Aisling is Gaelic for dream or vision. As a poetic genre, an aisling is an Irish vision poem popularized in the 17th century when Britain refused to permit the Irish any nationalistic expression. Aislings generally presented the vision of a woman as a metaphor for Ireland itself. Often the woman was young and lovely, symbolizing the majestic beauty of the nation. Sometimes she was an old hag, symbolizing Ireland's desperate state. In either case the woman bemoans the plight of the Irish under British rule, and holds forth the promise of a brighter day.

The Snake contains what may be the most Irish of all MacGowan's songs, "Aisling." He wrote it in 1989, but the Pogues inexplicably voted it off Hell's Ditch. When it was finally recorded for The Snake, Spider Stacy and Jem Finer sat in on the session. MacGowan's aisling works wonders with the metaphor of Ireland as woman. Amid images of the rural Irish countryside, rebels, and strong drink, the black haired beauty representing Ireland in MacGowan's song is actually named Aisling. The singer's longing to be reunited with his love applies eloquently to both the woman and the land: "Bless the wind that shakes the barley, curse the spade and curse the plow. Waking in the morning early, I wish to hell I was with you now."

MacGowan's use of a woman as a metaphor for Ireland is echoed in one of the album's traditional songs, but this time the woman represents another of his consuming loves: alcohol. "Nancy Whiskey," while not one of The Snake's highlights, suits MacGowan very well. The singer meets Nancy Whiskey in Glasgow and begins a seven-year affair during which he spends everything he has on his passion, eventually turning to robbery to keep the relationship going. In the end, he can't escape the woman's or the whiskey's grip.

> The more I held her, the more I loved her
> Nancy had her spell on me
> All I had was lovely Nancy
> The things I needed I could not see
>
> Whiskey, Whiskey, Nancy Whiskey
> Whiskey, Whiskey, Nancy Ohh
>
> As I awoke to slake my thirst
> As I tried crawling from my bed
> I fell down flat, I could not stagger
> Nancy had me by the legs

The rest of the album consists of love songs of one kind or another. As in "Nancy Whiskey," however without the metaphor, a woman and whiskey are at the center of "That Woman's Got Me Drinking," a track that vies with "I'll be Your Handbag" for the record's most dispensable. The remaining songs all fare better. MacGowan didn't write one of the best of them. Gerry Rafferty's "Her Father Didn't Like Me Anyway" is a perfect vehicle for Shane. Written as a sad lament over a relationship doomed due to parental disapproval, the song is transformed in MacGowan's hands. He spits it out with a fury that ends with Shane shouting expletives at the interfering father. His vocal is wonderful; his anger and resentment seethe. Still, it's hard not to take Dad's side.

The three other love songs, "Song with No Name," "Haunted," and "Victoria," are all excellent. "Victoria," which rocks the hardest, is a fitting tribute to Shane's long-suffering soul mate, Victoria Clarke. In addition to owning up to being a "lout," MacGowan's lyrics allude to Van Morrison, fame, opium, and his love's green eyes. The Pogues originally did "Haunted," a duet Shane sings here with Sinead O'Connor, using only Cait O'Riordan on the vocal. It was first recorded for the soundtrack of Alex Cox's film about Sid Vicious and Nancy Spurgeon, *Sid and Nancy*. MacGowan told the *Boston Globe* that O'Conner was forced upon him. That seems strange, given Shane's control over *The Snake*. If it is true, the pairing was a very fortunate coercion. The juxtaposition of O'Conner's and MacGowan's voices is mesmerizing. One critic said it sounded like a duet between Satan and the Virgin Mary.

The album's best love song, however, is "Song with No Name." Using the age old folk process, MacGowan appropriated a timeless Irish melody reminiscent of "Lilly of the West," "Tramps and Hawkers," and especially "The Hills of Donegal." Achingly sad, the music is a perfect frame for MacGowan's lyric of a passionate love affair gone wrong. In the months before *The Snake* was released, the press had alluded to Shane and Victoria's relationship as being on again off again, calling them "recently separated." I asked Shane if he thought that pain produced the best art. "When people have experienced a lot of pain, and are out of the pain, and then they look back at it, that's when the best art is produced," he told me. "Once you've got over the heartbreak then you can write about the heartbreak — well, when you're starting to get over the heartbreak. It's a way of getting over the heartbreak." With lines like, "I was brutal, I was ignorant, I was cruel, I was brash. I never gave a damn about the beauty that I smashed," it is easy to speculate that "Song with No Name" was born of pain. It stands as one of MacGowan's finest achievements.

The Snake garnered good reviews. It entered the charts at number 37 but failed to move up, falling off completely after only two weeks. The second single from the album, "That Woman's Got Me Drinking" did a little better, staying on the charts longer and reaching number 34. The publicity Johnny Depp brought to the song didn't hurt any. He played in and directed the song's video. When Shane and the Popes played the song on *Top of the Pops* Depp sat in on guitar.

In November Shane got to work on one of his least favorite aspects of the music business: media promotion. He and the Popes were about to start a European tour to support *The Snake*. He did the television and radio talk shows and newspaper and magazine interviews. Typically Shane would show up a bit higher than the average interviewee and give far more candid, frank responses to inane questions than the average interviewee. The press and the public were well entertained. The tour sold out. They played Glassgow, Paris, Dublin, Claremorris, Berlin, Cologne, Frankfort, and two shows apiece in Hamburg and London; nine cities and eleven shows in just under three weeks. The concerts were excellent. Old Pogues fans said they felt they had witnessed a resurrection. MacGowan was far from sober, but he was performing as he did with the Pogues prior to *Peace and Love*. The crowds loved it. It seemed like old times.

The show at Dublin's Olympia was particularly wild. The place was packed. MacGowan came on stage late, about 1.30 am. Several in the crowd promptly smashed up the first two rows of seats, about two dozen in all. By the time the show was over some 80 minutes later, ten security guards were crouched on the front of the stage, barely able to contain the crowd surge. One paper called the show "the first full-length Irish concert by MacGowan and his band," and wrote, "So wild was the dancing that several people were plucked from the audience and ejected." MacGowan was in top form all night. The set mixed old Pogues favorites with songs from the new album. Shane's sister dueted with him on "Fairytale of New York."

MacGowan may have been unwilling to resume a Pogues-like touring schedule, but he and the Popes worked hard to support the new release. In February there were four sold out shows in Norway and three in Sweden. Wherever they went, Shane seemed to be enjoying the performances. He often spent most of the night after a show drinking and jamming in a local pub. In Oslo he and some of the band treated the regulars to an impromptu version of Van Morrison's classic "Gloria." Early March saw them in Belgium and Paris. By St. Patrick's Day they were back in London for a show. The passion was back. On some nights when MacGowan drank too much he slurred his vocals, but he was still good. On other nights he was magnificent. "The early Pogues and what I do now is raw," he said at the time. "It's like what Irish music is really about, which is straightforward, no bullshit, raw, raunchy and quite messy. Or else slow, beautiful ballads. Sort of melancholy. But it gets you in the gut and the heart."

"Haunted" with Sinead O'Conner was released in April while MacGowan and the band took a break from touring. It made it to number 30 in the UK charts, the highest position Shane had attained in seven years. In May there were rumors in the press that Shane was working on a television talk show. Not as a guest, but as the host. It was to be a new Channel 4 series called *A Drink with Shane MacGowan*. The pilot was filmed in Johnny Depp's Hollywood club, the Viper Room, where the young actor River Phoenix took a fatal drug overdose two years earlier. Some bonified stars including Nicholas Cage, Bono, Sinead O'Connor, and of course Johnny Depp were said to have agreed to be on the show.

In the pilot Shane encouraged his guests to misbehave for the cameras as the drink and four-letter words flowed. They discussed controversial topics and traded outrageous gossip. *The Star*, characterizing the pilot as "a boozy, X-rated chat show," quoted an anonymous insider who was there. "Viewers can expect an orgy of bad taste gags, as the guests are let loose on the free-flowing alcohol. It was anything goes. Total mayhem. Shane goes out of his way to cause an upset. Late night TV hasn't seen anything quite like it. The stars are invited to drink as much as they like as the conversation flows. We're not sure whether the bad language will be bleeped out, but it's certainly bound to cause raised eyebrows among concerned parents." During the taping Shane performed with Los Lobos singing "Little Bitty Pretty One" and "We Gotta Get Outa This Place." Later in the evening he sang "Mellow Down Easy" and "Baby Please Don't Go" with a local blues band.

While he was filming in Los Angeles MacGowan stayed at the Chateau Marmont in the same bungalow where John Belushi died of a speedball overdose. The show, which some papers referred to as a documentary, never aired. MacGowan's memories of it seem fond, "Yeah, we made one episode of a chat show in LA. We had Chris Penn on it, and a real private detective, who wouldn't admit he'd ever killed anyone but obviously had. And a porn model who'd turned into a pop singer, and Johnny Depp was on it too. And we had Los Lobos on it. I thought it was a laugh. It was a good mixture of music and chat. The subject was violence. It was never shown."

Shane and the Popes spent the rest of the summer playing select gigs, mostly outdoor festivals in Europe. MacGowan's performances ran the gamut from magnificent to embarrassingly awful, depending primarily on his state of intoxication. In July he turned in an excellent set at the Montreaux Jazz festival. He was clearly drunk, but still in good form, blessing himself with the sign of the cross repeatedly during "Donegal Express" and shouting "Up the Republic!" at the song's end. He also took the opportunity to slag the "Brits" when introducing "The gentleman Soldier." His set was video recorded and is still available on DVD. But just a month earlier, at the Pink Pop Festival in the Netherlands, it appeared for a moment that the bottom was going to fall out again. During "I'll Be Your Handbag" the Popes realized the set was falling apart and tried desperately to cover for their frontman. When MacGowan introduced "Greenland Whale Fisheries" he slurred so badly it's unlikely anyone not already familiar with the song had any idea what he said. By the time MacGowan began singing he was several seconds behind the band. He never did manage to catch up. The lyrics were incomprehensible. Shane sounded more like a jazz singer doing vocal lines rather than singing actual words. Guitarist Paul McGuinness tried to help out on vocals but the number was still a disaster. For a moment things looked up as a lone fiddle beautifully played the slow, opening strands of "The Broad Majestic Shannon." Unfortunately, even the slowed down pace did little to enable Shane's performance. He hummed more than sang the lyrics, and he didn't even hum the right words at the right time. It was a sad, pitiful, heartbreaking thing to watch. The press said he was too drunk to sing, but any drunk plucked from the audience at random could have turned in a better performance, so Shane was probably not impaired by drink alone. Likely as not, heroin was a factor. It was Shane's bad luck that the Pink Pop set was recorded for Dutch television. If ever he did a worse show, fortunately it was not taped. Shane's last number was "Dark Streets of London." Having been unable to keep up with the band on the previous slow song, he never had a chance with the up-tempo "Dark Streets." McGuinness had to jump in on Shane's vocal from the outset. At the end of the first verse someone came out of the wings and led MacGowan offstage, and McGuinness finished the vocal. With Shane off stage, McGuinness introduced the next number saying, "We're gonna do one more song. Shane hasn't been well. We're sorry, but I'll sing it for you. This one's for Shane. It's called 'Fall from Grace.' You'll have to help me with the words." Remarkably, the audience seemed to love the set anyway. They danced and jumped about as at any MacGowan concert. The Popes, on the other hand, were less than pleased. Years later MacGowan said, "Quite a few times I was led off or carried off, not knowing where I was or what was happening… I didn't do that many bum gigs. That was grossly over reported that, you know. But I did do a few. And like, the band expected perfection. The audience was far more forgiving."

In August MacGowan took his new band to North America for the first time, doing 15 shows in the United States and Canada. On a Thursday night at Tramps in New York City he did nothing from the new album. His fans actually booed the nine-song, 30-minute set. On Friday night, in the same venue, he brought the house down. At the Great American Music Hall in San Francisco one reviewer said MacGowan was "wasted, nearly falling down drunk." He forgot lyrics and was out of time. The band seemed bored. One fan said Shane was "very intoxicated" and "fell on his face once… left the stage for 15 minutes…and told the crowd he was high on cocaine and heroin." None the less he made it through 19 songs, including seven from *The Snake*. He threw in a cover of Neil Diamond's "Cracklin' Rosie" and "Hippy, Hippy Shake" for good measure. It was the same in every city: Chicago, Boston, Providence, Toronto. Critics described the shows alternately as "frantic, slurry, shambolic, romantic, passionate, diffident, roughshod, and fantastic." In November Shane and the Popes returned for a second, short American tour and more of the same.

That August what was left of the Pogues released their final album. In what seemed a desperate attempt to show they were still the same band, they called it *Pogue Mahone*. One listen made it evident that they were not the same band. Jem Finer, Andrew Rankin, and Spider Stacy were the only ones left from the original line up. Within a year they would play their last gig in a London pub. Shane was supposed to sing a few songs with his old band at the farewell performance. In the event, it was clear there was still a little animosity left. David Coulter, a new Pogue recruited for the last album told an American reporter, "I don't miss Shane. I don't think anybody does. He was sort of made to walk the plank, you know? Who wants to pay $20.00 to see someone fall down drunk? Anyway, it's not my place to say more. I wasn't in the band then." Apparently, it escaped Coulter that even though the Pogues were still playing MacGowan songs at the time of their demise, more people were willing to pay to see MacGowan falling down drunk than to see a Shaneless Pogues. Especially one without Phillip Chevron, James Fearnley, and Terry Woods as well. Perhaps Coulter was just annoyed that five years after Shane was sacked fans were still chanting "We want Shane!" at Pogues gigs.

The reunion at the last Pogues show did not go as planned. According to the *Daily Mirror*, "It was a chaotic and emotional evening for some, and after a misunderstanding Shane was nearly thrown out and only allowed to sing one song by the group's minders." Shane said in the same article, "I didn't feel anything about them breaking up. They've had nothing to do with me for a long time. I don't know why people thought they'd outlast me."

CHAPTER 11

"Is it not possible that the ultimate end is gaiety and music and a dance of joy?"

James Stephens, The Crock of Gold

MacGowan and the Popes finished 1995 with a series of Christmas season shows in the UK. They continued to perform throughout Europe, although more sporadically, throughout 1996. That summer Shane released a cover of Frank Sinatra's "My Way" as a single. Thematically it was a perfect choice. Compared to MacGowan's, Sinatra's life looked conventional. Musically, the track left a lot to be desired, but it made money. It charted at a respectable number 30 in the UK, but the record really lined Shane's pocket when Nike used it in a television commercial. By the time Shane and the Popes played their next round of the usual Christmas gigs in England and Ireland, some new material was making its way into the set. After two scorching shows at the Olympia in Dublin, MacGowan retreated to Tipperary to spend the holidays with friends and family.

Shane kept a relatively low profile in 1997. Part of the reason was that he was spending time in the studio recording new songs that were increasingly showing up in his concerts. Part of the reason was that early in the year he fell off a barstool and broke his hip. Part of the reason was that heroin had become more of a problem. Long time fans complained that he was a stoned, heroin zombie for most of the gigs he did do with the Popes. That said, there were some top-notch shows mixed in. It was not unusual for the performances to run hot and cold. That summer MacGowan and the Popes concentrated on outdoor festivals. Ironically they replaced an "ill" Bob Dylan at three festivals in two weeks time. At the "Great Homecoming" open-air concert in Millstreet, County Cork, MacGowan's onstage comments on the political situation in Ireland sparked controversy. Politics in Ireland had been heating up for some time, focusing again on a peace process to bring the "troubles" plaguing Ireland for three decades to an end. When a reporter asked MacGowan about royalties he had donated to The Bannaside Children's Development Agency in Northern Ireland he said, "It helps those kids in the North and the North is very important to me 'cause all this is happening in my country. They're invading our country...I know that's not all there is to it. There's nothing simple about it, but if any other country did what the English are doing there'd be a UN force right in there. I don't know how the UK gets away with it. What I'm doing is no big deal. There's a lot of shit going down up there and there are people trying to do something constructive about it, but I've no faith in those peace talks unless Sinn Fein is involved. I mean it's so absurd to even consider the idea of peace without them. The British Government are being held to ransom by Unionists. They'd probably love to get out. I mean those families don't want bombs going off, they don't want their kids getting killed by the army either."

Although Unionist paramilitary groups in Northern Ireland had joined the IRA in the cease-fire resulting from the Downing Street Declaration, tensions remained. The Unionists wanted the IRA to give up their weapons and disband before they would enter into talks in which Sinn Fein participated. For their part, the IRA never had any intention of disbanding. Despite declaring the cease-fire, the IRA continued gathering intelligence and training volunteers. In rural Clonaslee, County Laois, they turned an old house into a bomb factory. The Provos had every intention of resuming military action if the peace process failed to go as planned.

The English government tried to appease the Unionists by getting the IRA to show some progress towards disarming as a condition for allowing Sinn Fein to continue participating in substantive talks. From the outset, The IRA refused to give up a single bullet until a negotiated settlement was reached. They did agree, however, to disarm when a settlement was agreed upon, providing that settlement included the removal of British troops from Ireland.

The impasse fueled tensions that led to protests. When an angry confrontation nearly got out of hand at Drumcree in July of 1995, it was clear the peace process was faltering. That summer the British government began to re-assess everything that had gone on up until that point. That fall the IRA, sensing a change in the air, decided to resume its military campaign if political progress was not forthcoming. The cease-fire may well have ended before the year was out if Bill Clinton hadn't intervened.

The American President came to Northern Ireland near the end of November. He got both parties to agree to continue negotiations with the help of an International Body lead by George Mitchell, an ex-United States Senator. The International Body would focus on finding a way to continue the peace process while simultaneously pursing IRA disarmament. It was like sticking a finger in the damn. On February 9th, 1996 the IRA declared that the war was back on, underscoring the announcement by bombing the Docklands' Canary Wharf in London. Two civilians died. The peace had lasted just over 17 months. The bombs manufactured in County Laois during the truce were taken off the shelf. In June the Provos destroyed a huge section of downtown Manchester, injuring over 200 people. It was the largest bomb to explode in England since World War II.

When MacGowan began airing his Republican views onstage during the summer of 1997, the renewed IRA military campaign was over a year old, but there was also renewed hope on the horizon. In May general elections were held throughout Great Britain. Sinn Fein did well in Northern Ireland. Increasing its share of the vote to 16%, it became the region's third largest party, winning two seats in Parliament. Gerry Adams and Martin McGuinness were their new MPs. In June Sinn Fein won a seat in the Republic of Ireland's Parliament, its first since the Irish Civil War.

Moreover, there were positive rumors of peace process progress coming out of Stormont, Northern Ireland's Parliament. Sinn Fein, which had been excluded from all talks because of the Provos renewed military campaign, indicated that the IRA was willing to lay down its arms again providing that Sinn Fein was admitted to the Stormont talks without further conditions, and that the talks were given a specific timeframe in which to reach an agreement. Both London and Dublin agreed to those terms, and the IRA announced a renewed cease-fire in July. The larger problem regarding IRA disarmament was, for the time being, resolved by what was dubbed a "twin track process." It provided that the decommissioning of paramilitary arms should take place during, rather than before or after, all-party negotiations. By September Gerry Adams, this time in tandem with Martin McGuinness, sat at the peace table in Stormont Castle.

That fall, anticipating the imminent release of his new album, Shane seemed to be regaining his focus. In late September he was in top form for three sold out shows at Dublin's Mean Fiddler. At the final show he greeted the crowd with "*Dia is Muire Dhuit,*" Gaelic for "May God be with you." He dedicated "Ceilidh Cowboy," a song from the new album, to Terry Woods, the Pogues' most traditional Irish musician. If it had been left up to Woods, the Pogues probably would have never turned from their Irish roots. In November, MacGowan released *The Crock of Gold* on his new label, ZTT Records. Unapologetically stressing an Irish Republican agenda, it is the most nationalist-minded of all MacGowan's recordings.

During the round of press interviews to promote *The Crock of Gold*, McGowan told *The Irish World* that one of his biggest gripes with the Pogues was that they balked when he tried to promote pro-Republican views through the music. He said that he wanted to do more rebel songs, and when the band refused there were angry confrontations. He complained, "They wanted to vote on everything. I couldn't do the kind of music I wanted to perform. They wouldn't let me do it....I hope the peace process (in Ireland) works, but I can see that it will be a long drawn out process. I think it should happen now. The English should get out. We've talked enough, they should let the Irish run their own country. I've always said the Brits have no right to be there. I believe in a Republic, a socialist Republic."

The Crock of Gold's title came from James Stephens' Irish novel of the same name. The book is an account of a philosopher's mythical journey. In his travels he encounters leprechauns who sometimes help and sometimes hinder him. The novel had been a favorite of Shane's since childhood. He painted the album cover, a depiction of the book's leprechauns dancing around a fire. He called them "Malicious fairies from hell." When MacGowan and the Popes first went on the road to support the record a blowup of the cover was used as a backdrop.

"I thought *The Crock of Gold* was a great title for an album," he told the *Irish Post*. "And the album does have that theme. The crock of gold is in Ireland, not over here. It's not a concept album, but it could be viewed as such... It's a comedy album, really. The songs are mainly comical, it's either light-hearted or funny, there's no heavy stuff on there. The crock of gold is a great sort of legend, and when I was in Ireland, living in the old farmhouse, I thought, hey, I've gone round the world looking for it, but the crock of gold was beneath my feet all the time... That's the main reason I called the album *The Crock of Gold*, because it's got a lot of songs about leaving London and going back to Ireland. It's internal. The crock of gold isn't really a crock of gold; it means that at the end of the rainbow there's peace and tranquillity. And the book happens to be one that I really like, a classic of Irish literature."

Before its release MacGowan had said the record was going to be called *The Paddy Album* and that the word Paddy would be in every song title. Paddy is a derogatory term used, especially in London, to mock the Irish. It derives from classic, unusual Irish names like Padraeic. MacGowan's intention was to defuse the insult by claiming it as his own, much like African-American rappers had done with the racial slur nigger. "It's a way of getting the English back for calling all Irishmen 'Paddy,' sticking it up their noses and then rubbing it in the dirt," he explained. "They used to call our music 'Paddy-beat' and 'Paddy-billy'.... If you want Paddy, I'll give you Paddy. At one point, I was hoping to get Paddy in every song title." In the end only three songs on the album used the word in the title.

The album is less electrified than *The Snake*. It makes better use of whistles, fiddles, and accordions than its predecessor did. Its 17 tracks cover several styles of Irish music. MacGowan said at the time that it "got back to the roots... back to pure Irish music." He called it his best work since the third Pogues album, the last one where he felt he had control. "I'm just part of a tradition," he said. "*The Crock of Gold* is my attempt at covering all aspects of Irishness. People still think there's only one type of Irish music. The album takes you through the whole spectrum. There's ceilidh, showband, punk, rock and roll, traditional."

Of the album's seventeen tracks all but two were either written by MacGowan or are traditional numbers arranged by Shane. Of the two, one is a 34 second, Irishy, banjo piece written by the Popes' Tom Macmanamon. The other is an old Lerner and Lowe song called "Wanderin' Star." It features a guest vocal by the late Charlie Maclennan, the long time Pogues roadie who followed Shane when he formed the Popes. It adds very little to the album.

The traditional numbers, all very Irish, fare better. Least notable is "The Spanish Lady." MacGowan's take on the old chestnut, while very enjoyable, brings nothing new to the song. "Come to the Bower" is a sentimental ode to Ireland bursting with references to the island's landscape and heroes.

> Will you come to the Bower
> Over the free boundless ocean
> Where the stupendous waves
> Roll in thundering motion
> Where mermaids are seen
> And the fierce tempest gathers

To love Erin the green
The dear land of our fathers

Sappy and a bit soft around the edges, "Come to the Bower" is sharply contrasted by the final traditional track, "Skipping Rhymes." It's as anti-British as anything MacGowan has ever recorded, but he downplays that. "'Skipping Rhymes'- all it is, is preserving traditional music. It's kids' street rhymes, which I've heard them singing," he says. "I didn't write the words, I overheard them. When you hear little kids singing it, 'First we put a hood around his head, then we shot the bastard dead,' it sends chills up your spine. But I suppose they don't know anything else. It's like 'Ring-a-Ring-a Rosie', which is about the plague, the Black Death in London. No, there's no way I'm trying to get people to go out and kill other people. I mean, it might annoy David Trimble and people like that, but then I suppose David Trimble is not going to listen to the album anyway." If David Trimble ever did listen to *The Crock of Gold*, it's unlikely he listened to "Skipping Rhymes" more than once. Not with the refrain "The nation's gonna rise again" and verses like this:

I shot one, I shot two, I shot three
That's more than you
With a nick nack paddy whack
Give a dog a bone
Send the stupid bastards home

The three songs that conformed to Shane's original plan of putting "Paddy" in every title ("Paddy Rolling Stone," "Rock 'N' Roll Paddy," and "Paddy Public Enemy No. 1") open the album. Naturally, all three are Irish to the core. "Paddy Rolling Stone," complete with its share of "tu-ra-lu-ra-lays," is done to the tune of the traditional "Jug of Punch." Not only does the music rock along much harder than its predecessor does, Shane's lyrics have a good bit more kick to them as well. The traditional song's "pretty wench" has been replaced by a "buxom Irish whore." Instead of "sitting with my glass and spoon," MacGowan "lays blasted in my room." His condition, one would suspect, has been helped along by his "junkie friends" and the gang from "Nenagh town" who, when they're not "howling at the ceilidh moon" pledge to "burn the whole place down." Overall, it's a solid rocker that would go down well in any Irish dance hall. The same can be said for "Rock and Roll Paddy." This song is done to the tune of the traditional "Barnyards of Delgaty." Here, however, the rewritten lyrics are even darker than those of "Paddy Rolling Stone." The singer, who admits to being "the lowest of the low" and "the sickest of the sick," is released first from an asylum and then from prison before being crushed "on the dole." By the song's end he is stalking some men intending to "Rape their women and scare their children, burn them in their brand new cars." When *The Crock of Gold* was released there was some speculation that the album's lyrics limited airplay. If that's true, "Rock and Roll Paddy" may have been a culprit.

"Paddy Public Enemy No. 1" could have been another. Given the peace talks going on in Northern Ireland at the time, the song was bound to raise controversy. Critics called it a tribute to the dead Republican leader "Mad Dog" Dominic McGlinchey. A former IRA gunman and one time leader of the INLA, McGlinchey was for years the most wanted terrorist in Ireland. When he was just 15 years old McGlinchey got involved in Northern Ireland's civil rights movement. Two years later he wound up in Long Kesh Prison where his Republicanism took a militant turn. After serving 11 months without a trial, he was released and immediately joined the IRA. McGlinchey claimed to have been eventually involved in over 200 terrorist operations including 30 killings. In 1993 he was severely wounded in an unsuccessful assassination attempt. The following February the assassins didn't fail. He was shot 14 times in a phone booth in Drogheda as his 16 year-old son watched from the passenger seat of their car. Seven years earlier, almost to the day, the same son and his brother saw their mother gunned down at home as she gave the boys a bath. MacGowan contended that "Paddy Public Enemy No. 1" was not written specifically about McGlinchey. "Yeah, 'Public Enemy' is an outlaw song about an IRA man," he said, "and like all outlaw songs, it ends in his demise, shot by his former allies. It seems to be a recurring story in the topsy-turvy world of the war in Northern Ireland. There does seem to be a lot of shootings and bombings of ex-IRA men. It's not specifically about Dominic McGlinchey, but it was, to a certain extent, inspired by him." It's not surprising that many of Shane's critics didn't buy his explanation since the Republican in his song, like McGlinchey, was at the top of the most wanted list, was in both the IRA and the INLA, and was gunned down in a phone booth.

Two of the album's cuts draw on MacGowan's experience in crossing the Irish Sea. "B&I Ferry" takes its name from the British and Irish Steam Packet Company, a firm that began in Dublin in the 1800s with a fleet of steam powered paddleboats. Lyrically, it's not as strong as "Boat Train," MacGowan's earlier song about ferrying across the sea. Musically, however, it fares very well with its simple but infectious reggae beat. MacGowan's connection to reggae goes way back. "When I was about ten I got into stuff like Desmond Dekker and Horace Faith," he explained. "There are a lot of musical connections between Irish music and reggae. A few old Irish tunes are very close to reggae rhythms, and there's a huge Irish influence in the Caribbean." "Mother Mo Chroi" is MacGowan's most personal song dealing with his recurring theme of the Irish Diaspora. It starts with the day he sailed across the Irish Sea to begin a new life in England. Having been forced "to leave dear old Ireland," he fondly remembers the homeland throughout the song before declaring at the end, "My kids will never scrape shit around here, and I won't be crying in my beer. I'm going back to Ireland and Mother Mo Chroi."

MacGowan finds himself back in London after a trip to the States in "Back in the County Hell." Despite having "missed the smack… the crack" and "the London Irish girls," he seems none too happy to be there. He fantasizes about using glue-sniffing kids to "kill rich Brits" before returning "back home to Nenagh" after doing his "patriotic chore" of burning London to the ground. The driver in "Truck Drivin' Man" is no less dangerous. Hopped up on moonshine, speed, morphine, and methedrine he blows a policeman's arm off with a twelve-gauge shotgun. When the initial blast fails to kill his victim a second shot "blew his guts out thru his back." Finally, for good measure, he puts the gun barrel in the cop's mouth and blows off his head. His personae in "More Pricks than Kicks" and "Ceilidh Cowboy" are not quite as perilous, being more interested in women, drinks, and drugs than in destruction and murder. "More Pricks Than Kicks" (named after a book by Dublin born Samuel Beckett) has the singer dancing and drinking in "country Irish" style and boasting that he can name a bar on any street one might mention. Since *ceilidh* is an Irish word for a big public dance, the wrangler in "Ceilidh Cowboy" can probably do a mean jig as well. He, however, seems far more interested in the ladies than in cutting a rug, bragging "Your women squeal with joy when I get their knickers down" and "fuck them half to death."

Despite the unabashed nasty bent to *The Crock of Gold's* lyrics, it is actually a very listenable, enjoyable album. Its major flaw is that it lacks a Shane MacGowan masterwork. There is nothing in the same league as "Rainy Night in Soho," "The Broad Majestic Shannon," "Sickbed of Cuchulainn," "Body of an American," "Fairytale of New York," "Song with No Name," or "Aisling." One gets the feeling that Shane meant for "Lonesome Highway," a slow ballad, to be *The Crock of Gold's* showstopper. It was released as a single, and he featured it prominently in his live shows for quite some time. Admittedly, MacGowan's vocal is excellent on the track, but the song's lyrics are rather mundane.

On the other hand, it is the simplicity of the lyric that makes "St. John of Gods" an album highlight. The Hospitaller Order of St. John of God is a Catholic group that ministers all over the world to people needing psychiatric care or counseling and therapy. MacGowan spent some time in their Dublin facility. He was involuntarily committed when, depending on who you believe, he indulged in either too much Ecstasy or too much poitín (illegal Irish moonshine). Perhaps it was both. He's called the place "kind of a loony bin for alcoholic nutters." The song is about "a crushed up man" who "doesn't seem to see or care or even understand." Pitiful yet defiant, we see him wielding a broken bottle in a bar room brawl, being beaten up and dragged away by the cops, and ultimately facing his day in court. Through it all, all he can say is "F yez all, F yez all." MacGowan's choice not to put the "F-word" in the drunk's mouth makes the tale all the more realistic and gripping. His defiance in the face of certain defeat is arresting. The song's slow, methodical pace is enhanced with some beautiful accordion lines and a finger picked banjo. MacGowan's vocal is perfect. Overall, "St. John of Gods" is powerful and brilliant in its simplicity.

The Crock of Gold debuted at number 59 on the UK charts. It fell off completely after one week. Poorly promoted in the UK, it wasn't even released in the United

States. The reviews, on either side of the Atlantic, were mixed. "Lonesome Highway," the first single from the album, didn't chart at all.

There is some confusion over why *The Crock of Gold* was not initially released in America. Some say there was concern over some of the lyrics and that concern apparently held back support over here. Those who hold this view are divided over whether the lyrics in question were too favorable to the IRA or too obscene. The latter is improbable since Warner Brothers had no problem with *The Snake's* "Donegal Express." Others say Shane's British label, ZTT, heard through the grapevine that he wanted to leave ZTT so they didn't look for a stateside label to handle his new release. Warner Brothers confirmed that it was ZTT and not them that showed no interest in an agreement to distribute *The Crock of Gold* in America. Other labels, Rykodisc for example, were also interested in doing business, but ZTT never negotiated a deal.

MacGowan and the Popes kept a busy schedule the rest of the year, playing in support of the album throughout the UK. The shows were very good, but of course Shane was better on some nights than on others. As usual he tore up Glasgow and Dublin. He also did a particularly good set at the Alleycat in Reading, but the tour was not without incident.

In Newcastle Shane was very late. The impatient, increasingly rowdy crowd threw bottles and glasses onstage in frustration while they waited for him to make it to the stage. In Manchester he was not that lucky. When MacGowan arrived, a bit shaky on his feet and over an hour late, angry fans shouted abuse and pelted him with plastic cups, most of them empty. An officer at the venue said, "He was barely able to speak, although when he eventually did start singing everyone was happy enough. But when people were kept waiting there was a near riot. A plastic glass hit him but he didn't seem to notice or care much."

MacGowan was even more unlucky in Liverpool. After the show he was arrested in his dressing room and spent a night in jail. A man who was in the audience had called the police complaining that he had been hit in the face by a microphone stand that Shane hurled into the crowd. The Liverpool police reported, "He spent the night in custody and was released at around 1:00 PM the following day. He's got to come back to St Anne's Street police station on January 21. It was alleged he'd thrown a mike stand into the crowd causing injury to a man." Shane admitted throwing the stand into the audience but said it hit the man by mistake.

By the end of the year MacGowan's luck improved considerably. A little crock of gold came his way. Aer Lingus, in a nice tie in with MacGowan's continuing fascination with emigration and the Irish abroad, featured Shane in an ad campaign launched during the holidays. There was a series of print ads where his face took up most of the page. The text touted the advantages of flying Aer Lingus to America, adding, "especially if you've got a reputation."

In January an album of Yeats poetry set to music was released featuring Shane doing "An Irish Airman Foresees His Death" set to an Irish jig. That March Shane's recording of "She Moved Through the Fair" was used in a Kilkenny beer commercial while MacGowan and the Popes reeled off a superb series of shows. Beginning in England and Holland, the tour ended up in Ireland with Shane giving some of the best performances of his career. He was outstanding at the Point in Dublin and even better at the Cork Opera House. His best show, however, could have been in the 1,000 seat Shinrone Community Hall just east of Borrisokane, the closest town to Carney Commons. The crowd were at least as well into their cups as Shane, and they loved it. Shane's dad Maurice MacGowan was there that night and seemed to enjoy talking with the fans that besieged him.

That Spring the BBC released *The Great Hunger*, a documentary about Shane MacGowan directed by Mike Connelly. It portrayed him as a troubled genius in the Irish tradition of Brendan Behan. Shane wasn't too happy with the film. "*The Great Hunger* is crap," he said when it came out. "It's a load of old po-faced BBC pathological rubbish...can't understand why anyone'd be interested, to be honest. They didn't get anything on me. I keep all my cards close to my chest, me. And all those nice words from people like Christy and that ...they're all good friends of mine, but they don't know the inner workings of my soul, so how revealing can it be?" He said that he only co-operated with the film makers for the money. Surprisingly, he wasn't as much annoyed that he was filmed drunk, often barely coherent, as he was that his girlfriend Victoria and his parents were on camera as much as they were. Overall, the documentary came across as very sympathetic. He was shown to be an alcoholic, perhaps even a tragic figure, but none the less a major figure in Irish art and culture. It raised his profile considerably and conferred further legitimacy on him.

The documentary took its title from a MacGowan song called "The Dunes." A highlight of the film came at the conclusion when Ronnie Drew sang the song acapella. Many MacGowan fans had never heard the song since he had never released a recording of it himself. That is unfortunate. It is one of the most powerful things he has ever written. It's about the people of County Mayo burying victims of the 19th century potato famine in sand dunes on the beaches. "I was up there, near Louisburgh, when I was about 18 or 19 with some mates and I heard the story about people burying their dead there on the beach during the Famine times," he told the *Irish Times*. "They had no earth to bury their dead. Think of it. The place was eerie, the atmosphere was kind of foul, dank . . . all these bones lying about. I'll never forget the place...It was one of the grimmest places I've been, and the bleakest feeling I've had. I used to think about it a lot. They are gone now, the dunes, they got blown away in a storm a few years back. When I wrote the song they were still there, though." In April Shane's manager, Joey Cashman, told the press that Shane was working "like a man possessed" on a volume of short stories. He said, "They're all like Charles Bukowski mini-stories, an extension of his song lyrics if you like." Nothing was ever published.

On April 10th a Northern Ireland peace treaty, the Good Friday Peace Agreement, was signed in Belfast. It was approved by popular vote in May. It was a complicated

agreement with several goals. For one, it provided a plan for a more inclusive government in Northern Ireland, and one that would gradually transfer power from London to Belfast. It created a 108-member Assembly and 14-member executive body in
which both Catholic and Protestant political representatives would govern together.
It was only the second provision for power sharing since 1920, the first being the ill-
fated Sunningdale Agreement 25 years before. Various commissions were established to
devolve British involvement in Northern Ireland. The agreement also provided for the
conditional early release of Irish political prisoners. This was to take place within two
years, but was tied to Republican organizations adhering to a cease-fire, and the IRA's
co-operation in decommissioning their weapons. Moreover, the treaty set guidelines
for the possibility of a future 32 county Ireland. The guidelines prescribed "exclusively
peaceful and democratic means." The status of Northern Ireland could not change without a majority vote of its people. In addition, the Irish Republic had to abandon its territorial claim to the six counties of Northern Ireland. Specifically, the Republic had to
change articles two and three of its 1937 constitution, which stated that "The national
territory consists of the whole island of Ireland, its islands and territorial seas." The
amended articles recognized "the entitlement and birthright of every person born on
the island of Ireland, which includes its islands and seas, to be part of the Irish Nation,"
with the caveat that it is "the firm will of the Irish Nation...to unite all the people who
share the territory of the island of Ireland...recognizing that a united Ireland will be
brought about only by peaceful means with the consent of a majority of the people,
democratically expressed, in both jurisdictions in the island." Put simply, if more than
half of the people of Northern Ireland wanted to join the Republic, England would let
them go, providing that more than half the people in the Irish Republic would have
them. Only 56% of voters in the South went to the polls to vote on the referendum to
amend the constitution and comply with the Good Friday Agreement. It passed with
a whopping 94% of the vote. In Northern Ireland, where the agreement stirred more
controversy, turnout was an impressive 81% of eligible voters. There the agreement
was approved more narrowly with a 56% affirmative result.

The same week, while the political talks in Belfast were going on, MacGowan's
political views made headlines, most of them unfavorable. The *Sunday World's* account
ran under this banner, "Wild MacGowan praises killer 'Mad Dog': Rock star sparks
political row at top awards do." The fuss was over comments Shane made at the Hot
Press Music Awards, Ireland's equivalent of the Grammy's, held in Belfast's Europa
Hotel. Receiving an award for being the quintessential Irish Rover, MacGowan dedicated it to the best known Sinn Fein negotiators, Martin McGuinness and Gerry Adams.
The writer, clearly not a MacGowan fan, called Shane Ireland's "ugliest man" and "a
rock star with an alcoholic past," and went on to report that "later, off camera and
out of earshot of the star-studded audience, he eulogized multiple murderer Dominic
McGlinchey, the former leader of the Irish National Liberation Army. Two years ago," it
continued, "McGlinchey was gunned down in Drogheda. He was a renowned terrorist

who murdered dozens of people in a bloody reign of terror." The piece concluded by saying that "McGowan sparked a walkout among those attending the rock awards when he described Mad Dog McGlinchey as one of his heroes."

Despite having been passed with 94% of the vote in the Irish republic, the Good Friday Agreement was seen by some members of the IRA as a betrayal of the Republican struggle for a united 32 county Ireland. Dissidents within the Provisional Irish Republican Army, which had co-operated with and endorsed the negotiations, split from the group and formed the Real Irish Republican Army (RIRA). Their goal was to undermine the peace process through what they called a military campaign. Everyone else called it terrorism.

Their first attempt came in early January of 1998 in Banbridge, County Down. They planted a 300 pound car bomb which was discovered and difused by authorities. The RIRA successfully detonated a car bomb in Banbridge that summer. Two weeks later, on August 15th, they were responsible for killing 29 people with a car bomb in Omagh, County Tyrone, Northern Ireland. Over 220 people were injured. It was the single worst terrorist attack in 30 years of "troubles." The tradgedy was condemned by leaders worldwide, including Sinn Fein's Good Friday Agreement negotiators, Martin McGuinness and Gerry Adams.

That afternoon a maroon Vauxhall Cavalier, which had been stolen in County Monaghan a few days earlier, had been loaded with 500 pounds of explosives. The RIRA intended to park it in front of Omagh's courthouse. Unfortunately, the closest parking spot they could find was about 400 meters down the street in front of a clothing store in an area crowded with Saturday shoppers. Three telephone calls were made that day warning of the blast. The warnings, which were probably intended to lessen casualties, were vague and confusing. The final phone call was made around 3:00 PM, shortly before the bomb went off. The police, in an attempt to clear the area around the courthouse, unintentionally herded people closer to the maroon Vauxhall. The carnage was terrible and indiscriminate. Among the dead were Irish Catholics, Irish Protestants, and foreign tourists. Nine children died. So did a woman pregnant with twins. Survivors suffered severed limbs, traumatic head injuries, and horrific burns.

The RIRA paid a price for the atrocity. The group was roundly condemned throughout Ireland and around the world. Moreover, the bombing at Omagh caused a wave of revulsion that rallied support around the negotiated peace process the attack was intended to derail. Even the Irish National Liberation Army, which was also opposed to the Good Friday Agreement, called a ceasefire in their campaign against the British government. Families of those killed in the Omagh bombing filed a civil lawsuit against the RIRA and several of its members suspected of having taken part in the attack. It took over a decade, but in June of 2009 four of those members (Michael McKevitt, Liam Campbell, Colm Murphy and Seamus Daly) were found responsible for the bombing and held liable for nearly $2.5 million in damages.

Against that summer's volatile political backdrop, MacGowan and the Popes played mainly outdoor festivals, including the first ever United States Fleadah, scheduled for four cities: New York, Boston, Chicago, and Los Angeles. Sponsored by Guinness, the Fleadh booked over 30 acts: Van Morrison, Elvis Costello, Wilco, Billy Bragg, Sinead O'Conner, Lucinda Williams, Paul Brady, John Martyn, the Saw Doctors, Alejandro Escovedo, Richard Thompson, Nanci Griffith, Lonnie Donegan, Altan, Liam Clancy, Tommy Makem, John Lee Hooker, and the Pretenders were all on the bill. Being an Irish music festival (despite the few American acts) sponsored by Ireland's premiere beer company, it's not surprising that MacGowan was the highlight for most of the 30,000 or so people that attended each show. In each city he headlined one of the three stage areas and packed it out. Although Morrison missed the Boston show, in New York, Chicago, and Los Angeles Shane was onstage at the same time as Morrison and Costello, outdrawing them every night.

Shane didn't disappoint the crowds. His Fleadah performances were usually on the money. He was, after all, really in his element. He explained the concept of the Fleadah like this. "That's what they call it when the towns back in Ireland get together to play music, dance, drink and celebrate life…As for these touring ones, they started in London, and they're a great way to spread Irish music around the world. I've played about 20 at least, and the audiences love them because they know it's irresistible dance music. Not like synthesizers and drum machines, but in the real traditional dancing sense…The Fleadah has become a wide-angled thing," he continued, referring to the stateside festival's diverse bill. "Besides, Irish music has very wide angles itself. It's been around for years. I mean, it's older than Christ, so along the way there have been many different styles coming off it."

That summer Shane's sister, Siobahn MacGowan, released her own album, *Chariot*. Siobahn had been involved in the music industry for some time. She had worked for the Pogues in various capacities and traveled with Van Morrison throughout the United States and Europe as his personal assistant. She took her first shot at making her own music in 1988 in Dublin with a band she formed called The Frantic. They performed her songs in clubs in the capital and on one tour throughout Ireland, but they never made any real headway. *Chariot* got off to a promising start, garnering some excellent reviews. The music sounded nothing like Shane's. There was no Irish folk feel to it. Most critics called the songs, all of them originals, "atmospheric." The disc was pleasant enough, and very listenable, but ultimately it sold poorly.

For the rest of the decade MacGowan kept a relatively low profile. The press, however, kept up an interest in him, but it was mainly to report on his self-destructive ways. His notoriety for missing gigs began to surpass the reputation of cancellation king George Jones. There were rumors of a new double album, but nothing was ever released. He and the Popes continued to play but at a less hectic pace. There were always short tours around St. Patrick's Day and in the Christmas season and festivals in the summer. Mick O'Connell joined the Popes on accordion near the end of the year adding a great deal to the band's Irish sound. As the century came to a close many things remained the same. MacGowan was still on the stage, the British were still on the Emerald Isle, and Shane still wasn't afraid to let people know how he felt about it. He seemed less than enthused about the prospects for the new century. "Fuck the millennium," he growled. "It's just another year, y'know? Another year the Brits are in Northern Ireland. When's it gonna end?" In a particularly good Christmas season show at the Forum in London, he chided his English fans repeatedly. In the introduction to "Paddy Public Enemy No. 1" MacGowan told an anti-British joke about a new school curriculum in Northern Ireland. When he finished "Skipping Rhymes" he shouted at the audience, "It's your' fuckin' government and your fuckin' army."

As he faced the new millenium Shane MacGowan was confronted with one concern more personal than Irish politics. In November, his lingering problem with heroin came to a head. Sinead O'Conner turned Shane in to the police for heroin possession when he snorted the drug in front of her while she was visiting him in his flat. He only had a small amount but admitted possessing the drug to police and was arrested. O'Conner, who had recently become Mother Bernadette, a sort of Catholic priestess, said at the time, "I love Shane and it makes me angry to see him destroy himself selfishly in front of those who love him." MacGowan denied that he was addicted to heroin. In response to O'Connor's action he said, "I might as well clear up the fact that she's made out I was lying on the floor in a coma, whereas in fact I was sitting on the sofa having a G and T and watching a Sam Peckinpah movie, *Cross of Iron*." Shane later told the media that O'Conner turned him in because she wanted to generate publicity for herself, a charge she denies. "I reported him to the police for his own good," she said. "I never wanted him put into prison, because drugs are freely available there, but ordered into a rehabilitation program." MacGowan didn't show for his first court date at Highbury Magistrate Court. The charges were dropped in March 2000.

"Hell, I only drink so much so people won't think I'm a dope fiend."

Willie Nelson

As the new millenium started, Shane MacGowan had not released an album of new material in over two years, and as it turned out, wouldn't for the remainder of the decade. Despite the creative drought, he managed to stay in the public eye. The media was obsessed with MacGowan, not for his music, but for his uncompromising lifestyle. Having outlived the frequent predictions of death by substance abuse, MacGowan's constitution had taken on a near mythical status. A tongue in cheek Irish travelogue which actually had little to do with him was published with the title *Is Shane MacGowan Still Alive?*

While MacGowan was able to defy predictions of his demise, a number of his friends had not been so fortunate. An article in the March 26, 2000, *Sunday Independent* entitled "Death in Shane's Orbit" referenced three MacGowan friends who died as a direct result of substance abuse: Robbie O'Neill, Brian Ging, and Dave Jordan. O'Neal and Ging actually died in Shane's flat.

O'Neill was the son of Terry O'Neill, the Pogues' former publicist. Robbie had once worked for Vince Power as a soundman in the Irish music mogul's various venues. That experience, and just being his father's son, kept O'Neill around the music business for most of his life. In the early part of 1999 he quit working for Power. Newly unemployed, he took up MacGowan's offer to live rent free in Shane's flat at 82 Savernake Road, Gospel Oak, in North London.

Given O'Neill's connection to the music business, it's little surprise that he dabbled in drugs. Friends say, however, that he did not do heroin. No doubt they were surprised when he died of a heroin overdose in MacGowan's apartment on May 17, 1999. Speculation was that he snorted a line of heroin believing it was cocaine. He quickly fell into a coma and was dead within the hour. The coroner said that since rigor mortise had already set in, O'Neill must have been dead a few hours before the ambulance was called. The postmortem report revealed that he had taken four times the lethal dose of heroin, but since there was no heroin detected in his urine, he couldn't have been a heroin addict. That was little consolation to his family.

Terry O'Neill, who considered himself a friend of MacGowan's, was particularly upset that Shane didn't attend the inquest, sending a written statement instead. "On Monday May 17 between midnight and 2:00 AM Robbie came home and he was happy and he was messing about," Shane's account read. "We chatted and watched a video, *The Wild Bunch*. I went to bed because I was tired. Robbie was still awake. I slept for 22 hours as I was awake two days [previously] wrestling and trying to do work. Then

Robbie seemed happy enough, mucking about. On Tuesday, May 18, at around 1:00 AM I woke up and found Robbie in the living room. I thought he was asleep and I tried to wake him up but he did not respond. I could not see him breathing and noted that he felt cold. I tried to move him but he was stiff."

The *Independent* quoted Terry O'Neill as saying, "I don't believe Shane's statement. It's a disgrace that he did not have the courtesy to come here (to the inquest) himself." O'Neill felt there were unanswered questions surrounding the tragedy that Shane could have cleared up at the inquest. His skepticism arose in part because one of his son's friends insisted that he spoke with MacGowan during the 22-hour period Shane claimed to have been asleep. "On the night of his death I rang Shane McGowan's place to make contact, because I had not seen him (O'Neill) since before the weekend," the friend said. "The time was about 10:50 PM. When I asked him where Robbie was he replied, 'Robbie? No. No he's not here, he's not here. I saw him yesterday.' I asked him to leave a message that I had called, and he said quickly, 'Yeah, yeah.'"

The *Independent* article included Shane's response. "I did not have to turn up at Robbie O'Neill's inquest," he said. "I went to the police and they told me that I would have to give a statement, but I did not have to turn up. I use heroin only very occasionally. To be honest I prefer poitín to heroin, and poitín is illegal. There would be nothing about this except Sinéad O'Connor went around to the police and hassled them all day. I know the police, all the young guys are fans. I got no favors, they had to do their job. But they knew the score and that's why I got off with a caution. I did not have to turn up at Highbury court... I do not know what got into her [Sinéad]; she was ranting and raving about me being in a coma, and all these paramedics arrived. It was a waste of their time. I was pissed but I wasn't in a coma.

"I don't want heroin in my place. My place is my place, I don't want any of this shit [heroin] in my house. I told Robbie that he could do drink and dope. I mean I was doing him a favor. I put him up and he didn't have to pay rent. He came in and he said he was stoned on heroin. I was pissed off and told him, 'you idiot, don't do it again.' I went to bed and slept for a long, long time. There could have been phone calls but I don't answer the phone in my sleep. The phone was in the sitting room, but it is a big flat, you would have to shout to get someone's attention on the other side of the room. I was sound asleep. I can't recall any calls. If I was on the phone, I was on the phone to God."

Robbie O'Neill was not the first MacGowan acquaintance to die in Shane's home. In July of 1995, Dublin born Brian "Ginger" Ging overdosed on a combination of alcohol and morphine in MacGowan's flat on Blackstock Road in North London. Ging had been a regular hanger-on around the Dublin and London music scenes since the 1970s. In the 1980s he endeared himself to the Pogues, particularly MacGowan. The friendship continued after Shane went on to form the Popes.

Details on the incident are sketchy at best. According to hospital and police records, an ambulance was dispatched to the house in response to an emergency phone call. Ging was found dead on the floor, propped up against a chest of drawers. A paramedic said there were two other men in the flat, both of whom "seemed to be under the influence of drugs or alcohol or both." Apparently, neither of the men said much as the body went unidentified for several days. North London police stopped by the flat several times over the next few days but nobody ever came to the door. They also left notes but received no replies. The police finally traced the number from the emergency phone call made the night of Ging's death. They found it had come from the home where the body was found and that Shane MacGowan resided there. Evidently, the police gave the phone number to Anne Sheridan, a friend of Ging. She called the number and whoever answered the phone affirmed that MacGowan did live there but was not home. MacGowan didn't make Ging's inquest either. Shane's comments on the incident were included in the *Independent* article.

"I remember Bryan Ging," Shane began. "He was a multi-drug user. This night I met him in a pub and he came back to the flat later. You know how a crowd goes back after the pub closes; to drink, listen to music and chat. At one stage someone said that Ging was not looking too well. He was like crashed out. They noticed but I didn't notice. I mean Ginger always looked dead. We tried to wake him up but he was not responding. So we called an ambulance to the house. They came in and carried him out on a stretcher. I heard he died a few hours later, 'cause we rang up the hospital. I didn't know any of his relatives so how could I tell them? Nobody else knew his family. I didn't attend his inquest, 'cause I was busy at the time. I mean I loved the guy and I was one of the few people who did like him. A lot of people thought he was a prick; you know, he could tell a good story, like Behan, but you know the way people think of those characters as obnoxious. Bryan was a larger-than-life character. I liked him because he used to cheer me up. I was very upset about his death. It's a tragedy. I am beginning to feel that a lot of people are dying in my flat. There was this other guy, but he died of alcoholic poisoning. He was our lighting man. Big into drink, not drugs. Yeah, he died too."

Four months earlier, Dave Jordan, the Popes soundman and producer of *The Snake*, died in a Paris hotel room while on tour with MacGowan and the Popes. While the tour promoter was dealing with the police, Shane and the rest of the band packed up and left for London. The *Independent* article was critical of Shane for leaving Paris without contacting authorities, contending that he could have expedited the return of Jordan's body to England by providing pertinent information. In the end, some of Jordan's friends enlisted the British Embassy's help to get Jordan home. Shane told *The Independent*, "Dave Jordan, the sound engineer, died in a hotel in Paris while we were on tour. Yeah, I think it was an overdose of heroin. It's all too depressing. He died suddenly while on tour. But I really don't want to discuss it. All these people... but most people that worked with The Pogues and The Popes are still alive. I am still alive and I think I am in good shape. I drink to relax but not to get drunk. I am a slow drinker, not a desperate drinker."

The Independent article failed to mention the death of two other MacGowan friends who had worked with him on the road. Paul Verner, the Pogues' lighting man, drank himself to death. Cirrhosis of the liver took him shortly after MacGowan left the band. Charlie Maclennan, who had been with the Pogues from the earliest days, died after joining the Popes' road crew. Officially, MacLennan died of a heart attack, but Joey Cashman pulled no punches in attributing the heart failure to drug abuse. According to Cashman, "Charlie got a huge amount of heroin and cocaine and he put out these massive lines, and that's what really killed him." The first of MacGowan's bandmates to die was Popes' banjo player Tom McManamon. He passed away on December 15, 2006, "after a long battle with illness." The "illness" was exacerbated if not caused by years of substance abuse.

In February Shane became the first Irishman to be satirized in *VIZ* magazine. In a comic strip titled "The Adventures of Little Shane McGowan" (sic) the magazine gave his drink and drug consumption a pass but lampooned his notoriously bad teeth. The cartoon depicts Little Shane frustrating his mother's attempts to get him to practice good oral hygiene, chomping away at big bags of gobstoppers, candy floss, and pouring cola over bowls of curly-wurleys. When his teeth rot, Shane visits a new dentist: blind Stevie Wonder. Wonder finds no cavities, and this good report prompts Little Shane's mom to reward him with a huge bag of sweets.

That same month MacGowan checked into the $600.00 per day Priory Clinic for what was to be a two-week detoxification program. It wasn't his first trip to the clinic, nor would it be his last. His previous visits ended with him being thrown out for various indiscretions including having booze in his room and threatening a nurse. He didn't fare any better this time and was asked to leave after "a few sharp words" with the staff. He told reporters that he wasn't terribly impressed with the Priory. "It had a love cross outside, it was full of priests. They were buggering each other," he said, adding that he stayed sober "as long as it took to get to the nearest bar."

MacGowan continued to play gigs with the Popes, but not enough for their liking. Like the Pogues before them, Shane's new band couldn't afford to stay home and live off royalties. In March they released their own album, *Holloway Boulevard* and began booking dates in support of it. MacGowan was a guest on the album, co-writing three songs: "Pump Action Paddy," "Jukebox," and "Chino's Place." He also did the vocal on "Chino's Place." The Popes, for their part, realized their bread and butter was still being Shane MacGowan's back-up band. They played when Shane was willing and worked their own gigs around his schedule. That spring MacGowan and the Popes played a few European festivals. At a show in Smithfield, Ireland, MacGowan joined George Harrison and Donovan to perform "Raglan Road" and "Dirty Old Town."

Meanwhile, slowly but surely, the provisions of the Good Friday Peace Agreement were moving forward. On July 28th Maze Prison, known to locals as Long Kesh, was officially closed. It had been opened in 1971 on a Royal Air Force airfield, about 10 miles west of Belfast, to house political prisoners arrested under Britain's internment policy. At one time it held over 1,700 inmates. The site of the hunger strikes and the Blanket Men's "dirty protest," Long Kesh was to Irish Catholics what Abu Ghraib is to Iraqi Muslims. As part of the Good Friday Agreement, nearly 430 political prisoners were released, 143 of which were serving life sentences. Among those being freed were Sean Kelly and James McArdle. Kelly was convicted of planting the Shankill Road fish shop bomb that killed 10 people in 1993. McArdle was imprisoned for the Dockland's Canary Wharf bombing in London in 1996. While the vast majority of those released were Republicans, not all were. Loyalist Michael Stone was among those freed. He had killed six Catholics, three of them during his solo gun and grenade attack on a 1988 IRA funeral in Belfast's Milltown Cemetery. When he was freed he told the media, "I realize those in the Nationalist and Republican community will view my release with anger. In a similar way the Loyalist community will be saddened and angered at the Republican prisoners who will be released. But times do move on and now we need to support the peace process. My war is over." Apparently he meant over for now. In November of 2006 he was arrested for breaking into the Stormont Parliament buildings and attempting to murder Martin McGuinness and Gerry Adams. In December of the following year he was convicted and sentenced to 16 years.

Before the year ended MacGowan was back in the recording studio doing a guest vocal on a Dropkick Murphy's album. He sang "Good Rats," a song about the Guinness brewery. He also did two short North American tours with the Popes. Bootlegs of most of those shows were widely circulated. Generally, MacGowan was very good when he finally made it to the stage. He was always late, however, very late (three and a half hours late at the House of Blues in Los Angeles). Worse yet, his tendency to not show up at all was getting worse. He missed shows in Vancouver and Seattle. The night after a cancellation in Dallas, Shane and the Popes played La Zona Rosa in Austin, Texas. When he walked on stage that night he addressed the crowd in a Southern drawl saying, "Hello, San Francisco! I hope there's no Mexicans or niggers out there," and laughed adding "I hope everyone checked their guns at the door." Naturally, the comment caused some controversy. Some called Shane a racist because of the comments. His defenders believed he was trying to be funny by mocking the American obsession with political correctness. In any case, he did a good show that night.

Things began to get ugly at a show in Philadelphia. The opening act was through by 9:00 PM. At 11:30 MacGowan still hadn't appeared. The crowd was getting impatient. Several fans started chanting "asshole, asshole" and pelted the stage with drinks. A lot of pushing and shoving was going on in the pit. People at the front of the stage were getting crushed by the crowd behind them even though there was no band onstage. For awhile it looked like a riot was a real possibility. The club's management closed the bar for security reasons, and that didn't make the fans any happier. By midnight the crowd was furious, getting uglier and more violent by the minute. One fan jumped on the stage, grabbed a microphone, and started cursing the absent MacGowan before a security guard drug him off. A few minutes after midnight the Popes' guitarist, Paul McGuinness, came out and said, "Look, Shane's not in the building right now. It looks like he's not going to be here." The crowd responded with a barrage of cups, some full, some not. Standing his ground, McGuinness continued, "Look, the rest of us are here. Do you want us to play for half an hour? We'd be happy to if that'll make you shut the fuck up." Some in the audience cheered, some booed, and the Popes began to play a MacGowanless set.

Around half past midnight a roadie came out of the wings and spoke into McGuinness' ear. "Guess what?" the guitarist reported, "He's fucking here!" The crowd went wild as an unshaven, pale, sweaty MacGowan, looking dazed and confused, shuffled out in a stained shirt and crumpled suit. One reporter said Shane looked like he had just been sick and might be ready to heave again. With a drink in one hand and a cigarette in the other, he wobbled to the mike as the band broke into "If I Should Fall from Grace with God." Remarkably, MacGowan launched into the song transformed and went on to give an outstanding performance.

For the rest of the year Shane made a few more aborted trips to the Priory Clinic and performed occasionally. He ended the year in the UK with the usual round of Christmas season shows. In London, on a rainy night, in Soho of all places, Spider Stacy's new band was the opening act. Stacy sat in on whistle and some vocals for about half of Shane's set.

Sometime in 2000 MacGowan did something he had wanted to do for a long while. He moved back to the old home place in Carney Commons, Tipperary. Two years earlier Shane had told *Rock and Reel* he was going to make the move soon. "Ireland's my home," he said, "it always was. I love getting on the boat. It makes me happy. In all my school holidays I used to go back. I left school at the age of fourteen and I'd work for about six months over here, to make money to go back. Then I'd come back over here for nightlife. I never lost contact with Ireland, even when we were touring the world...I go home as often as I can. But at the moment I haven't made enough money to go home permanently. The record company is here, the agents are here, most of the gigs are here. But I hate living in England. It's a horrible country."

Back in Carney Commons, MacGowan quickly settled into the quiet, country life. He'd walk down the road to Ryan's, the nearest pub, for a pint. He was said to be writing quite a bit about one of his primary passions, Irish history. His focus was on the Blueshirts, a right wing group active in the 1930s, which began as part of the Army Comrades Association (ACA). During the period leading up to World War II there was considerable, if unfounded, concern that the group intended a fascist takeover of Ireland. Hitler had his Brownshirts, Mussolini had his Blackshirts, and O'Duffy had his Blueshirts. Moreover, the Blueshirts had adopted the Roman salute, raising the right arm in the air at a 45-degree angle, as the Nazis did. Eoin O'Duffy, their leader, fought with the IRA in the Irish Revolution, eventually rising to Chief of Staff. In the subsequent Irish Civil War, O'Duffy was a general in the Free State Army. He eventually became a prominent member of the Free State government. When De Valera booted him out of his position as Irish Police Commissioner in 1933, O'Duffy took over the ACA and galvanized opposition to the IRA's socialist leanings. The Blueshirts clashed frequently with the IRA, politically and physically. De Valera eventually outlawed the Blueshirts. MacGowan started work on a historical novel based on O'Duffy. MacGowan also wrote songs. "The last song that I wrote is a sad little ballad called 'Little Irish Blue Shirt Boy,'"he said at the time. "It is a haunting ballad. It is about a broken hearted mother worrying as she sows the patch onto the blue shirt of her little Irish Blue Shirt boy as he is going out to defend what he believes in." Shane also visited with his parents in nearby Silvermines village. He talked about starting a herd of wild horses. He gave interviews to the *Guardian*, the local paper in Nenagh. "This is the only fixed address that I have ever had," he told the paper. "I will stay here for the rest of my life. This has always been my home. However far I wander this is where I belong. This is my home, this is the only place where I ever lived in and it is where I am living now and it is the last place that I will ever live."

MacGowan liked the peace and quiet, but apparently not all the time. Perhaps the sight of Carney Commons' unused dance floor irked him. Nearly every small, rural, Irish community used to have an outdoor wooden dance floor built for summer *ceilidhs*. Dance and music were so important to the people of Carney Commons, they had made their dance floor out of concrete. By the time Shane had moved back home it had been long neglected and grown over with brush. At one point he had his home phone number published in the *Guardian* and asked people to contact him if they were interested in helping him put on "acid house hooleys" in the field behind his house. "It will be like the spirit of punk," he said. "Anyone can just turn up and DJ or whatever. You don't have to have a fucking degree in music. I am doing this because I am bored shitless waiting for somebody else to do it. If Geldof wants to make a difference to the starving millions, he should have saved the money on the four album set of his greatest stuff he just put out. He's always been fucking slagging Ireland. I don't think Ireland is a fucking banana republic! It is a community thing that kept rural Ireland going for years when there were hard times and not a lot of money but you could always go out dancing and drinking. Ireland wasn't about how rich you could get or how many houses you could buy. We can get to enjoying ourselves again. Apart from America and London, Ireland is becoming one of the dullest places you can go. The committees and the town councils are taking over. I am excited about this! Everybody in Ireland just can't sit on their arses counting their money and ripping each other off, do you know what I mean?"

Perhaps the thing that MacGowan enjoyed most about moving back to Tipperary was the success of Tipperary's hurling team. Hurling, the oldest field game in Europe, is said to have been played in Ireland in one form or another for nearly 2,000 years. Apart from MacGowan's reference to the game in "The Broad Majestic Shannon," few outside Ireland are familiar with it. The game is similar to field hockey, but a player can pick up the ball with the stick (called a hurley) and carry it in his hand for four steps. Then if he bounces it on the ground he can carry the ball another four steps. A player is allowed two hand-carries per possession, and he can also run while balancing the hurley ball on the hurley. The goal posts are a cross between rugby and soccer goals. Tipperary has a rich tradition of great hurling teams, having won the All Ireland Championship regularly in the late 19th century. In what could well be the most famous hurling match of all time, Tipperary beat Wexford in the 1899 All Ireland Hurling Final. That Tipperary team was mostly from a little village called Horse & Jockey, named after the pub that the village grew up around. The Horse and Jockey was a favorite of Theobald Wolfe Tone, the legendary Irish rebel. He was a regular there in the 1790s. Shortly after MacGowan moved back to Carney Commons, Tipperary won the McCarthy Cup (the All-Ireland Hurling championship) by beating Galway. Some fans wrote a song called "The Sons of Knockagow" celebrating the Tipperary hurling tradition. An article in the *Guardian* featured a picture of Shane holding a hurling stick and wearing a Tipperary hurling jersey. John Quirke, one of the song's writers, claimed Shane was recording the record's B-side and that he and Shane were working on an album together. Neither the B-side nor the album ever materialized.

In February of 2001 there was a new round of speculation in the press concerning MacGowan's health. It started with a review in the *Irish Mirror* of Shane's gig at Eamon Doran's pub in Temple Bar, Dublin. McGowan had been spotted drinking in Bloom's Hotel on several nights in the days leading up to the concert and a source close to Shane was quoted as saying he feared that "Shane was slipping back into his old boozing ways," adding, "He looks like an ill man. Anyone can see that." The night of the show, as usual, Shane was late. He didn't take the stage until two in the morning. The *Mirror's* reviewer said MacGowan "looked haggard... had dark rings under his eyes...looked the worse for wear... had put on a lot of weight," and "looked tired and unwell." His description was reinforced by an incredibly unflattering picture of Shane taken at the concert. In Shane's defense, he had just finished a show at Dublin College's annual ball earlier the same night. Despite his appearance, most fans at the show agreed that MacGowan chain-smoked his way through a terrific hour long set in Doran's pub.

In March MacGowan and the Popes flew back to the States for a two-month tour. He missed the first gig at the Vanderbilt, a large club in Long Island, New York. There were rumors that once again he wasn't allowed on the plane, but others claimed he had been seen drinking all night in a bar called The Irish Rover in Queens. He also missed a scheduled show in Pittsburgh. The club owner there said Shane's people called her at 8:30 the night of the gig to say that he was still in New York but that he might be able to make it sometime after midnight. She told them not to bother. Shane was also booked to play New York's annual Bartender's Ball at 10:00 PM the night after St. Patrick's Day. He didn't show up until 2:30 in the morning, long after most of crowd had gone home. At Chicago's Vic Theater two weeks later, MacGowan put on a good show despite having puked on stage as he finished "Sally MacLennane." The fans didn't mind a bit. After cleaning up the mess, a roadie threw the nasty towel into the audience, who promptly began fighting over it. MacGowan took it all in stride. "It wasn't unpleasant," he said. "I just did it and carried on. In the early days with the Pogues a lot of us used to puke onstage, because we used to drink a helluva lot before we went on. We used to practice puking at the right time, you know, 'Where's the stop?' Between words, you know what I mean? Or in-between a chorus and a verse."

In May, on the anniversary of Bobby Sands' death, MacGowan and the Popes did a concert in Northern Ireland. It coincided with the beginning of two months of violence in the streets. Northern Orangemen marked the Sands' anniversary with a rally protesting the government's decision to ban them from parading down the predominantly Catholic Drumcree Road. Parades had long been a sore point between Protestants and Catholics. During the marching season from Easter Monday to the end of September over 3,500 parades are held in Northern Ireland, most of them in the summer. The majority is staged by the Protestant Orange Order. For the most part, they celebrate Protestant military victories over Catholics. The July 12th parade, for instance, celebrates the victory of the Protestant English king, William of Orange, over the Catholic king he deposed, James II, at the Battle of Boyne in 1690. So, it's not surprising that the parades are onerous and insulting to Republican Nationalists, especially when they are routed through Catholic neighborhoods. The parade tradition is over 200 years old. The first one was held in 1796, the year after the Loyal Orange Institution was formed in honor of William of Orange.

The rally to protest the parade ban kicked off the violence. Catholics pelted the Protestant marchers with stones. Before the summer was over Belfast had suffered its worst rioting in years. It peaked in late June. Tensions had been mounting for several days, with each side blaming the other. Catholics had thrown stones at a Protestant Order march. They threw more when Unionists erected flags on streets adjacent to the Holy Cross Primary School for girls in Belfast's Ardoyne section. The school is near an intersection separating a Catholic and a Protestant community. When school got out, and students were leaving the building, Protestant youths threw stones at them and the parents who had come to pick up their girls. To protect the students Holy Cross was temporarily closed. When it reopened a crowd of Protestants blocked access to the school, setting the stage for an angry confrontation. Amid that tension a bomb was detonated in the yard of a Catholic home. Before it was over an estimated 600 rioters took to the streets. Stones, bottles, and gasoline bombs were hurled. Shots were fired. Cars were set on fire. Sixty policemen were injured.

The riots provided a dramatic backdrop underscoring the urgency of the peace talks going on in Belfast's Stormont Castle. June 2001 had been set as the deadline for full implementation of the Good Friday Agreement. As part of the agreement, the IRA had promised to put their weapons "completely and verifiably beyond use." The Ulster Unionists, however, contended that the IRA had not done so and demanded that the IRA's weapons be turned over to the authorities. Unionist leader David Trimble and Republican leader Gerry Adams were engaged in a fresh round of talks aimed at breaking the Unionist and Republican deadlock over IRA disarmament. A year earlier the power sharing government in Northern Ireland was resuscitated when the IRA announced it was in fact going to disarm. Trimble said, "The IRA promised a year ago that they would put their weapons beyond use...they were given a whole year to do something. They haven't done it." It was reported that the IRA had amassed 1,700 weapons including 50 heavy and general-purpose machine guns, 40 rocket launchers, grenades, mortars, flame throwers, booby traps, ground-to-air missiles, and an estimated two tons of explosives. Speculation was that the weapons were hidden in the Irish Republic in deep bunkers, the exact locations known only to a few. Also on the Stormont negotiating table were plans for police reforms and the scaling back of British military bases.

The June deadline was missed. Ultimately an agreement was reached that, while it didn't satisfy a great many Unionists, moved the peace process forward. By October the IRA allowed international monitors, including Cyril Ramaphosa, former Secretary General of the African National Congress, to inspect three sealed arms bunkers to prove its weapons were not in use. The bunkers were secured very much like bank safety deposit boxes are. Each was fitted with a two key, dual-lock system. The international weapons inspectors held one of the keys for each bunker, ensuring that the IRA could not unilaterally open the arsenals. Ramaphosa said in his report, "We inspected a number of arms dumps. The arms dumps held a substantial amount of military material, including explosives and related equipment, as well as weapons and other material. We observed that the weapons and explosives were safely and adequately stored. We have ensured that the weapons and explosives cannot be used without our detection." In November Northern Ireland's police force, the Royal Ulster Constabulary, was replaced by the Police Service of Northern Ireland. Since its formation in 1922 the RUC was roundly hated by Republicans who alleged that it discriminated against Catholics and colluded with Unionist paramilitary groups. The new police force was recruited with the goal of attaining a 50% Catholic and a 50% Protestant membership. It was originally going to be called the Northern Ireland Police Service (the NIPS), but some thought that wouldn't be appropriate. As the year came to an end it seemed a real possibility that peace was on the horizon.

Through it all, MacGowan and the Popes continued to play sporadically, mostly in clubs and on the summer festival circuit. There were particularly good shows in Dublin and Limerick. He returned to Tipperary for the "Ned O' the Hill Festival" in Upperchurch, about half an hour from Thurles. There was tremendous excitement in that small village. Upperchurch consists of a handful of houses, three pubs, and miles of green fields. The festival began with a parade led by the Tipperary Camogie team. Camogie is a women's sport similar to hurling. The team was going after their third consecutive all Ireland championship. It was an outdoor festival, and light rain fell throughout much of the day. Of course MacGowan was late. By the time he arrived, the crowd had knocked down the security fence in front of the stage. By 11:00 PM rumors circulated that Shane was not going to show. Some said a friend of his had died earlier in the day. Others said he was drunk in some pub. When he did turn up, At 1:30 in the morning, he was clutching a nearly empty vodka bottle and told the wet fans, "This gig is dedicated to my friend Tex who died today." He was pretty wasted. It was far from his best show, but most of the audience didn't seem to notice. Few in Upperchurch will ever forget it.

Throughout the year speculation continued about a new album. MacGowan continued to insist that one was in the works, but nothing materialized. He did appear on two records, however. He sang "Plaistow Patricia" on an Ian Dury tribute album and was featured on Danny Pope's (the Popes' first drummer) EP *Acid Teeth*. Shane's contribution was a dub taken from the Popes' recording of "B&I Ferry." There was also the enticing rumor that MacGowan, Liam Clancy, Ronnie Drew, and Terry Woods were forming a band. One columnist joked they were going to call themselves the Publiners. Nothing came of it, but two years later Shane did appear on the Eamon Dunphy show with Drew, Woods, and Eamon Campell as the Hellfire Club.

That Fall Ingrid Knetsch, the director of Shane MacGowan's fan club, posted an open letter to Shane on the Friends of Shane website. She announced that she was going to stop running the fan club, something she had been doing faithfully for 12 years. She cited Shane's lack of co-operation as the reason, saying it had become next to impossible to get any information about shows or any of his other activities from MacGowan or his management. Knetsch said she had spoken to Shane and his father about the lack of communication during the previous two years, but since nothing had been done she was giving up.

In October, Pogues fans' dreams came true. A Christmas season Pogues' reunion tour of the UK was announced. Billed as "The Pogues for one week only," tickets sold out quickly. They were gone two months in advance. Still, there was considerable skepticism that the shows would ever take place. As late as October 15 Spider Stacy still seemed uncommitted to the reunion. He was quoted in the press as saying, "I'm good friends with everyone but I have made a decision not to play with Shane anymore because there is nothing left of the person I used to know. He's an angry, unhappy wreck and I feel sorry for him but I really don't have the time anymore...Chances are the reunion will never happen because Shane can't be trusted not to fuck it up and certainly his comments (in *A Drink with Shane MacGowan*) about Jem and James finished it for me." MacGowan, too, seemed less than enthused, fueling speculation that he might not show up. In October Ingrid Knetsch said he got unpleasant when she asked him about the reunion gigs. "I got the impression the whole reunion thing is already getting on Shane's nerves," she said. A fan that saw him in Bloom's Hotel bar in November said Shane wouldn't talk about the reunion, saying he preferred to do Popes' gigs instead.

Anticipation was high, probably higher than expectations. Rumor had it that the Pogues had only managed four rehearsals. It was enough. Most critics and the vast majority of fans felt the shows were sensational. Nearly all of the material came from the band's Irish period, prior to *Peace and Love*. "Tuesday Morning" was the only post-MacGowan Pogues' song performed. Most of the classics were there: "Streams of Whiskey," "If I Should Fall from Grace with God," "Boys from the County Hell," "Broad Majestic Shannon," "Rainy Night in Soho," "A Pair of Brown Eyes," "The Old Main Drag," "Body of an American," "Dirty Old Town," "Lullaby of London," "Sick Bed of Cuchulainn," "Sally MacLennane," "Fairytale of New York," and "Thousands are Sailing." Of the set's 26 numbers, all but five were written and/or sung by Shane. Moreover, MacGowan was focused and in command. Night after night, he was clearly the center of attention. The *Guardian's* review of the Manchester show was typical. "The Pogues musicianship is fearsomely impressive...but this is MacGowan's two-hour show. Paunch aside, he looks better preserved than most of the band." One reviewer said MacGowan "looked like crap," and had "put on 50 lbs." but was very playful, far more so than in the past. Shane taunted the crowd when some of them began chanting "You fat bastard!"

For most of the fans it was just like old times. In Glasgow an old man was drunk and leaning on speakers before the opening band even came out. He eventually passed out and security removed him while the crowd chanted, "F yez all," the chorus from "St. John of Gods." When the Pogues took the stage the crowd began chanting, "There's only one Shane MacGowan!" That night, and every other for that matter, it was Shane's show. He was clearly the reason the reunion was a smash. The Pogues were tight, magnificent by all accounts, but it was MacGowan that rekindled the magic.

The shows closest to Christmas were probably the best. One venue played Christmas songs before the Pogues came out, including, appropriately, "All I Want for Christmas Is My Two front Teeth." A chant of "Shane-o" filled the hall for several minutes before MacGowan came onstage greeting the faithful with a gruff "Merry fuckin' Christmas." His mother did the duet on "Fairytale of New York." Just when it seemed that it couldn't get any better, some of the Dubliners walked out for an encore of "The Irish Rover."

If there was a downside to what was by all accounts a fantastic reunion tour, it was the release of a "new" live Pogues' album. An outfit called Castle Records released *Streams of Whiskey* to capitalize on the Pogues' reunion tour. It was a live recording of a concert in Leysin, Switzerland, from July 12, 1991, which had long been available as a bootleg called *Bad Lieutenant*. The Pogues were very pissed off and asked fans not to buy it, but to wait instead for an official new live album recorded during the reunion gigs. Eventually, the reunion show recorded at the Brixton Academy was released as half of yet another "Best of..." compilation. Spider Stacy said this at the time, "That *Streams of Whiskey* album is a bit of a sore point. To cut a long story short, they acquired the rights through very dubious means and it's not really worth our while going to court for a long, expensive battle. Companies like this operate on that assumption and they get away with it. We decided we had to let it go and get on with having fun doing Pogues gigs rather than tie ourselves up for god knows how long in legal shit."

The Pogues' reunion shows were a tremendous success in every regard. Anthony Addis, formerly the Pogues' accountant, put the tour together and in effect became the band's new manager. For once, things ran smoothly and professionally. MacGowan was inspired and responded with a passion his performances hadn't had for some time. Moreover, he was relatively sober and, by his standards, reliable. Shane had gotten pretty much what he had longed for a decade before: occasional high profile, high paying Pogues gigs without constant touring.

The reunion also had the effect of raising MacGowan's profile in regard to his solo career. Unfortunately, the efficiency and professionalism that permeated the reunion shows didn't follow Shane in his solo endeavors. In early February he appeared on Pat Kenny's *Late, Late Show*. His actual performance of "Mother Mo Chroí" was not bad at all, but his demeanor was a bit unbecoming. He was very drunk and had his fly unzipped before pulling it up half way through the song. He ended the performance with a half-hearted, clumsy attempt at trashing the set. The television station got telephone calls from irate viewers complaining that it was a disgrace to let him on the air so drunk. The print media jumped on the story. The *Irish Times* ran a column saying he shouldn't have been allowed on in his condition writing, "Here was one of the finest songwriters of our age, a person of obvious wit, intelligence, and imagination, and he was unable to string five words together to form a coherent sentence."

MacGowan and the Popes continued to play short tours and one-off gigs. In February they released two albums, but neither contained new material with the exception of live versions of Hank Williams' "Angel of Death" and the traditional "Granuaille," a song that Ernie O'Malley said was a Republican favorite in the free state internment camps during the Irish Civil War. *The Rare Ould Stuff* (on ZTT Records) was made up half of tracks taken from *The Snake* and *The Crock of Gold* and half of singles' B-sides. *Across the Broad Atlantic* (on Eagle Records) was a live album recorded on the previous St. Patrick's Day in both Dublin and New York, surely a first in recording history. The album's liner notes say the New York set was recorded on March 17th, but the Dublin show was recorded on May 19th. Dublin's official celebration of the holiday was moved to that date, according to the notes, because of an outbreak of foot and mouth disease. It's a good live recording. Shane is in good form and the Popes rock. The album contains 20 tracks, 11 of them Pogues' numbers, all predating *Peace and Love*. Four tracks came from *The Crock of Gold*, and two from *The Snake*, including "Aisling." There's also a Popes instrumental and the two previously mentioned covers, neither of which stands out. The album's notes also alerted fans to look for a Shane MacGowan album with "all brand new material" in the summer of 2002. It never arrived.

St. Patrick's Day 2002 turned out to be somewhat of a wash. The holiday has always generated festivities in America, affording Irish Americans an excuse to celebrate their heritage. Until recently it had not been that big a deal anywhere else. In the past the Irish typically observed the Saint's feast day as a quiet family holiday, usually by attending mass and sitting down to a nice meal. It has never amounted to much in England. In 2001, however, Dublin's St. Patrick's Day celebration drew 1.3 million people to an outdoor festival. In 2002 London's Mayor Ken Livingstone, perhaps inspired by the belief that the saint came to Ireland from England, but more likely jealous of the economic boost Dublin's celebration brought to that city, revealed his idea for a London St. Patrick's Day festival. Flanked by two supporters wearing giant inflatable Guinness costumes, the mayor announced plans for a parade starting at the Roman Catholic Westminster Cathedral that would end in Trafalgar Square with a festival of Irish music and dance. At one point MacGowan and the Popes were said to be the festival's headliners. Livingstone's plans caused an immediate controversy. The Royal Society of St. George (England's patron saint) was livid. They had recently asked the mayor for $15,000.00 to put on a St. George festival on his feast day, April 23, but they were turned down. Arthur Naisbitt, the St. George Society Vice-chairman, said, "We have been trying to get a festival for years. We are appalled. We cannot believe it." In the midst of the controversy it was announced that MacGowan and the Popes were going to do a short St. Patrick's week tour in the United States. In the end, MacGowan had no concert scheduled on the saint's holiday. The American tour was cancelled, and the Popes played their own gig that night in Kentish Town, London. After the Popes finished their set Shane came on stage and sang a few tunes acapella including "Spancil Hill," "Kitty," and "Boys of Kilmichael." The crowd loved it. When Shane was through the Popes came back on and they did a pretty full set with Shane.

The cancelled American tour caused problems with MacGowan's fan base. The official word for the cancellation was "visa problems." There were rumors that after a Dublin concert either Shane or someone in his entourage tore up a hotel room, and when he refused to pay for the damages the hotel confiscated his passport. Another story had Joey Cashman at the problem's root, blaming him for not getting the proper P-2 Work Visa, a temporary green card that has to be applied for a couple of months in advance. Speculation was that Cashman was going to have Shane enter the States as a regular tourist, but that didn't work. In any case, it is true that musicians at that time were increasingly having problems entering the States. In June of 2002 Luka Bloom got very vocal in the press about the situation saying, "They're making it very difficult for guys like me to come over. People say it's 9/11 stuff, but I don't think that's true at all. It has more to do with a new philosophy since the Bush administration came in which seems to say that any foreign musicians are taking gigs away from American performers."

Mick O'Connell, the Popes' accordion player later posted a message on the Friends of Shane website that blamed Cashman for the cancelled tour. "We missed going to America for Paddy's Day as Joey had not made the calls to firm the dates that Mick (McDonagh) had fixed for him with the American agent so the tour was put off till May," O'Connell wrote. "That meant that the American record company were fucked off as well. They had loads of promotion set up to promote the album (*Across the Broad Atlantic*) around Paddy's Day in New York with a big gig. They had to cancel it all and it meant that we had no real dates for Paddy's Day... We were all really pissed off but Joey told Shane that we had not gone to America in March as our visas had not come through. That was bollocks. I know for a fact Mick had collected my passport from me in Chiswick around Christmas, well early, but he could not put the visa stuff in until the dates had been signed by Joey. The dates were falling out in America as Joey did not get around to dealing with it."

Whatever the reason for the cancelled tour, fans on the Friends of Shane website blamed Cashman first and heroin second. The consensus was that a professional manager should have been on top of the details. Ingrid Knetsch suggested that Cashman was more MacGowan's drug dealer than his manager, and that Shane needed to get into a methadone program. Most fans that weighed in agreed that heroin was part of the problem. Those who said they had seen Shane around the time reported that he was no longer friendly or fun to be around.

In April MacGowan and the Popes did a quick tour of the Netherlands before finally making it to the United States. As usual, the shows were terrific some nights, not so good on others. Generally, the crowds were smaller than in the past. Many fans stayed away because of MacGowan's reputation for no-shows. Indeed, this time around he cancelled in Chicago, Toronto, and Detroit. In Chicago Paul McGuinness came out and said, "Shane's not here and that's all we'll say about that." Some, however, had plenty to say. Official word was that he was in a Boston hospital. Others reported that he had missed his flight or was seen drinking in a Boston bar. One fan on the MacGowan website wrote, "Fuck Shane. I'm done supporting that drunk's drinking habit. Four fucking times I've traveled at least 200 miles just to be let down. Not anymore though." When MacGowan didn't show in Toronto, the Popes, as usual, played without him. A fan there complained that he had taken two days off from work, booked a hotel, and drove to Toronto for nothing. A roadie selling T-shirts in Toronto said that he hadn't seen MacGowan since Boston. He did say that Shane was suffering pretty bad from heroin withdrawal since arriving in the States, but he didn't know if that was related to the no show.

In the same internet post cited earlier, Mick O'Connell said, "When we did go to America that May it could still have been a good tour except Joey decided to stay in Boston and fly up with Shane instead of going on the tour bus with us. He just stayed in Boston so we had to face the fucking promoters in Toronto, Detroit, and Chicago when he and Shane did not show up. It was a disaster, especially as Joey was supposed to give us money in Toronto. I knew then that it was all going to shit and that it would never go anywhere with Joey around."

Back in the UK MacGowan teamed up with the Pogues again for a few lucrative festival dates. In June he showed up unannounced at a local dance in Tipperary and had a great time singing several songs with a local band. The Popes banjo player, Tommy McManamon, took a leave of absence to deal with health problems, so MacGowan and the Popes didn't play as much that summer, although there were sporadic shows. In August Shane was hospitalized in Dublin for a hairline fracture in his previously broken hip. The official word was that he sustained the injury while running for a plane, although there was much speculation he had fallen when in his cups. Whatever the cause, the fracture didn't slow him down for long. He began an Irish tour opening in Letterkenny. Once the Popes came out a roadie wheeled an empty wheelchair to the front of the stage. A moment later three or four bouncer types carried Shane to the stage, placed him in the wheelchair, and handed him a pint of clear liquid and a cigarette. That done, the microphone was maneuvered into position, and MacGowan launched into a wonderful set. It was reported later that he thought he was in Kilkenny. By the time the tour reached Carrick-on-Shannon, McManamon was back on banjo looking 20 years younger.

On a Friday night in September MacGowan appeared as a guest disk jockey with BF Fallon's Death Disco at Eamon Doran's in Dublin. He obviously enjoyed himself singing along to Elvis' "I Was the One" and playing tracks all night. Among other things he played Bob Dylan, the Sex Pistols, Eddie Cochran, Junior Parker, and Led Zepplin. The next night he and the Popes did a concert at the Ambassador in Dublin. Completely wasted in his wheelchair, Shane threw up profusely half way through the set setting off another round of media speculation as to his health and life expectancy. There were numerous discussions about the incident on radio shows. On Sunday night a show in Waterford was cancelled. On Monday, MacGowan was admitted to a Dublin hospital. He had collapsed at home after a whiskey and heroin binge. He had been on a downward spiral since Victoria Clarke left him the previous year. Sinead O'Conner was one of the many who worried publicly, commenting to the press about her concern for Shane's condition. The papers reported that O'Conner took him into her home to nurse him back to health. A few days later MacGowan posed for photographers throwing down a pair of crutches proclaiming and demonstrating the healing powers of Mother Sinead.

Having made somewhat of a recovery, MacGowan spent a little more time recuperating in Carney Commons before finishing out the year playing a handful of shows with the Popes. The shows were far from his best. He performed on crutches. Unfortunately, the Popes had by now become a four-piece rock band playing traditional folk influenced music on guitar, bass, drums, and banjo. Despite Tom McManamon's considerable banjo skills, without an accordion, fiddle, or even a whistle it was getting difficult to achieve the Irish infused sound MacGowan's fans craved. Shane's performances that December were lackluster. He seemed disinterested. Three days before Christmas 2002, Shane's birthday, Joe Strummer died of a heart attack after walking his dog. An undiagnosed congenital heart defect was the cause. He was 50 years old, an age that looked increasingly unlikely that Shane MacGowan would reach.

CHAPTER 13

"The appeal was to capture him for the future, because you do get the impression spending time with him that he could drop dead at any minute."

Sarah Share

Musically, the New Year began as the last ended. MacGowan fronted the four-piece Popes in small venues on a very irregular basis. When he finally discarded his crutches, he began performing sitting in a chair. On some nights he stood, and on those nights the shows were usually better. He also continued doing the Death Disco thing with BF Fallon. One night in Belfast's Front Page Bar a drunken "fan" got annoyed that Shane wasn't playing any Pogues tracks. Having gotten his fill of Margaret Barry, Tom Waits, Jacques Brel, Hank Williams, and Bobby Sands' poem "The Rhythm of Time" set to music and recited by Gerry McGrogan, the drunk chucked a glass at Shane. One witness swore it was an empty vodka bottle. Fans in the club more loyal to MacGowan promptly beat the crap out of the culprit. Ten minutes later, having tasted blood, they wrecked the stage.

In late January MacGowan accepted an invitation to attend the premier of a documentary in Wurzburg, Germany. The film, *If I Should Fall from Grace*, was the story of Shane MacGowan's life thus far. Directed by Sarah Share, it debuted in America on the Sundance Channel the following St. Patrick's Day. The film's genesis was serendipity at its best. MacGowan was scheduled to do a television appearance in County Galway. He stopped in a pub on the way to the station and never made it to the show. The no-show generated a lot of negative press around Galway, causing MacGowan a good deal of embarrassment. Share, a friend of Joey Cashman, had contacts at the television station. She was invited to do a short documentary on MacGowan for the Irish language TG4 in order to smooth things over a bit. Originally Share was not even a MacGowan fan, but she said she became obsessed with "trying to get behind the way he was." She ended up spending six months with Shane while directing the feature length theatrical release. The first time she met MacGowan Cashman brought him by her home for Shane to give her the once over. They arrived around midnight, drank everything in the house, and didn't leave until daybreak when an exasperated Share told them, "You got to go, boys. I can't take this anymore."

By most accounts Share did a brilliant job. The film is powerful and even-handed, managing to portray MacGowan as a gifted genius without glossing over his troubled, self-destructive side. Key to the documentary's success was the filmmaker's decision to forego narration and let the camera, Shane, his family, and friends tell the story through interviews. Share herself stayed off camera. That brought a sense of intimacy to the film, giving the feeling that those interviewed were speaking directly to the viewer. In a round of interviews to promote the film, the director was candid about the difficulty she had working with MacGowan. "The appeal was to capture him for the future, because you do get the impression spending time with him that he could drop dead at any minute," she told the *Irish Herald*. "He is difficult, he is sick. In some ways it's like being around an invalid. He does a lot of drink and drugs. On many occasions we sat outside his flat waiting for hours for him to answer the phone or the door. I'd arrive at 12 noon and finally get him out to do something at 12 at night. Plus he was frequently incoherent. I have hours and hours of incoherent footage. In the end it was best to just follow him around waiting to get a little nugget of something. My cameraman described it as being like wildlife photography. He is sociable - he does like going out at night and he'll stay up all night. Some of the interviews were done at three or four or five in the morning. Then at six in the morning he wondered why we wanted to go home... I think there is an extent to which he hides behind his persona, which he adopted to kind of protect him from people. He's basically very shy, and frequently seems more out of it than he is. There are some interviews where he's perfectly coherent, and those are probably the ones where he's more defensive, more aggressive. It was when he was together and lucid that he'd argue with me."

When MacGowan returned from the film's German premier, he was one of over 50 Irish musicians to sign an open letter of protest to the *Taoiseach*, Ireland's Prime Minister, Bertie Ahern. The Irish government had agreed to allow American troop transfer planes on their way to Iraq to refuel at Shannon airport in County Clare. Shane's friends Christy Moore, Sinead O'Conner, and most of the Dubliners had also signed the letter, which was published in the *Irish Times*. It read in part, "In the event of war in the Middle East, the Irish people would be implicated in any unjustified civilian losses and humanitarian crisis that would ensue." The letter went on to say that the government's action undermined Ireland's traditional neutrality and constitutional commitment to the peaceful resolution of international disputes. A week later protesters organized an anti-war rally in Dublin, hoping to draw 20,000 people. On the Saturday of the event 90,000 protesters turned out. MacGowan was more passionate than logical about the situation with an interviewer from *Hotpress*, simultaneously venting about the American military while seemingly agreeing with Ahern's decision to let the planes land at Shannon.

SM: *Do you know what happened at Shannon Airport? The security was so tight, but two women demonstrators got in and irreparably damaged two airliners. Have you seen security at Shannon?*

HP: *How do civilians go about disabling military aircraft? Where do you start?*

SM: *You just slash the fuck out of it, and the Yanks are such shit-heads they won't fly a plane that's even got a dent. That's why you get cheap Yank cars if they've got a dent in them... and then some stupid reporter asked Bertie, Mr. Ahern, the Taoiseach, the leader of our nation, what about America? And he said, "America is America."*

HP: *That sounds profound.*

SM: *Well, it's true isn't it? What do you want him to do? Declare war on America?*

HP: *No, but he could've told them to go and use somebody else's airport.*

SM: *It would've lost us 45 billion. I don't think it's an argument. If you want to be a bunch of wankers, be a bunch of wankers.*

That spring and summer MacGowan and the Popes may not have played as frequently as the Pogues used to, but they covered just about as much ground. There were the usual bad nights. He was very drunk at festivals in Budapest and Serbia, and his performance suffered. But, when Shane was good, he was very good. Shows in Dublin, London, and the Netherlands went down extremely well, as did his set before 15,000 fans at the Holidays in the Sun Punk Festival, in Morecambe, England. Perhaps the best concert, however, was a raucous show in front of 1,900 soccer fans at the Barrowlands in Glasgow, Scotland. The Barrowlands had always been a great venue for Shane, but on that particular night fans had gathered early to watch an important soccer match between Celtic and Porto televised on big screens before Shane played. Shane was a fan of Celtic, if not soccer itself, because he considered the team a "flagrant" example of Republicanism in the UK. By the time he took the stage the crowd was at a fever pitch.

MacGowan returned to Glasgow about a week later to receive the McGinn Lifetime Achievement Award. Matt McGinn was one of Glasgow's finest. A poet, folk singer, songwriter, play-write, and humorist, he died of smoke inhalation in 1977 when he fell asleep with a cigarette and his flat caught fire. Reporting on the awards ceremony *The Living Tradition*, a Scottish folk music magazine said, "The most poignant moment came during a shambling Shane MacGowan rendition of McGinn's take on "Loch Lomond." Wearing an expression which had long since passed through drunkenness to serenity, and framed in a hazy blue halo of cigarette smoke, as he sang 'and I'll be in heaven before ye,' few would have been inclined to disagree."

MacGowan and the Popes also did a short Australian tour, but the media was not quite as impressed down under. He was in pretty bad shape when he played the Byron Bay Blues and Roots Festival. One paper said much of the audience was "appalled" and reported that 200 to 300 people walked out. If they did, they probably made a big mistake. Another critic said that while MacGowan did get off to a very shaky start, he pulled it together about half way through the set and that the final 30 minutes were "the most electrifying of any of the performances this year." While the band was still touring the country, Australian playwright Brendan Delaney staged a one-man play about Shane in Melbourne's Celtic Club.

That September, there was a buzz among MacGowan fans. Many that had followed his career for two decades said his current performances were as good as any they had ever seen. Just prior to starting an Irish tour in late summer, he had added a young Irishman named Brian Kelly on mandolin, beefing up the traditional element in his set. But it was more than that. Shane had stopped doing heroin. Years later he told Victoria Clarke, "I would say that nobody can handle heroin…It was incredibly hard to kick.

I was terrified, all the time, of cold turkey. It is unbelievably horrific. The physical bits are so horrific that they blank out the screaming depression, though. It's the loneliest feeling in the world." With heroin behind him, MacGowan was invigorated. Whereas he had spent most of the last year singing from a chair, he was now dancing around, animated and in top form. That month on *The Dunphy Show* on Ireland's TV3, Shane gave his most coherent interview in years. On the Ray Darcy radio show two days earlier he was brilliant, talking intelligently and lucidly for the full hour. In response to a question about Victoria Clarke he said that they were still dating but living separately. "It was totally unexpected when she left," he told Darcy, " but at least it forced me to clean up my act." Long time fans exulted in a new Shane MacGowan.

There were also new recording projects. There still was no sign of the promised new album, but at least there were some guest appearances. MacGowan contributed three vocals on *Every God Damned Time*, the new Lancaster County Prison album. He did duets on "The Town I Loved So Well," which got some airplay, and "Satan Is Waiting for Me." He also sang the lead vocal on "Long Black Veil," which was a real joy. To be honest, he flubbed that vocal a bit, but Shane doing anything with a folky, country feel always works for me. He even flew over to sing about eight songs at the CD's launch party at the Irish Rover in Queens, New York. Shane did another recording for Jools Holland's third *Friends* album, contributing "Just to be With You."

By December MacGowan was certainly on a roll. His December tour of Ireland was the best he'd done in years, maybe ever. At the Elk Nite Club in Toomebridge, County Armagh, he sang "Roddy McCorley," a song he rarely performed live, in honor of the bridge of Toome were McCorley was executed. A few nights later at Dolan's in Limerick, a fan requested "Sean South." Shane introduced the next song as "Sean South" and then did "Roddy McCorley" again, which he does to the same tune. The shows at the Olympia in Dublin were particularly good. Ex-Pogue Cait O'Riordan showed up one night and sang "A Man You Don't Meet Everyday" and dueted with MacGowan on "Fairytale of New York." The year's end brought MacGowan some valuable media exposure. Two days after Christmas BBC Radio2 aired a one-hour special called "Pogue Mahone: The Story of the Pogues." Four days later, MacGowan appeared on Jools Holland's annual New Years Eve show. When Holland asked Shane for his 2004 predictions he answered, "Judgement Day."

If Judgement Day comes at the end of the road, then Shane's prediction was close to right in regard to his relationship with the Popes. Although there was no formal dissolution of Shane MacGowan and the Popes, they played together a great deal less beginning in 2004. There were one-off gigs in MacGowan strongholds like Glasgow, the usual March tour of Ireland and the UK, and summer festivals in Europe. Most of the concerts were quite good. At a free outdoor festival in Turin, Italy, 20,000 fans were treated to the most unique, if not the best performance ever of "Rainy Night in Soho." MacGowan was joined by a dozen black-suited musicians playing an assortment of horns. It was beautiful. Although he fronted the Popes less than in previous years, Shane stayed busy. He found many things to distract him.

Early in the year he showed up and sang "Born to Lose" and "Loaded" as a guest performer at a few Primal Scream concerts. He sang with Jools Holland in the Royal Albert Hall at a Teenagers Cancer Trust Benefit, dressed in what was described as "a shabby buccaneers' outfit." The outfit was probably the costume he wore on a film shoot a few weeks earlier with Johnny Depp. MacGowan was frequently seen hanging out with celebrity friends and performing, often informally and spontaneously, at a pub called the Boogaloo on Archway Road in Higate, North London. Arguably, it has the best pub juke box selection on the planet. Shane generally stayed in a flat over the Boogaloo whenever he was in London. His old friend Jerry O'Boyle opened the pub when he sold Filthy McNasty's Whiskey Cafe in 2000. The Boogaloo is a small place, so it was packed in January when 100 fans were invited to see Shane do an unusual set backed by a band of young, unknown musicians that included a stand-up bass and steel guitar. He did covers of "Cupid" and a few other Sam Cooke tunes, Elvis' versions of "Blue Moon of Kentucky" and "That's All Right Mama," Jonathan Richman's "Road Runner," and about half a dozen Pogues' numbers. At the Boogaloo's birthday bash for Irish poet William Butler Yeats, MacGowan sang with fellow Irishman Bap Kennedy's band. At the pub's release party for the single "Road to Paradise" Shane danced with supermodel Kate Moss and drank with Johnny Knoxville of *Jackass* fame.

"Road to Paradise," written by MacGowan, was a charity single to raise money for the Motor Neurone Disease Tribute Fund. It featured Scottish soccer legend Jimmy Johnstone who was diagnosed with the disease in 2001. He died five years later. At age 13 Johnstone was courted by both Manchester United and Celtic scouts but chose to play for Celtic. He spent 14 seasons with the team. Celtic's fans eventually voted him the team's all time best player. Along with the new MacGowan song, the single included Johnstone and Simple Mind's Jim Kerr singing "Dirty Old Town." Released under the moniker The Bhoys From Paradise, it sold pretty well, especially in England and Scotland. MacGowan was tireless in promoting the single. He told one journalist, "I am a Celtic fan, although I have no interest in the game itself. But they are a stalwart of flagrant Republican bigotry in the so-called British Isles." MacGowan did record signings in music stores and was extremely gracious to fans. When word got out that he was in Dublin's Tower Records the store was mobbed. Fans in the long line to meet him called friends on their cell phones alerting them to Shane's presence. The line kept growing, so MacGowan stayed until 8:00 PM despite having arrived in Dublin at six that morning on the 3:00 AM ferry from England. He autographed every disc with a personal note. On some days he did two or three press interviews, historically one of his least favorite activities. When interviewers brought up the subject of heroin MacGowan said he was off drugs and "Clean as a whistle," adding "I genuinely got incredible enjoyment out of it for years, but towards the end it really fucked me up. Giving it up was the closest thing I've been to hell on earth. It was like my own personal Iraq. I didn't give a fuck about wasting any talent I had. It broke up my relationship with the only woman I ever loved and that's all I give a fuck about."

In a related development Shane was asked to write a song for the Dali Lama's upcoming visit to Scotland. The holy man was coming to Glasgow to see a Celtic soccer match. If that sounds a little strange, it is. In a *Sunday Independent* article Victoria Clarke asked Shane what the Dali Lama had to do with soccer. "We are Catholics and we are warriors and we have an oppressive force driving us out of our own country," he explained. "That's what he's got in common with the Irish, the fact that he comes from a wonderful, beautiful Garden of Eden, which his place was until imperialism struck. He's got nothing to do with football, but that's what people do, they go to football matches. The matches between Rangers and Celtic are where the politics are acted out and the Dali Lama can explain to these eejits that there is one god governing all men. And he is a manifestation of that god, because he is a reincarnation of Buddha. Buddha said we will all be reincarnated, but he didn't make any rules about it."

The film shoot that provided MacGowan with his "shabby buccaneers' outfit" took place in March at Hampton Court, in West London. He and Johnny Depp were filming *The Libertine*, a movie about Lord Rochester, a 17th century rake played by Depp. MacGowan's part was that of a rowdy bard, a ballad singer who makes up a song to ridicule the King, Charles II, played by John Malkovich. Unfortunately, when *The Libertine* made it to theaters Shane's performance was on the cutting room floor.

That same month MacGowan was a guest on *This Week,* a BBC political talk show hosted by Janet Street Porter. He appeared with Labor MP Diane Abbot and Tory Michael Portillo. Shane was invited to discuss the smoking ban that Ireland had just instituted in public buildings. He was wasted, drinking and smoking in the studio. Porter said later that the program's floor manager was cowering in a corner, afraid to tell MacGowan that he couldn't smoke on the set. The gist of Shane's argument, what could be deciphered of it, was that the ban could never be enforced in pubs because the majority of the community was against it. Certainly MacGowan was against it. When the Pogues played Glasgow about a year later he was reminded backstage of Scotland's new ban on smoking in public buildings. Unconcerned about the $2,500.00 fine, he smoked throughout the concert throwing his unextinguished butts on the stage. Throughout the television show, Abbot and Portillo, unaware of Shane's tendency to drift and hesitate in mid-thought, kept trying to finish his sentences. Every time he said something incomprehensible they looked uncomfortable and said, "Yes, well…" Porter kept reiterating that the ban would indeed be enforced. It turns out that MacGowan and Porter were both right. The government did indeed ban smoking in public buildings, but Irish smokers have found ways to get around the law. In Shane's beloved Carney Commons, Ryan's pub has built a large addition on the back where smoking is allowed. The room has pool tables, a video jukebox, and most anything else a person out for a few pints might require in an evening. What it doesn't have is a seal between the roof and the walls, which apparently makes it an outdoor facility rather than part of the pub. It also makes it cold in winter. When I was last there, in December, the owners had installed two huge gas fired heaters, the kind the NFL uses on the sidelines, to keep off the chill.

In October MacGowan received the *Q Merit Award*. Held at the Grosvenor House Hotel in London, the press called it the most prestigious award ceremony of the year. Sponsored by Greenpeace, *Q Magazine* picked the winner. Bono did the presentation. Backstage after the program, Shane was reportedly goofing off, dancing around the dressing room balancing the award on his head when somehow he accidentally caught Bono's hair on fire. It was not the only mishap involved in the event. Later, MacGowan was kicked out of London's posh five-star Connaught Hotel where he had been staying while he was in town to attend the ceremony. The Connaught's management said that Shane's unnamed, bearded companion pissed himself on an expensive antique Queen Anne's chair in the lobby. Shane and his hirsute friend claimed it was white wine.

Of all his distractions, one really seemed to annoy MacGowan. It concerned Joey Cashman. Cashman, who managed the Pogues' touring schedules, became Shane's personal manager when the band fired MacGowan in 1991. He took care of all of Shane's business. Criticism of his old friend and manager had come to a head around the time of Shane and the Popes' most extensive round of shows in the weeks before and after St. Patrick's Day. Fans circulated a petition, primarily through the Friends of Shane website and at MacGowan concerts, to have Cashman ousted as manager. Even Shane's father, Maurice MacGowan, was part of the movement, vowing to stop attending his son's shows unless things changed. On the website the senior MacGowan wrote, "I think the time for change has come and Cashman must be removed for change to occur. Shane is now at best a middle ranking artist (and declining all the time) when he should be up there with the majors. He still has the huge talent that brought him fame. It just needs to be unlocked and a fresh start with a new set-up might be the key. I hope that Shane will bring in an expert, or team of experts, to look at and eliminate very serious weaknesses in the current set-up."

Shane's father was the first to sign the petition. Over 1,300 more signed, including the Dubliners' Eamon Campbell, within the first two weeks. It read in part, "There are times when we have felt ripped off. Yet we have continued to support you. We now feel that things have gone too far. Many fans have stopped attending your shows. This pattern is destined to continue unless something changes. It's up to you, Shane. Please get yourself the management your undoubted talent deserves."

The failed project with the Hellfire Club (Ronnie Drew, Eamon Campbell, Terry Woods, and MacGowan) seemed to trigger the fan uprising. Jim McKee, the booking agent, said he had confirmed Hellfire Club concert dates with Cashman in late January. Shane had been heard at the Boogaloo talking enthusiastically about shows scheduled for the Netherlands and Belgium. There was talk about new material. Tickets had already been sold. Then, without any clear explanation why, everything came unraveled. According to McKee, Cashman called him and said that Shane had never agreed to do the shows and that the dates conflicted with shows Shane and the Popes were booked to do in Poland. Cashman blamed the misunderstanding on mobile phones! MacGowan's father was unmoved. "The disastrous decision to cancel the dates, approximately two weeks after confirmation by Shane personally, is symptomatic of weaknesses in the current set-up, such as financial control and gig management," he said. "These gigs were the first break into something new, they might have been a new chapter for him...It exhibits a breathtaking contempt for the fans and is bound to limit gig opportunities. ... I'm delighted that fans are showing their teeth and long may they continue to do so."

The situation played in the media for weeks. The Popes original drummer, Danny Heatley told *Hotpress*, "The set-up at the moment under Joey Cashman is the most unprofessional since Spinal Tap. His Dad, Maurice, is 100% correct when he says that Shane's career is being strangled by Joey and that he deserves better...Everybody in the music industry knows that merchandising is a huge part of an artist's income, but rarely was there any available when we were on tour. Why is there no career strategy, with proper tours and albums? The list of questions is endless...When Joey's in town with Shane, he even sleeps in the same room as him. He answers the phone and nobody who's trying to help Shane can get to him...The amount of people who died around that band while I was in it was unbelievable - Charlie McLennan, Dave Jordan, Robbie O'Neill, Paul Verner, Mo O'Hagan, Paul Rowland's girlfriend and a handful more than that as well. The rot really set in after Charlie died. He was the one person that Shane loved and trusted completely. Joey hasn't got Charlie's heart. He's in it for himself. Shane's a very trusting person but it's to his own detriment where Cashman's involved. I was a founder member of the Popes, and know where the fuck-ups are coming from." In a post at the fan website Heatley called Cashman, "at best inept, and at worst a liar," adding that during a confrontation after a gig in Liverpool, "he jumped up, grabbed a beer bottle, tried to break it and came at me."

Cashman contacted *Hotpress* offering to respond with an interview with himself and Shane. They seemed to underscore the petition's point when he and Shane were no-shows. The magazine reported that they were able to reschedule the interview, but Cashman and MacGowan stiffed them a second time and never returned the magazine's calls. Cashman eventually faxed *Hotpress* a statement, supposedly from MacGowan, saying, "No business matters relating to Shane MacGowan should be conducted or discussed with Mr. Maurice MacGowan or any other person claiming to represent him." Maurice retorted, "The response to the petition has a very poor command of English so Shane could not have been the writer. Shane's people have a perfect right to express their views on the petition but have not chosen to exercise that right because they don't want to make themselves more ridiculous than they already are. I notice on the statement that yet another job has been created for Cashman, which is Shane's 'representative and long-term manager.' I would suggest a kick upstairs as a final appointment. Shane should appoint him as his ambassador to the Holy See (the Vatican), a job no more imaginary than the others he has held. He'd fit in perfectly in that web of intrigue.

Obviously he must retain his long-term perks such as full-time hotel accommodation, taxis ad-lib, and first class air travel...Shane says he has no reason to sack Cashman. Let me help him with a few that spring to mind – Shane's career decline, absence of an album, late arrival at gigs, cancellation of gigs, no proper administration, no financial controls, no merchandise."

Mick O'Connell, who like Danny Heatley says he quit the Popes because of Cashman, was perhaps the most virulent in his denunciation of MacGowan's manager. His post on the fan website said, among other things, "All that about the crap that is going on and the lies that Shane gets told, well what they have said is all true. I should bloody know. I was in the friggin' band...I have done tours of America as well as loads of Irish and European dates and I am still waiting to be paid. I am owed thousands. I have been trying to get hold of Joey for ages but he just disappears and won't ever call me back. I'd love to get my hands on the scheming bastard...The big fuck ups came in America when Cashman arrived and took all the money so apart from the money for the record we never did get paid properly. We got back and Joey stayed in America with the money... It was all OK, apart from Joey...We were supposed to tour to promote the live album in Ireland in the spring then in America for Paddy's Day but Joey fucked all that up. Our live album eventually came out really well, but it got beaten to the shops by that bootleg Pogues album. I heard that the record company went mad. Joey had said he knew nothing about it but I found out that he had done his own deal for that album to get some money in on the side and he knew it was coming out. He ballsed up Shane's new record deal and could not give a shite. There was a good bloke called Mike from Eagle (Records) who nearly lost his job over it... The last few gigs I did were some festivals in Europe. It was just more trouble and shite with Joey missing planes and us all being stuck facing the promoters and getting the shit waiting for them to show up. It was so embarrassing facing decent people who had put a lot of work in. Joey would always snatch the money, give a bit to Paul or Sarge to give some to us, but he would always vanish with our full money so we never get paid. Tommy is owed money and I am sure the others are as well.... I hate to say it but I think Shane's career is bollocked as long as Cashman is around. If I could get my hands round his throat I'd squeeze my money from the fucker." O'Connell was careful, however, to say he didn't believe MacGowan knew anything about the mishandling of the money.

In the end Maurice MacGowan knew little could be done. "It's Shane's decision at the end of the day," he said. "We just give our views. Joey Cashman is an old friend, and Shane is very loyal to his friends." Shane repeatedly made his position very clear. When a reporter with the *Sunday Times* asked about the petition he replied, "I don't want to discuss this. My family is nothing to do with you. I am not going to sack Joey Cashman. It's none of your business, but I'm not. My Dad has no control over who works with me. Me, and me alone has to take responsibility for anything. Petitions are ridiculous." During that March's tour MacGowan regularly trotted Cashman out on stage to show his support for his friend. In Dublin, the night before the saint's feast day, the first words out of MacGowan's mouth when he grabbed the microphone were, "Who's been signing the bloody petition?" Throughout the evening he introduced Joey several times saying, "This is Joey Cashman. He's my manager and he's the Popes' manager." MacGowan and the band made a point of hugging Joey to show their support. Shane tried to get his fans to acknowledge Cashman, calling him "the indispensable Joey Cashman," but they were having none of it. The crowd booed Cashman and chanted "Cashman out! Cashman out!"

The scene was repeated in nearly every venue, marring what was otherwise a wonderful string of concerts. With the exception of the show at the Academy in Manchester, where MacGowan was extremely drunk and nearly two hours late, he performed with a furious, captivating energy equal to any point in his career. Press and fans alike raved about his performances. One high profile dissenter, however, was Belfast's Lord Mayor Martin Morgan. MacGowan and the Popes did their first of two Saint Patrick's Day concerts in the afternoon at the city's free outdoor festival outside City Hall. People called radio stations complaining about Shane being drunk. The mayor was very vocal about Shane appearing drunk and drinking onstage at this "dry family event." He called it "an outrageous public act." Perhaps his outrage was fueled when at the end of his afternoon set Shane shouted, "Up the Republic!" before leaving the stage.

The mayor's rage was nothing compared to what was unleashed on MacGowan in April. He was beaten up in a pub. It happened on a Monday about 6:30 in the evening in the Joiner's Arms in Belgravia, a good section of London. Two men, aged 20 and 21 were held for questioning. Liam McInerney, a scaffolder, was subsequently charged with inflicting "grievous bodily harm." Reportedly high on drugs, McInerney apparently punched a woman in the face in addition to attacking MacGowan. He was eventually sentenced to three years in prison for the crimes. Court records say that Shane was attacked in the men's room. McInerney kicked and punched him after hitting him with a metal bar. Shane suffered a fractured cheekbone and a black eye. He was admitted to St. Thomas Hospital but left before being treated. A hospital spokesman confirmed, "The patient came in, registered and left before he was actually seen. He didn't receive any treatment and we don't know the extent of his injuries." A witness in the pub said, "It was a totally unprovoked attack. He was just having a quiet drink with his mates and had even been chatting to one of the blokes who jumped on him." At one point McInerney followed MacGowan into the men's room.

Shane told Victoria Clarke, "Me and a couple of friends were having a drink and we got to talking to this Irish guy. And he bought me a drink. Later on, I saw him talking to this other bigger guy who followed me into the toilet and hit me with what felt like a knuckle duster. I couldn't believe the pain! I've never experienced pain or suffering like that in my life. It was really horrible. I just took the punches and then I slid down the wall. He kicked me with his foot a few times, but that was like someone applying bandages compared to the metal." When a reporter asked Clarke about the incident she said, "He wasn't happy about being beaten up. But he wasn't angry either. He wasn't

176

looking for revenge. He was simply bemused. After all, what had he done to these guys? Absolutely nothing. Sadly, he just lost two more teeth, which doesn't leave him with many." McInerney told the judge that Shane propositioned him, offering to pay for gay sex. Nobody, least of all the judge, believed the claim. MacGowan's doctor prescribed a month of complete rest causing shows in Holland and Spain scheduled for May to be cancelled.

To recuperate MacGowan took a holiday in Malta. Despite their having been separated for a few years, he asked Victoria Clarke to come along. Shane arrived at the airport using a paper bag for luggage. For the most part it was filled with books, including ,biographies of Gerry Adams and Che Guevara. Clarke made him buy a carry-on in the duty free shop and some clothes once they'd arrived in Malta. When they got to the Kempinski Hotel, he headed straight for the bar rather than checking out his room. That's where he was found asleep when the sun came up. Despite the precarious start, the vacation went well. Shane described it as "total and absolute serenity." They spent time getting ayurvedic massages, sunning on Gozo Island's beach, and visiting churches; including the cathedral and another one where the Virgin Mary was supposed to have appeared. They even attended Mass. Shane took communion.

In July Clarke's assertion that they were not back together was confirmed by a story in the press that Shane and an unnamed "new girlfriend" had adopted a Tibetan orphan. The article went on to say that Shane's old friends didn't like his new flame and felt that she was using Shane to generate publicity for "her charities." In fact, Shane hadn't adopted anyone, but the girlfriend had. "She has adopted a Tibetan boy through a charity, basically rescuing him from a life of starvation and providing him with an education," he told the *Irish Mirror*. "I've seen photos of him and I plan to go over there and meet him soon. I think he's 20, or then again he could be 18, but he looks very well. It's a great thing she's doing."

MacGowan and the Popes finished the summer with a handful of shows in Ireland and the UK, including a few festivals. The dates included four consecutive Sunday night gigs at Ronnie Scott's Jazz Club in London. While he was there he said he had new material and would start recording next month. The new material wasn't included in his sets, and seven years later no new album has surfaced. At the end of October MacGowan performed with the Dubliners at a Luke Kelly tribute in Dublin's Gaiety Theatre. He sang "Roddy McCorley," "Freeborn Man of the Traveling People," "Irish Rover," and "Molly Malone." During "Molly Malone" he grabbed his crotch every time he sang the words "cockles and mussels." A few weeks later there was good news for Pogues' fans: there would be another Christmas season reunion tour, and the entire Pogues' back catalogue was going to be remixed, remastered, and released in conjunction with the tour.

This time around Cait O'Riordan was invited along. She did vocals on "Fairytale of New York" and "A Man You Don't Meet Everyday." It was the first time that the original Pogues lineup performed together in nearly two decades. There were shows in England, Ireland, and Scotland. Reviews were uniformly excellent. Once again, critics noted how professional the Pogues were compared to the old days. As they did during the first reunion tour in 2001, the crowds chanted "There's only one Shane MacGowan" night after night.

As the year closed things were looking very good for Shane MacGowan. The reunion tour was a smash, and it spurred sales of the five reissued Pogues' albums. On top of that, an English poll named "Fairytale of New York" the best Christmas song of all time. As if that weren't enough, MacGowan came in first in an international internet poll to find out what people liked best about Ireland. He beat out James Joyce, St. Patrick, Irish whiskey, and Guinness.

Christmas 2004 was good for MacGowan, but not for the people of Indonesia, Sri Lanka, India, and Shane's beloved Thailand. On December 26th an undersea earthquake with a magnitude of 9.3, the second strongest ever recorded, occurred off the west coast of Sumatra. It caused the entire planet to vibrate and triggered a massive tsunami with waves over 100 feet high devasting the coastlines of countries bordering the Indian Ocean. More than 225,000 people in eleven countries were killed. It was one of the deadliest natural disasters in recorded history. A worldwide relief effort began almost immediately, eventually raising more than $7 billion in aid. In early January Irish musicians held a benefit in Dublin. MacGowan sang "Sayonara" with the Hothouse Flowers, and then Cait O'Riordan joined them on "Fairytale of New York." Shane and Ronnie Drew did Johnny Cash's "I Walk the Line" and, with the rest of the Dubliners, "Irish Rover."

CHAPTER 14

"Always, you get more than you expect, with Shane."

James Fearnley

MacGowan continued giving impromptu performances sitting in with bands at the Boogaloo. In January and again in March he sang Desmond Dekker's old reggae hit "Israelites" with Yeti, a band led by former Libertines bassist John Hassell. Yeti had recorded a song called "Shane MacGowan" on their album, *The Legend of Gonzales*. In February MacGowan recorded "On the Mighty Ocean of Alcohol" at the pub. The track was for Bap Kennedy's new album. Kennedy asked him to do the guest vocal knowing it would be easier to get Shane to agree than to actually show up at a studio. "We had to record his vocal in the kitchen in the back of the pub," Kennedy explained. "We needed what they call a pop shield to put in front of the microphone. In the end we borrowed a pair of tights from this girl in the bar. She wasn't keen at first. But I bought her a triple tequila and told her Shane MacGowan needed her. That seemed to do the trick." On St. Patrick's Day, Shane did a short set at the Boogaloo with Pete Doherty, before hurrying over to Shepherd's Bush for his show with the Popes. They sang Hank Williams' "Lost Highway", "A Pair of Brown Eyes," "Cupid," and "Dirty Old Town." Doherty, the frontman for the Libertines and Babyshambles, had a reputation for substance abuse that rivaled MacGowan's. The two had become close. On several occasions Shane showed up at Babyshambles shows to sing "Dirty Old Town" with the band. The press was fascinated with the pairing of two singer-songwriters seemingly defying death with each stoned performance. Their tipsy appearances weren't the only thing that attracted the media. Doherty had begun dating Kate Moss.

The super model's presence inevitably drew the paparazzi to the Boogaloo. They were out in force and security was high for the St. Patrick's Day show. They were back in April when Moss showed up to see the Lancaster Bombers play at the pub. That night MacGowan sat in with the band on a punked up version of Bobby Darin's "Beyond the Sea." Having Kate around certainly did nothing to hurt Shane's public profile. He was regularly mentioned in the press for being seen with Doherty and Moss at celebrity functions. In July the media besieged the Boogaloo expecting to see Moss. Shane, Doherty, Spider Stacy, and Mick Jones of the Clash were scheduled to do a photo shoot for Italian *Vogue* magazine, but Pete and Kate were no shows.

MacGowan's public profile had risen to the extent that he often made the news whether he was doing a concert or not, and whether Moss and Doherty were around or not. In May Shane's presence brought attention on wealthy Tunbridge Wells. His sister Siobhan was married there in what was intended to be a relatively private ceremony. The media showed up, reporting that Shane sang Frank Sinatra's "I've Been a Rover" and that his mother gave a short speech in Gaelic. In June the press spotted him in Dublin's Croke Park at a U2 concert. He was said to be grinning widely when Bono dedicated "Dirty Old Town" to MacGowan. Shane also made the news just by attending a White Stripes show at the Hammersmith Apollo in London.

MacGowan's concerts with the Popes were getting less and less frequent. "I mean I did my best for year's to make the Popes pay," he told Martin Roddy, "but at the end it couldn't possibly pay. All sorts of things happened in the end, shit happens, you know? We used to play two or three nights at the Olympia, and we were losing money because it wasn't the Pogues. It's the name itself. I'm not saying that me and the Popes are the exact same thing as me and the Pogues, but it's just the magic of the name or whatever. Plus the fact that playing two gigs at the Olympia doesn't make you as much money as playing one as the Pogues at The Point." In July he got together with the Pogues again for what was getting increasingly difficult to call a reunion. A major reason the Popes were ebbing was that the Pogues had in effect become a very successful part time band. After two days of rehearsal they played a festival at Guilfest. It was beginning to seem like old times. MacGowan was a bit more than tipsy and changed the set list just before they went onstage, but the band coped and turned in a fine performance. At one point MacGowan told the crowd, "It's nice to play in Denmark again," before launching into the graveyard soliloquy from *Hamlet*. Guilfest was just a warm-up for a short five-day tour of Japan, the Pogues' first Japanese concerts since they sacked Shane there in 1991.

The Pogues were still huge in Japan, and the tour was a tremendous success. This time around, however, things were very different. MacGowan, showing up at the airport in a new sharkskin suit he called his "Bobby Darin" outfit, quipped that they were a bunch of "angry old men." They had indeed matured. This time Jem Finer brought his wife and two teenage daughters along. Victoria Clarke came along as before, but she and Shane were still officially not a couple and she insisted on having her own room. Still, past problems were in the back of several minds. James Fearnley, remembering the Dylan tour fiasco, was concerned that MacGowan might not be allowed on the plane. Shane was, but the long flight was apparently not without incident. Shane managed to spill no less than three drinks on Victoria, who sat with Cashman and MacGowan away from the rest of the entourage. A woman sitting near them was overheard saying she had "never been so disgusted" in her life. At the Narita Airport outside of Tokyo, it was Cashman, not Shane who was detained by authorities. On his first night in Tokyo Shane went out drinking all night, returning at six in the morning with a Japanese ska band. They all went up to his room and continued to swizzle sake.

The first concert was in Tokyo. It went down extremely well. Shane missed the sound check, but no one seemed to mind. Fearnley commented in his tour journal that the sound checks actually went a lot better when MacGowan failed to show. After opening in Tokyo the entourage boarded the bullet train for Osaka. It was the same train that MacGowan fell off during the ill-fated 1991 tour. As before, Shane swigged from a tall white carton of sake, but this time he didn't fall off the train. He did, however, manage to get out of pocket somehow between the station and the hotel. Cashman was with him. Fortunately, they made it to the gig on time. The concert was a repeat of the Pogues' Tokyo triumph. They turned in a fine set enthralling the Japanese crowd. As had become their custom, the Pogues encored with "Fiesta." At its end Fearnley was on his back on the floor. Leaving the stage, MacGowan managed to spill what he said was a mixture of "gin, vodka, and fucking sake" on Fearnley's accordion. James was okay with that. He wrote that MacGowan was "amazing" that night, high praise from a man with an alcohol soaked accordion. Before flying back to London the Pogues played to 100,000 people at the Fuji Rock Festival. They ended the summer with one last gig, the Azkena Rock Festival in Spain. After the Pogues' tour Shane and the Popes cancelled their appearance at Solfest, a festival in England, in addition to some other gigs. The press called it a "string of cancellations and missed appearances."

Shane told the media he was going to use his money from the tour to get a set of false teeth. He had recently worn false teeth on the Frank Skinner show as a joke. "I'm going to get my teeth fully sorted this year," he said. "People seem surprised to hear it, but it's something I've wanted to do for ages. In the recent past I never had the money, but the cash from the Pogues' shows has come through. I put in false teeth on Frank Skinner's chat show and thought I looked rather handsome." In the end, he passed on the dentures at that point, but did get a set of false teeth in Spain in 2009.

That fall MacGowan attended a party commemorating the 50 year anniversary of *The Ginger Man*, a novel he admired by J.P. Donleavy, who also wrote the novel called *Fairytale of New York*. Donleavy was born in Brooklyn to Irish immigrant parents. He grew up in the Bronx before emigrating to Ireland after World War II to attend Trinity College in Dublin. *The Ginger Man*, which was initially banned in Ireland and the United States due to the author's handling of sexual content, follows the exploits of Sebastian Dangerfield, a heavy drinking adulterer. Most of the Irish bars named The Ginger Man throughout the English speaking world can probably be attributed to Donleavy's character. The anniversary party was held at one of them in New York, The Ginger Man on 36th Street. Shane sang "Boys of Kilmichael" and "Peggy Gordon" as part of the festivities. Plans to make a movie of the book were announced. It was to be directed by Laurence Dunmore, who also did *The Libertine*. Johnny Depp had agreed to play Sebastian Dangerfield and MacGowan was slated to play one of his heroes, Brendan Behan. Behan was the first to read Donleavy's original manuscript of *The Ginger Man*. He raved about it, proclaiming "This book is going to go around the world and beat the bejaysus out of the Bible." It was reported that Donleavy had agreed to alter the story in order to expand the Behan role. That was more than a bit curious, since Behan does not appear in the novel. So far, the movie has not materialized. After having met MacGowan, Donleavy was quoted in the media as not believing all the stories about MacGowan's excesses. The elderly author opined that it was part of Shane's act. Apparently Donleavy had not spent too much time around him. None the less, his comments did reflect Shane's vastly improved state. There were other questionable press reports about MacGowan at that time. One said that Pete Doherty had brought a "stunning art student" named Nuha to a Shane MacGowan dinner party while Kate Moss was abroad. The story was questionable not so much for the suggestion that Doherty would step out on Moss for an art student, no matter how stunning, but that Shane MacGowan would host a dinner party.

In November another honor came MacGowan's way. He was one of the original 12 Irish musical heroes immortalized on a Wall of Fame erected in Dublin's Temple Bar area. Van Morrison, Thin Lizzy's Phil Lynott, Luke Kelly, Christy Moore, and Sinead O'Conner were also honored. Other than MacGowan, none of the Pogues made the list. The following month he was scheduled to present rather than receive an award. At London's Musos awards he was to present an award to Primal Scream. Before the presentation he came out to sing with the Lancaster Bombers. He was pretty drunk and fell down on stage. Someone helped him up and Shane sang, of all things, "She'll Be Coming Around the Mountain." It wasn't very good. When he was through Shane left the stage, forgetting to present Primal Scream's award.

As usual, the Christmas season was good for MacGowan. The BBC aired a special called "The Story of Fairytale of New York" a television documentary on the making of the song. To no one's surprise the Pogues re-released the song as a single and did another "Reunion Tour," this time doing six shows in the UK. When the Pogues began rehearsals for the tour in early December, MacGowan was vacationing in Tangier, Morocco, with Dickon Edwards, a London friend he had met a few months earlier at the Boogaloo. Some of his bandmates began referring to Shane as the Caliph and were less than pleased that the Caliph was still in North Africa. Actually, they were lucky MacGowan's weeklong excursion didn't extend much longer than it did. Edwards, who calls MacGowan "the most well-read man I've ever met," said that Shane spent most of the trip in his hotel room reading, drinking gin, and smoking kif, a narcotic similar to hashish that is readily available in Morocco. At one point the hotel staff suggested that Edwards should get MacGowan a doctor. When they were ready to return to England, officials at Tangier's airport refused to let Shane on the plane, contending that he was too drunk. They told him to come back sober the next day. Edwards called Jerry Boyle at the Boogaloo for advice. Boyle assured him that the next day would be no different and suggested an alternate plan. Boyle advised that they board a ferry to Algeciras, Spain; from there take a taxi up the Spanish coast to Malaga; and finally get a plane from Malaga to Stansted, England. If need be, Edwards was to get Shane a wheelchair for the flight, assuming airport officials wouldn't keep an invalid off the plane. In the end, the final ruse wasn't necessary.

The day Shane finally made it to rehearsals he surprised everyone by being there on time for the arrival of Katie Melua, who was brought on board to sing the "Fairytale of New York" duet. Her manager was a bit concerned about the dancing bit Shane and the female singer always do at the end of the song. He thought it should be rehearsed. MacGowan, ever the leader of an Irish dance band, blew him off saying, "It's not difficult or anything, comes naturally, that sort of thing." Perhaps the manager was right. When Melua and the Pogues made it to the sound check for Jonathan Ross' television show Shane lost his balance during the dance. Melua tried to hold him up momentarily before letting him go, crashing into the monitors and landing face down on the floor, shaken but unhurt. It happened again on the tour during the Brixton Academy show. That time however, Jem Finer's daughter Ella was Shane's partner.

The Christmas tour was short and sweet, but covered the UK fairly well. It started in Wales and ended in Dublin. Shane's problems flying back from Morocco apparently annoyed him to the extent that he took a train to Glasgow rather than fly with the rest of the band. At the Glasgow concert Dominic Behan's 78 year-old widow and son came backstage to meet Shane. He seemed just as pleased to meet them as they were to meet him. The show at the Brixton Academy in London featured a welcome surprise. At one point Andrew Rankin had to leave the stage to answer nature's call. In a "the show must go on" move, Shane lead the band into an impromptu performance of "Boys of Kilmichael." At the tour's grand finale in Dublin, Victoria brought out a cake while the band played "Happy Birthday." An overflow crowd sang along. The icing on the cake - the Irish tri-color flag with *Eire* written on it.

In 2006 MacGowan probably performed less than he had since he began his career. The larger paydays for infrequent Pogues' gigs moved the Popes to the back burner. Despite the lack of concerts, Shane got mentioned in the press more than ever. His celebrity was such, especially in Ireland, that a simple MacGowan sighting was deemed newsworthy. Simply showing up at an event got him in the papers. In January he was reported attending a star studded opening of Neil Jordan's *Breakfast on Pluto*, an event that doubled as a UNICEF fund raiser, at Dublin's Savoy Theater. In February he attended the Meteor Awards, Ireland's Grammys, in Dublin. The Pogues received the Meteor Lifetime Achievement Award and performed "Irish Rover" with the Dubliners. The same month a three-hour BBC documentary called "Folk Britannia" acknowledged MacGowan's contributions to British folk music. The press noted his presence at ex-Sex Pistol's Glen Matlock's gig at the Boogaloo; at a Boogaloo barbecue party; at a Babyshambles show in Spain; at the London premiere of *Pirates of the Caribbean II*; with Nick Cave at a Bobby McGees' gig in a Brighton pub; with Victoria Clarke, Pete Doherty, and Kate Moss at a Jerry Lee Lewis gig; and at the *Irish Post* Awards at the Park Lane Hotel in London.

Not all of the press attention was welcome. In January there was a flurry of stories about an incident involving the police. French police had stopped a 59 year-old Irishman trying to bring $444,000.00 across the Spanish - French border. The money, which turned out to be hot, was stuffed in a bag. The man was carrying an Irish passport bearing the name Shane Patrick MacGowan. When questioned by the cops, Shane said that he had lost his passport some time ago in London. It was determined that MacGowan had indeed reported his passport missing sometime back and had since applied for and received a new one. Apparently, the man with the moneybag had either found the old one or purchased it on the black market.

In the spring the Pogues got back together for their first American tour since 1989. As usual there was anxiety over MacGowan's problem with airports. Rather than cross the Atlantic with the band, he made the flight with Joey Cashman. They had a layover in Chicago, but managed it without incident and made it on time to Washington, DC, for the first concert. In fact, to everyone's astonishment, Shane and Joey arrived an hour early at the first gig. It had been fifteen years since this Pogues' lineup had played the States, and their fans were more than ready. They did nine shows in ten days. Every one of them sold out. The crowds were exuberant, and MacGowan fed off their energy. On most nights he was excellent: animated, playful, and talkative. *Brokeback Mountain*, the gay cowboy film, was big at the time, and Shane often commented on it, calling it "Sex Pistols." In Boston he went on about there being only one law, and that was "God's law." In New York on St. Patrick's day Shane wore a tri-color sash. That night during the "Fiesta" encore he wrapped a cord around his neck pretending to kill himself, but he got a bit carried away. His face turned bright red, his eyes bugged out, and his veins nearly popped. He began changing the words to "Dirty Old Town" singing that he consummated his relationship with, rather than just "met" his girl by the gasworks wall. Everyone, fans and Pogues alike, agreed the shows were some of the band's best.

Once in America they toured by bus. They passed the travel hours watching DVDs: *Cream's Farewell Concert*, *A Mighty Wind*, *Hannibal*, and *Dirty Harry* among them. When the DVD player's heads needed cleaning, MacGowan authoritatively assured everyone that gin would do the job perfectly well. MacGowan and Cashman staked out an area of the bus that Fearnley described as "the cacophonous, contentious, smoke-filled, and sometimes squalid den" having a table "covered in materials - ashtrays, a bottle of white Zinfandel, a plastic cup of I don't know, gin or vodka, hotdogs and a shed-load of cheese." Shane frequently fell asleep on the bus while watching TV and smoking. Often he woke up when his cigarette burned down to the point that it burned him.

It's not surprising that MacGowan did a lot of sleeping on the bus, since he did very little of it in the hotels. Most nights he stayed up all hours talking to fans in the hotel bars. In Atlantic city Shane and a few of the others stayed up all night talking with friends of Patsy O'Hara, the third hunger striker to die in Belfast's Long Kesh Prison in 1981. Shane also spent time with family members of a man who was killed in the Bloody Sunday riots. In Baltimore he met the Mayor, Martin O'Malley, who was absolutely elated to shake Shane's hand. A long time Pogues' fan, the Mayor plays guitar in O'Malley's March, his own Irish music band. When the ten days were over the Pogues returned to England without their singer. Shane stayed behind in his New York City hotel room for the next three weeks with a "Do not disturb" sign on his door.

In the fall they returned to Japan for a few shows and followed that with a short tour of the West Coast in the States before returning home. Once there, they took nearly two months off before doing what had become an annual Christmas season tour in the UK. On the last leg of the American tour, they played Las Vegas where Spider Stacy got married. Shane was his best man and sang "Love Me Tender" dressed up in an Elvis impersonator outfit. Cait O'Riordan wasn't invited back for these shows. A reporter wrote that she showed up at one of them and "pleaded" to join the band on stage. They refused. None of the Pogues were willing to comment on the incident. All they would say was that it was due to "personal reasons." A few years later, O'Riordan told a journalist, "I rejoined the Pogues in 2004 for a two-week tour, but they didn't ask me back and I don't blame them. They're older guys; most of them don't drink now. I was toxic and dysfunctional. I told a doctor that I was either developing schizophrenia or possessed." She said that after her career with the Pogues and her marriage to Elvis Costello she was financially secure, but unhappy, and started drinking heavily. (Some have reported O'Riordan and Costello never actually married.) She had a breakdown at 38 and was admitted to a psychiatric hospital for depression. Eventually she improved and went back to school to become a psychologist, but added, "I desperately miss playing. If anyone needs a bass player, call me. When I was doing my exams, there was a poster up for the Pogues, who were playing in the same building. I thought, 'I wish there was someone I could talk to about how weird this feels.'"

In October there was good political news coming from Scotland. The multi-party Northern Ireland peace talks taking place there had produced The St. Andrews Agreement. It restored the power sharing Northern Ireland Assembly and set a timetable for the devolution of police and justice powers from England to Northern Ireland. In addition, Sinn Fein agreed to fully accept the Police Service of Northern Ireland. Reg Empey, Leader of the Ulster Unionist Party, described the agreement as "the Belfast (Good Friday) Agreement for slow learners." Martin McGuinness, who had worked closely with Unionist leader Ian Paisley, told the press, "Up until the 26th of March this year, Ian Paisley and I never had a conversation about anything – not even about the weather – and now we have worked very closely together over the last seven months and there's been no angry words between us. ...This shows we are set for a new course."

On December 15th, 2006, Tom McMannamon, the Popes banjo player, died. He was only 45 years old. He was buried in jeans and a leather jacket, holding his banjo. Shane didn't attend the funeral. A source said he didn't want to distract from the proceedings. He did, however, eulogize McMannamon on the fan club website saying, "He gained a lot of personal problems and it's none of my business to discuss them, stuff like his parents dying when he was young and stuff like that. The most brilliant banjo player I have ever played with. He was undoubtedly one of the nicest guys, he was always brilliant, but there was a high emotional price to pay, that sort of genius comes with a price, and he drank too much basically. Tommy took a sabbatical, to try and get healthy, cause the last thing I wanted was for another person to die, for the sake of us playing gigs. He went off and we made an agreement that we would all try and get ourselves together, and I wouldn't see him and he wouldn't see me until he was okay. It seemed to be working, and it certainly worked for me and the rest of the gang, but the band broke up eventually. Tommy was already very ill by the time. It was only meant to be a sabbatical he was taking. He never left the band or we never threw him out or anything. Unquestionably, in the banjo stakes he was in the same category as Terry Woods, a really inspired musician…Tommy never played a bad gig. He was absolutely brilliant, and a brilliant human being, it's a pity that staying off the road didn't work."

The now annual Pogues UK Christmas tour got off to a good start. MacGowan showed up for the first rehearsal sporting a new pin-stripe suit and leather coat. Everyone was in good spirits. James Fearnley also had a new suit. In his tour diary he wrote that Terry Woods told him that it was the same color as the old Free State Army uniforms. James made the mistake of mentioning that to Shane, who took umbrage at the assertion, knowing that his British band mate wasn't quite sure what the Free State Army was. Fearnley, much to his relief, narrowly escaped a lecture on the fine points of the Irish Civil War. During rehearsals the Pogues decided to add some tunes that they hadn't performed in awhile to the Christmas set. They rehearsed "Hell's Ditch," "Kitty," "Boat Train," and "The Auld Triangle," but they had to listen to them on an Ipod first to remember how the songs went.

MacGowan even showed up for the sound check on opening night in Glasgow. Backstage before the show Fearnley observed him performing strange physical maneuvers. He was sitting in a chair, lifting his feet into the air, and twirling them around. He also whirled his arms around in the air. At one point he grabbed his ankles, one at a time, and lifted each foot onto his lap in a sort of half lotus position. Shane claimed it was an oriental exercise routine called *Chu Ki*. He said it was similar to *Tai Chi*, the major difference being that it's done sitting down instead of standing up. He swore that it was all the rage in Ireland. Fearnley said he was, "amazed at his suppleness…I mean, I've seen him walk from the hotel door to the bus, from the side of the stage to the mike, and I'm amazed."

MacGowan sported a new stage look in concert. He wore the buccaneer shirt he got from the *Libertine* film shoot along with what he called a Stasi trench coat. It was a full length, black leather coat similar to the ones Nazi SS officers wore in World War II. After a desperate search to fulfill Shane's request, Cashman found it for $45.00 in a Glasgow second hand store. During that night's set MacGowan ignored Scotland's recent ban on smoking in public buildings. He smoked throughout the set, throwing his still lit cigarette butts on the stage. No one dared stop him. Afterwards, back at the hotel, he wasn't as lucky. Earlier in the day Shane had smoked in the hotel bar. The hotel manager, while adamant to put a stop to the outrage, was no less hesitant to confront Shane. Instead, he closed the bar before the Pogues got back from the gig. From his hotel room Shane called Dickon Edwards, who helped him blog about smoking on the Friends of Shane website. "I can't believe how severely the smoking ban is enforced up here in Scotland, where I've been playing a gig with The Pogues," he wrote. "The ban is simply incredible up here. The enforcement is tougher than you could believe.

Certainly compared to Dublin. Back there the fuss has comparatively died away. There are areas divided up into smoking and non-smoking and so on, and there are a lot of blind eyes being turned for the sake of the 'auld boys.' And rightly so – it's all about personal freedom and personal choice, and city air is damaging enough as it is, so you might as well choose your own filter. But in Glasgow the police really go for the ban in strength. Some of us were smoking onstage on account it being part of our time-honored performance, as it were, but the audience was clearly feeling the eyes of the ban upon them. It was tangible. The moment we left the stage for good, the crowd dashed outside purely to smoke. And it's not as if the Scots were pressurized into the ban in the first place. I think it's that tough, gutsy Scottish will-power thing – 'We can jump about pissed to Irish rock and roll music AND we can do it without smoking!'"

Despite the promising start, the Pogues' 2006 Christmas tour was probably the weakest of their second incarnation. One problem was the sound. They couldn't quite hear each other right, and sometimes they had trouble keeping the beat. They lost it repeatedly during "Sunny Side of the Street." In Birmingham Shane was out of time on "Paddy Works on the Railroad." Fearnley came over to him and stomped his foot loudly to the beat in an effort to get MacGowan back on time. Shane either misunderstood the effort, or perhaps he was just annoyed by it. It made him mad enough to splash wine from his bottle of Retsina onto Fearnley's new accordion. James was not pleased. Part of the audio problem was that they had a new sound engineer. It was Tim Sunderland's first time on the road with the band, and apart from hearing a few of the Pogues' records, he wasn't all that familiar with their material. Each night he had a stack of note cards to help him cope with instrument changes and the like. The worst show was in Manchester the night after Tommy McMannamon died. Although he didn't say anything about it, Shane was surely affected by his friend's death. He went onstage noticeably drunker than he had been at any of the previous reunion concerts and seemed adrift. The next night in London he showed up at the Brixton Academy sound check to try and sort things out. The Brixton shows were noticeably better. The last night at the Academy, however, MacGowan barely made the show. Backstage shortly before the concert, an assistant entered the dressing room to announce that Shane hadn't arrived yet. He had locked himself in his hotel room and was still asleep, or worse. Apparently, no amount of commotion outside the door was able to wake him. The hotel passkey was useless since Shane had fastened the security latch from the inside. With 4,500 fans expecting their hero to take the stage any moment, the band, not to mention the promoter, were getting more and more anxious. MacGowan later blogged on his fan website, "Last Tuesday I was woken by hotel security breaking down the door. It was minutes before I was due onstage with The Pogues at Brixton Academy, and people were understandably concerned that I hadn't yet emerged. It's fair to say I'm not much of a day person. I'd been up all night talking with friends, holding court, then overslept somewhat." In good Taoist form, MacGowan went with the flow, arriving at the hall oblivious to the consternation just as the Pogues were scheduled to go on. Fearnley said it was a fine show and Shane was in "remarkably good form." When the Pogues closed the tour in Dublin they seemed to have ironed out the audio difficulties, and MacGowan turned in a great performance.

On Christmas day Shane MacGowan, against all odds, began his 50th year. He spent his 49th birthday at the old home place. "I've been down in Tipp since Christmas day," he said. "We had a lot of drink over Christmas, a few rows with the old man, and it has been mainly friendly so far… I am looking forward to New Year's Eve. That will be a good one. We are going to spend it at the old house, which is right out in the country where I was brought up, her mother and her mother you know? It's nearly 400 hundred years old. It's where I got it all from; obviously I didn't scrape it off the floor! It should be a good night. What's left of the family will be there, we will have a few drinks, and sing and play music. I still mess around on guitar or whatever is there, but on New Year's it will be more the Sean Nos type of thing mixed with playing the old records like Elvis and Rock 'n' Roll."

In January Ireland's channel 4 aired a show called *The Ultimate Hellraiser*. It listed the top 25 rock and roll hell raisers of all time. Shane came in at a disappointing #7, finishing among others behind Keith Moon, Ozzy Osbourne, and Keith Richards. MacGowan, Clarke, and Cashman were all interviewed for the program. They spoke mostly about the time Maori spirits enticed Shane to paint himself blue in New Zealand, and the time he dropped 15 to 20 tabs of acid and ate a Beach Boys album to demonstrate the United States' cultural inferiority.

The Pogues returned to America for another round of sold out concerts in the spring. MacGowan missed a show at New York's Roseland Ballroom, his first no-show with the reunited Pogues. Word was that he had fallen and injured a knee. He was back onstage in a wheelchair the following night. He was still in the wheelchair in Philadelphia. The show took place at the Electric Factory during a rare March snowstorm. The roads were treacherous, but the Factory was packed. The Pogues opened with an instrumental before MacGowan was wheeled out. The crowd went wild. In a word, he was sensational. Incredibly focused and intense, he just sat there, tapping his left arm on the side of the wheelchair. It was spellbinding. After every third song or so Shane was wheeled offstage. While he was in the wings, the Pogues did one number, and then he was wheeled back out again. Most of the crowd knew all the songs and sang along. On the slower numbers they put their arms over each other's shoulders, rocking back and forth in unison to the tune. One reviewer said, "The crowd's enthusiasm, the Pogues' exuberance, and Shane's flat-out brilliance resulted in one of the finest concerts the city of brotherly love had ever seen."

In June Deirdre Drew, Ronnie's wife, died of cancer. Ronnie himself had been receiving cancer treatments and had just gotten the all clear when Deirdre was diagnosed. She was gone within six weeks. Shane and Victoria attended the funeral in Greystones, County Wicklow, Ireland. Ronnie Drew followed his wife to the grave a little more than a year later, leaving an estate of $1,636,448. Irish folk music had been as good to him as he had been to it. He was 73 years old. The week after the funeral Shane participated in *The Forest of No Return*, a night dedicated to songs from Disney movies, at London's Southbank Meltdown Festival. He sang a punk version of "Zip-A-Dee-Doo-Dah." It was an unforgettable sight: a disheveled man in a rumpled black suit, drink in hand, singing Disney! The crowd roared its approval. He also joined Jarvis Cocker, Pete Doherty, and Nick Cave in a three-minute dog-howling chorus from *Lady And the Tramp*. The following week MacGowan participated in the Hoping Foundation's celebrity karaoke night benefit. Attendees bid to hear celebrities sing to raise money for Palestinian kids. The top bid of the event was a staggering $573,000.00 for Elton John to sing Elvis' "Are You Lonesome Tonight?" Sir Elton paid $52,000.00 to hear Shane sing Billy Joel's "We Didn't Start the Fire."

MacGowan videotaped "Dirty Old Town," "The Irish Rover," and an interview for American television's *Henry Rollins Show* in July. Only "Dirty Old Town" made it onto the show. He was backed by an acoustic rhythm guitar, an electric bass, drums, and Joey Cashman on whistle. No Pogues or Popes were in the band. Before beginning "Dirty Old Town" he had some choice words for American President George Bush and American voters. Obviously drunk, before beginning the song Shane slurred into the microphone, "Fuck Bush! You're fucking doing the same thing all over again like you did in Nam. Fucking get rid of him." In the unaired interview Shane had more to say about Bush's policies. "It's a crazy thing to do, declaring war on Islam," he said. "It's so many different countries, so many different types of people. And then to hit the wrong country. I'm not going to go off on an Oliver Stone conspiracy plot, because you don't need conspiracies because the whole thing is an obvious fucking conspiracy. All governments are a conspiracy. In Ireland we got a transparent conspiracy. Everybody knows people are on the take and that's the way it works. I think it works like that in America. The English, they'll never admit it, but the Americans they're admitting it, but they're not doing anything to make it any better. They're not trying to fucking cool it out. They're trying to make it worse."

Throughout the summer MacGowan got some R n' R in preparation for yet another Pogues tour of the States. He was back with Victoria Clarke, and everywhere they went Shane and Victoria made the papers. They were seen at the 15th annual gay and lesbian film festival in Dublin, at the opening of the *Golden Age of Couture: Paris and London 1947-1957* exhibit at London's Victoria and Albert Museum, and at the Berkley Square Ball to support the Prince's Trust. In August MacGowan did a charity appearance in a television ad promoting the *People in Need* telethon. He was filmed in a dentist's chair pretending to get his teeth worked on.

In the fall Shane and the Pogues returned to the states for another short, successful American tour. They played one show in San Diego and two each in Seattle, San Francisco, Los Angeles, and Las Vegas. At the second of the two shows in Vegas, in response to a request shouted from the pit, MacGowan delighted the crowd with an impassioned take on "Boys of Kilmichael." The Pogues were back in the UK by December for their annual Christmas tour. They did 10 shows in Scotland, England, and Ireland. Each concert got great reviews, but Shane's best performance was the tour's last. It came two nights before Christmas in Dublin in the main hall of the Royal Dublin Society. Next to that hall was another room, nearly as large, which served as the bar. Both rooms were filled to capacity. There was a half hour long line to get into every restroom. The sold out crowd was decked out in Santa Claus hats, tri-color shirts, and green, green, green. The *Independent* reported, "The sense of Irishness just managed to stay on the right side of overwhelming." MacGowan came out after the rest of the Pogues to thunderous applause. He wore his full-length leather Stasi coat and a black tophat. The set lasted an hour and a half. Highlights? There were none. The show was sensational from start to finish. The crowd went especially wild over "Dirty Old Town." During "Sickbed of Cuchulainn" someone threw the Irish tri-color flag onstage. Appropriately, Shane finished the song literally wrapped in the flag. Phil Chevron missed the tour due to a battle with cancer. As awful as that was for Pogues' fans, it provided the audience the rare opportunity to hear MacGowan sing "Thousands Are Sailing" in concert. There were several encores. The best was "Fairytale of New York." As Fearnley's piano played the opening notes to the Christmas classic, Sinead O'Conner entered from the wings dressed in a skimpy Santa Claus suit. The crowd roared. It wasn't Kirsty MaColl, but nobody was complaining. If the night had a more emotional moment, it was the sold out crowd singing happy birthday to MacGowan. In two days he would be 50 years old. Surely the County Hell would freeze over.

MacGowan celebrated the big day over a relatively quiet Christmas dinner with friends and family in Cork. His sister gave him an assortment of Sun Records memorabilia she had ordered from America. The raucous party took place more than a week earlier in London at the Boogaloo. It was a private party, but it was well covered in the press, which dutifully reported that Shane partied hard with his pals. Victoria called it, "…warm, friendly, totally unpretentious and really good fun. We danced all night, and laughed a lot, and most importantly," she added, "even though he hates birthdays, Shane really enjoyed himself."

When the *NME* asked him about his birthday MacGowan said, "Yeah, it bothers me a lot. It's very hard to get used to the idea of not being a young man. I find it very depressing, but I try to be positive about it." That was in 1997 when MacGowan turned 40. He was far more upbeat a decade later. "To be honest I never thought too much about getting to 50. But if everyone is making bets that you are going to die at 4:30 tomorrow afternoon you just tend to think, fuck it, I'm not going to die as long as those fuckers are alive." The press worked overtime cranking out stories on Shane's ability to defy the odds, outliving the plethora of predictions of an early death on the alter of hedonism. Victoria Clarke said she was grateful that he had made it to 50, especially in light of "his legendary alcohol and drug consumption," adding that, "he had been run over several times, been attacked and kicked in the head countless times, he had overdosed, been in intensive care, been in loony bins, jumped out of moving cars, pretty much any way a person could endanger their own life he had tried." Victoria admitted that most of the time she was terrified that she'd awake in the morning to learn he was dead. She often pictured herself attending his funeral. MacGowan dismissed all the talk of his life-style being detrimental. With, one would like to believe, tongue in cheek, he attributed his 50 years to his passion for the wildside. "Smoking, drinking, partying - that's why I've stayed alive as long as I have," he declared. "I party my way through life, it's what I like to do… Booze is definitely good for your voice - it greases the whistle. And I've got better with age. That's what's meant to happen."

EPILOGUE

**"I know that I'm going to live to a very old age. I've always known that.
Call it a superstition or call it something else. My whole family thinks that.
Of course, I could be wrong, but I believe strongly that I am going to be here
for a long time. When I'm actually dead, you'll have to convince me otherwise."**

Shane MacGowan

At one point I considered calling this book *Shane MacGowan: The first 50 years*. When he left the Pogues in 1991, I wouldn't have wagered much that MacGowan would celebrate a 35th birthday. Somehow, he just keeps on going. Amazingly, he's more popular than ever. Since Tommy MacMannamon's death and the Pogues resurgence, it's unlikely we'll ever see MacGowan tour with the Popes again. He did vocals, however, on three tracks on the Popes 2009 release, *Outlaw Heaven*. His only lead vocal on the album, "The Loneliness of the Long Distance Drinker," was a bit rough. He plays several shows each year as a "special guest" on Sharon Shannon tours. More often than not Shane brings the house down just by walking onstage when Shannon is well into her set. It's fair to say that at least as many in her concert audiences have come to see Shane as have come to see Sharon. His real bread and butter, though, are the Pogues tours. The boys generally come together for short American tours in the fall and around every St. Patrick's Day. They usually do a handful of European summer festivals, and inevitably a short Christmas tour of England, Scotland, and Ireland. The Christmas tour of 2010, however, may have been the last. That August Spider Stacy announced that it was "the last Christmas tour for the foreseeable future," adding, "we're tired of dragging our weary, freezing carcasses around these drowning islands every December, so we're going to give it a rest before you get tired of it too." Chevron called it the "first farewell tour." The second farewell tour, dubbed "A Parting Glass" happened three months later. In ten shows it covered six American cities. "I think we are basically pretty certain this is the last tour of this type we'll be doing in the States," Stacy told *Billboard*. He attributed their packing it in to band fatigue, economics, and MacGowan. "We can't always entirely trust Shane to deliver the goods," he said. The tour closed in New York, after three shows, on St. Patrick's Day. We saw all three shows, and the Pogues were brilliant. So was Shane. He commanded the stage. His vocals were superb. He was as unimpaired as we'd ever seen him. If he can maintain that form he's got a few miles left in him. The Pogues planned to continue playing summer festivals. Time will tell.

The remarkable catalogue of songs MacGowan penned as a Pogue seem sure to outlive him. Even if he lives to be 100. Or 200. Or 300. The last time I saw him he was on his way to see a Hilary Swank film called *P.S. I Love You*, which features some of Shane's songs in the soundtrack. It had just become the largest box office hit in Irish history, passing Liam Neeson's *Michael Collins*. While that may not say much for Irish film taste, it did wonders for MacGowan's bank account. When I mentioned that to him Shane flashed his unforgettable grin, cackled his famous death rattle laugh, and gave me the thumbs up. Since then the soundtrack of *The Wire*, a hit American TV series, has used several MacGowan songs. An increasing number of television shows, films, and advertisements feature his material. His work is slowly but surely becoming part of the aural lexicon on both sides of the Atlantic. His royalties alone should keep Shane in the money for the rest of his life. In 2009 he finally used some of that cash on a new set of teeth. He spent that May in Spain having the dental work done. One British paper speculated that his new smile could have cost Shane as much as $80,000.00, an unlikely sum unless it included his hotel bar bill. It wasn't long before he abandoned the dentures.

In May of 2008 MacGowan surprised everyone by reuniting with the Nips, a quarter century after they had disbanded. They did one show, opening for the Seattle punk group the Cute Lepers at the 100 Club in London. The band rehearsed without Shane, so it was clear it was never meant to be more than a lark. MacGowan came on stage in his top hat, clutching a bottle of Bulmer's, and snarled "Fuck you," into the microphone. He forgot some lyrics that night, at one point singing "I don't know the fuckin' words la la la." The Nips played for half an hour. By all accounts the band was tight. One critic called the set "raw, ragged, loud, and brilliant." The crowd loved it. The Nips performed again the following August at an unannounced gig at Philly Ryan's Bar in Nenagh, just down the road from Shane's old homeplace.

What little recording MacGowan has done in the last few years has been primarily as a guest vocalist on other artists' albums. He contributed "Rake at the Gates of Hell" on a Sharon Shannon CD, "Love Is A Casino" for Mundy, and Townes Van Zandt's "Waiting Around to Die" for Mighty Stef. He was also involved in tributes to Ronnie Drew and Liam Clancy. For Christmas in 2010 he did a guest vocal on "Drummer Boy" for the Priests. The recording that most excited MacGowan fans, however, was *Just Look Them Straight in the Eye and Say...Pogue Mahone!!*, a five disc box set released in 2008. It consisted of studio outtakes, rehearsal recordings, live recordings, and hard to find B-sides. Of the set's 111 tracks, three-quarters was unreleased material. Like most "posthumous" collections culled from recordings that had been left on the shelf, there are no long lost masterpieces included. Still, there are many good tracks and several hidden gems. "NW3," a precursor to "Mother Mo Chroi," "Something Wild," and "Driving Through the City" are all worthy additions to Shane's body of work. The set's most outstanding track, "Aisling," was recorded for *Hell's Ditch*. The Pogues' acoustic version is softer and considerably slower than the recording Shane did with the Popes on *The Snake*. Another delight is a portion of a fantastic set, six songs in all, recorded in Scotland's Barrowlands in 1987.

In March of 2010 MacGowan recorded Screamin' Jay Hawkins' 1956 classic "I Put a Spell on You" to raise money for victims of the earthquake that devastated Haiti. Victoria helped him put the charity single together, managing to get Nick Cave, Bobby Gillespie, Chrissie Hynde, Mick Jones, Cait O'Riordan, Glen Matlock, Paloma Faith, Eliza Doolittle, and Johnny Depp to participate. Actually, Shane has used his celebrity to become something of a philanthropist. In addition to giving of his own wealth, he regularly shows up and performs at charity events. He did a benefit for Haiti's poor months before the earthquake hit the island. He's performed at fundraisers for the Aisling Project, an African aids project, Dublin's Temple Street Children's Hospital, and others. At a Hopping Foundation benefit to help Palestinian refugee children he knocked out a quick painting for auction and sang "Fairytale of New York" raising nearly $65,000.00 for his efforts.

Many MacGowan fans have become resigned to the idea that they may have to settle for charity singles, guest recordings, and old outtakes from now on. Shane frequently says he's working on new material and that a new album is in the works, but he's been saying that for over a decade. In 1999 he told the *Irish Voice* he was working on his most political album yet, a double CD about "the history of paddys in Ireland, England, and America." "It's called *Twentieth Century Paddy*," he said. "It's going to be about IRA men, lonely farmers that hang themselves because they can't get a wife. One is based on my mother who got into modeling and was then voted Colleen of the Year in 1954." Three years later one of the Popes said that Shane had eight songs finished for the new CD, including "The Loneliness of the Long Distance Drinker." Two years after that, during a round of four consecutive weekend gigs at Ronnie Scott's Jazz Club in London, Shane told a reporter that he had new material and would begin recording the following month. In 2005 the *Herald* reported Shane was writing a song called "Bible John" for his new CD. It was supposed to be about one of Scotland's most infamous serial killers from the 1960s. The Scottish press had dubbed him Bible John because he quoted Bible verses. The unsolved case had recently been reopened when Glasgow police collected DNA samples from some of the suspects in the original investigation. Ironically, the killer preyed on women attending the Barrowlands dance hall where Shane and the Popes were scheduled to play as the story hit the press. When word got out that Shane was going to debut the song at the Barrowlands concert, three families of Bible John's female victims complained that it would glamorize the killer. The song has yet to surface. MacGowan tends to get a bit touchy if you bring up his lack of productivity. "It's not my fuckin' fault," he told *Hotpress*. "It's the business. I've been here all the time; I could be putting out as many albums as Costello, y'know what I mean? But I won't put out shite, y'know? But there is another album." Fans continue to wait and hope. Even Phil Chevron, who's in a position to know more than most, has not given up. "I think he is still writing, but I don't know why he has a problem in presenting the results," he said. "Maybe he needs a sympathetic environment to bring it out, one that is not there at the moment. Maybe he just needs to bounce his ideas off someone, and I don't think the present situation is conducive to that, but I think it will be again."

Shortly after Spider announced the end of Pogues' Christmas tours, hope of that "sympathetic environment" began to surface. In September of 2010 Shane played two well-reviewed Dublin shows with a new stripped down band billed as "Shane MacGowan and Friends." The sound was more Popes than Pogues, although the sets mixed songs from both bands in addition to covers. There was no new MacGowan material, but in a piece previewing the shows, the *Irish Independent* reported that Shane was "keen to get away from just doing the greatest hits format and back to more creative ways and has put a new band together for this solo project." It went on to say that the two shows were "aimed at getting the band to gel before he starts writing and recording new songs." The Clash's Mick Jones was said to have committed to involvement with recording a new album in February. In November Shane was reportedly in the Canary Islands working on new songs with his new band, by then being called "Shane Gang." Moreover, there was outside corroborating evidence that MacGowan is indeed working on a new album. Just after Christmas, Scottish producer John McLaughlin's car was stolen. He told a reporter that two new Shane MacGowan recordings were in the CD player. They were made after the Pogues' Glasgow show on December 13th.

As they have for nearly three decades, family, friends, and fans remain concerned about MacGowan's health. Every tour brings fresh anxiety as to what kind of condition he'll be in. When the Pogues toured America in the spring of 2009 he was in great shape. "Everybody was in top form, including, of course, Shane," Phil Chevron said, adding that MacGowan was "more consistent than I've ever known him." He was just as good on that year's Christmas tour of England, Scotland, and Ireland. In between those tours, however, on a fall tour of the States, Shane turned in some of the worst performances of his career. A few shows were good, Denver and Texas in particular, but on several nights he was beyond wasted. The press began speculating about his demise all over again. He performed without his new teeth and was invariably described as being pale as a cadaver. In Los Angeles he fell to floor three times. One writer quipped, "forget the pension, this tour is to pay for the wake." The bottom fell out at the Voodoo Festival in New Orleans. Shane went AWOL. He was last seen one evening in a Bourbon Street blues bar. When he failed to return by the following afternoon the tour manager, tour bus driver, and Victoria mounted a search. They scoured the French Quarter inquiring in every bar and voodoo shop. They called all the hospitals. They even checked dumpsters, fearing he may have been murdered and disposed of. Eventually, with Victoria in a panic and Shane still missing, the Pogues took the Voodoo Festival stage with Spider handling the vocals. Halfway into the fourth song, Shane staggered onstage in no condition to perform. He'd been delivered to the festival site by a fan who discovered him that afternoon in the lobby of the wrong hotel. If the fan hadn't had an extra ticket Shane wouldn't have made it onto the grounds. The next day he vomited continually on the flight to London. At one point an Irish paper reported that during a concert in Ireland MacGowan told the audience he had hepititus. The article went on to quote his father, "He has had a very good run on the drink, but he must remember he is mortal," Maurice MacGowan said. "Shane must heed the doctor's advice. He's had scares before but hepatitis is serious." Weeks later Shane denied he had hepatitis, claiming that he had the disease many years ago but had been cured.

One can only hope MacGowan will heed his doctor's advice. He has a lot to live for. He has a beautiful woman who loves him deeply, he has more money than he needs, and if he lives as long as he says he will he just might see a 32-county Ireland. When he was asked about the prospects for a united Ireland in 1996 he said, "I've gone beyond predicting what's gonna happen at this stage, but I do believe that it will be resolved in my lifetime. I reckon I've got long enough left to see it. I'm gonna grow to be a fine old age." As the millenium ended he said, "In this century we got the 26 counties. In the next we'll get the six more. Then there won't be any need for the IRA anymore. The British Army can go home, shag their wives, look after their farms, whatever. And the only ones who'll be pissed off are Trimble and Paisley and the madmen of the UDA… the majority of the regular people, all they want is safety, peace, and work. And that's what they'll get if the border goes, the Brits draw out, and there are 32 county elections. And the government doesn't have to be in Dublin. Fuckin' move it to Dundalk."

In March of 2010 the Northern Ireland Assembly voted to accept an agreement reached after nearly two weeks of round-the-clock talks at Hillsborough Castle in County Down. The agreement came at a time when politicians in the North, South, and England warned that Northern Ireland was staring into the "abyss" again, after a decade of peace. In the previous year there had been riots, bombs, and murders. In one instance two dissident Republican snipers with automatic rifles ambushed four British soldiers at the main gate of the Massereene Barracks as they were accepting a pizza delivery. After the initial volley of shots left the soldiers lying on the ground, the gunmen moved forward and opened fire again, deliberately turning their weapons on the civilians. Two soldiers were killed. The other two soldiers and two pizza deliverymen were seriously injured.

The Hillsborough Agreement was a major milestone in achieving the goals of the earlier Good Friday Agreement and the St. Andrews Agreement. It set a timetable for transfering police and judicial authority from London to Belfast. It also dealt with the problem of parades, mandating that the local people, both those doing the marching and those living in the communities being marched through, would come up with the solutions for managing parades. There were timetables set for this as well. It was particularly encouraging that the agreement passed with a healthy majority, 105 to 88, with only the Ulster Unionist Party voting no. It was also encouraging that the usual dissident violence intended to derail the agreement failed to gather any support. And there was violence. In the weeks leading up to the vote on the agreement, in Northern Ireland dissidents were responsible for a mortar attack on a police station, a car bomb explosion outside a courthouse, and a murder in Derry. The actions were roundly condemned and only increased support for the agreement. The response of John O'Dowd, a Sinn Fein assembly member, was typical. He said, "This attack was wrong and should not have been carried out. I would challenge those who claim to speak politically for these factions to tell the Republican and Nationalist community exactly how these sorts of activities, or indeed the recent murder in Derry, advance the cause of a united Ireland one iota."

Passage of the Hillsborough Agreement put optism for a united Ireland at the highest level it had been since the Irish revolution. It set the seal on a 15-year process that brought Republican leaders into the heart of Northern Ireland's power structure. In addition, the vastly improved economy in the South, even with the effects of the global recession, has persueded many Unionists that Irish unity is in their own economic interest. As 2010 began median earnings in the South were about $800.00 per week compared with $535.00 in the north and $595.00 in Britain. Moreover, in the last few decades there has been a demographic trend towards Nationalism in the North. The 2001 census reported 45% Protestants, 40% Catholics, and a surprising 14% identified with no religion at all. Given historically high Catholic birthrates and a general lessening of religious fervor, that gap will likely continue to close. According to recent surveys, 36% of Northern Ireland's population identify themselves as Unionists, 24% as Nationalists, and 40% as neither. Given the disparity in income and standard of living between the North and the South, it is likely that the 40% will gravitate towards the Nationalists. Of course the Irish question is not that simple. Among other things, voters are divided between conservative and liberal policies. Traditionally, Unionists are far more conservative than Nationalists, who tend to lean to the left. If the trends seen in most of the Western world holds true in Northern Ireland, however, that too should favor Nationalists. In a statement given just prior to the Hillsborough vote, Martin McGuinness shared his optimism for a 32-county nation. "There are a number of identifiable trends leading to Irish unity within a meaningful timeframe," he said. "Ireland is too small for two separate administrations. Partition is costing communities across our island. There is a draw towards the greater integration of services, structures and bodies on an all-Ireland basis in order to deliver quality services and economies of scale. I am encouraged that many Unionists support the development of these types of structures on the basis that they are mutually beneficial... These all point towards the realisation of reintegration of both states presently on the island of Ireland into one independent country. It is particularly important that people in Britain, and in particular the huge Irish Diaspora, are part of this discussion. Governments and all interested sections of society should consider and begin to plan for reunification."

Chances are, whether North and South Ireland reunite or not, Shane MacGowan will remain happy for the rest of his life. He and Victoria never did marry, but they continue to share a Dublin home. The 350 year-old cottage in Carney Commons remains a cherished getaway. Shane doesn't seem likely to give up drinking anytime soon. He lives the life of a celebrity, but doesn't seem to be adversely affected by the adulation. Last year he and Victoria did a reality TV show called *Victoria and Shane's Secret Garden*. Supposedly they were to live for a period of time off the produce they grew. There were recent major features stories about MacGowan in both *Mojo* and *Q* magazines. When he attended the London premiere of Tim Burton's *Alice in Wonderland*, MacGowan drew as much media attention as the film's stars. He takes it all like a good Taoist, going with the flow. "The thing is that Shane doesn't give a fuck," Darryl Hunt says, "and that really helps. He is the only rock star in the world who doesn't give a fuck."

"I have very little ego," Shane once told a journalist. "I intentionally destroyed my own ego, which stopped me becoming an arsehole rock star, as much as it could. Well, I did become a bit of an arsehole rock star at one stage, when the Pogues were really going strong. But I didn't feel that it was what I was doing that was making us a big, big thing. I always thought the music was more important than us. Like, I've never felt arrogant or better than anybody else. I believe in humility." Once in a discussion with Shane about the increasing number of bands doing Irish music, I said that he and the Pogues were primarily responsible for the increase. He was having none of that. "Well, basically the Clancy Brothers were pretty popular," he said. I tried to explain that there was a huge time gap between the Clancy Brothers in the early 1960's and the Pogues in the 1980s, that the Clancy Brothers popularity was brief and nowhere on the Pogues' 'scale, and that the current generation of performers enamoured with Irish music were Pogues fans, not Clancy Brothers fans. It was fruitless. He changed the subject and went off on a tangent that began with Liam Clancy and went on to various aspects of Ireland, Tipperary, the Gaelic language, the British occupation, and the Irish revolution. "Liam lives on the border of Tipperary," he began. "Actually, he was brought up on the border of Tipperary in Waterford. But he moved further east into the Irish speaking area of Waterford. The area of Waterford where most of the people speak Irish as a first language. But Tipperary, Waterford, they're the same. Tipperary's got nine boarders and they were all put there by the Brits. Ireland's Ireland. There are parts of Ireland — there are neighborhoods and the rest of it — Waterford is right next to Tipperary and it's right under Wexford. That's another very famous area for rebellion and revolution against the English." No wonder the Irish love Shane MacGowan. Long may he live.

"I've had a very, very happy life," he says. "If they stuck me in a box tomorrow I'd know I've had a bloody whale of a time. How many other people have made loads of money and done every drug under the sun, and gone out every night, and been all over the world before they're 30? A few maybe. I'm one of the lucky few."

ABRIDGED DISCOGRAPHY

The following is an abridged discography meant merely as a reference for this book. For a more complete discography including Pogues/Popes singles and MacGowan's many guest recordings see any of many Pogues/MacGowan Internet sites.

The Nipple Erectors and The Nips

Singles

King of the Bop/Nervous Wreck
Soho (SH 1) 1978

All the Time in the World/Private Eye
Soho (SH 4) 1979

Gabrielle/Vengeance
Soho (SH 9) 1980

LPs

Only The End Of The Beginning
 Love to Make You Cry, Vengeance, Gabrielle, King of the Bop, Ghostown, Fuss 'N' Bother, Venus in Bovver Boots, Happy Song, Stupid Cow, I Don't Want Nobody to Love, Infatuation, Maida Aida, Hit Parade, Can't Say No
(Recorded live, March 1980 in Wolverhampton)
Soho (HO HO 001) 1980

Bops, Babes, Booze & Bovver
King of the Bop, Nervous Wreck, So Pissed Off, Stavordale Road N5, All the Time in the World, Private Eye, Gabrielle, Vengeance

Big Beat (WIKM 66) 1987

The Tits Of Soho
Studio tracks: King of the Bop, Nervous Wreck, So Pissed Off, Stavordale RD-N5, All the Time in the World, Private Eye, Gabrielle, Vengeance, Happy Song, Nobody to Love
Live tracks: Love to Make You Cry, Vengeance, Gabrielle, King of the Bop, Fuss 'N' Bother, Ghostown, Venus in Bovver Boots, Happy Song, Stupid Cow, I Don't Want Nobody to Love, Infatuation, Maida Aida, Hit Parade, Can't Say No

Bovver Boot Company (BB-ST-8247) 2000

Pogue Mahone and The Pogues

LPs

Red Roses For Me
Transmetropolitan, The Battle of Brisbane, The Auld Triangle, Waxie's Dargle, Boys
From the County Hell, Sea Shanty, Dark Streets of London, Streams of Whiskey, Poor
Paddy, Dingle Regatta, Greenland Whale Fisheries, Down in the Ground Where the
Dead Men Go, Kitty
Stiff (SEEZ55) 1984
(The following tracks are included on the remastered reissue on Rhino, 2005)
Leaving of Liverpool, Muirshin Durkin, Repeal of the Licensing Laws,
The Band Played Waltzing Matilda, Whiskey You're the Devil, Wild Rover

Rum, Sodomy & the Lash
The Sick Bed of Cuchulainn, The Old Main Drag, Wild Cats of Kilkenny, I'm a Man
You Don't Meet Every Day, A Pair Of Brown Eyes, Sally MacLennane, Dirty Old
Town, Jesse James, Navigator, Billy's Bones, The Gentleman Soldier, The Band Played
Waltzing Matilda
Stiff (SEEZ58) 1985
(The following tracks are included on the remastered reissue on Rhino, 2005)
A Pistol for Paddy Garcia, London Girl, Rainy Night in Soho, Body of an American,
Planxty Noel Hill, Parting Glass

If I Should Fall From Grace With God
If I Should Fall From Grace With God, Turkish Song of the Damned, Bottle of Smoke,
Fairytale of New York, Metropolis, Thousands are Sailing, Fiesta, Medley, Streets of
Sorrow/Birmingham Six, Lullaby of London, Sit Down by the Fire, The Broad Majes-
tic Shannon, Worms
Stiff (CDNYR-1) 1988
(The following tracks are included on the remastered reissue on Rhino, 2006)
The Battle March Medley, Irish Rover, Mountain Dew, Shanne Bradley, Sketches of
Spain, South Australia

Peace & Love
Gridlock, White City, Young Ned of the Hill, Misty Morning Albert Bridge, Cotton
Fields, Blue Heaven, Down All the Days, USA, Lorelei, Gartloney Rats, Boat Train,
Tombstone, Night Train to Lorca, London You're a Lady
WEA (Pogue Mahone NYR2) 1989

(The following tracks are included on the remastered reissue on Rhino, 2005)
Star of the County Down, Limerick Rake, Train of Love, Every Man Is a King, Yeah
Yeah Yeah Yeah Yeah, Honky Tonk Women

Hell's Ditch

Sunnyside of the Street, Sayonara, The Ghost of a Smile, Hell's Ditch, Lorca's Novena,
Summer in Siam, Rain Street, Rainbow Man, The Wake of the Medusa, House of the
Gods, Five Green Queens and Jean, Maidrin Rua, Six to Go
WEA (Pogue Mahone 9031-72554/2) 1990
(The following tracks are included on the remastered reissue on Rhino, 2005)
Whiskey in the Jar, Bastard Landlord, Infinity, Curse of Love, Squid Out of Water,
Jack's Heroes, Rainy Night in Soho

Essential Pogues

The Sunnyside of the Street, If I Should Fall From Grace With God, Lorelei, Thousands Are Sailing, White City, Fairytale of New York, Fiesta, Rain Street, Turkish Song
of the Damned, Summer in Siam, Misty Morning Albert Bridge, Blue Heaven, Honky
Tonk Women, Yeah Yeah Yeah Yeah Yeah
Island Records (314-510610-2) 1991

The Best of the Pogues

Fairytale of New York, Sally MacLennane, Dirty Old Town, The Irish Rover, A Pair Of
Brown Eyes, Streams of Whiskey, A Rainy Night in Soho, Fiesta, Rain Street, Misty
Morning Albert Bridge, White City, Thousands Are Sailing, The Broad Majestic Shannon,
Body of an American
WEA (9031-75405-2) 1991

The Rest of the Best

If I Should Fall From Grace With God, The Sick Bed of Cuchulainn, The Old Main
Drag, Boys From the County Hell, Young Ned of the Hill, Dark Streets of London, The
Auld Triangle, Repeal Of The Licensing Laws, Yeah Yeah Yeah Yeah Yeah, London Girl,
Honky Tonk Women, Summer in Siam, Turkish Song of the Damned, Lullaby of Lon-
don, The Sunnyside of the Street, Hell's Ditch
WEA Records (9031-77341-2) 1992

The Best of the Pogues, Vol. I

Fairytale Of New York, Sally MacLennane, Dirty Old Town, The Irish Rover, A Pair
Of Brown Eyes, Streams of Whiskey, A Rainy Night in Soho, Fiesta, Rain Street, Misty
Morning-Albert Bridge, White City, Thousands Are Sailing, The Broad Majestic Shan-
non, The Body of an American

WEA Japan (1371) 1997

The Best of the Pogues, Vol. II
If I Should Fall from Grace with God, The Sick Bed of Cuchulainn, The Old Main
Drag, Boys from the County Hell, Young Ned of the Hill, Dark Streets of London, The
Auld Triangle, Repeal of the Licensing Laws, Yeah Yeah Yeah Yeah Yeah, London Girl,
Honky Tonk Woman, Summer in Siam, Turkish Song of the Damned, Lullaby of Lon-
don, The Sunnyside of the Street, Hell's Ditch
WEA Japan (1372) 1997

The Very Best of the Pogues
Dirty Old Town, The Irish Rover, Sally MacLennane, Fiesta, A Pair Of Brown Eyes,
Fairytale Of New York, The Body of an American, Streams Of Whiskey, The Sick Bed
Of Cuchulainn, If I Should Fall From Grace With God, Misty Morning-Albert Bridge,
Rain Street, White City, A Rainy Night in Soho, London Girl, Boys From The County
Hell, The Sunnyside Of The Street, Summer In Siam, Hell's Ditch, The Old Main
Drag, The Band Played Waltzing Matilda
WEA 2001

Just Look Them Straight in the Eye and Say…Pogue Mahone!!

Disc One
The Kerry Polka, The Rocky Road to Dublin, Boys from the County Hell, NW3,
The Donegal Express/The Hen and the Cock Are in Carrickmacross, Do You Believe
in Magic?, Hot Asphalt,   Danny Boy, Maggie May, Haunted, The Travelling People,
Eve of Destruction, My Baby's Gone, North Sea Holes, Garbo (aka In and Out), The
Last of McGee, Afro-Cuban Be-Bop (1), Young Ned of the Hill (Dub Version), Pinned
Down / I'm Alone in the Wilderness, When the Ship Comes In, Waxies Dargle

Disc Two
Repeal of the Licensing Laws, Dark Streets of London, Greenland Whale Fisheries,
Streams of Whiskey, The Auld Triangle, Poor Paddy on the Railway, Sea Shanty, Trans-
metropolitan, Kitty, Boys from the County Hell, Connemara, Let's Go! (aka Down
in the Ground Where the Dead Men Go), Billy's Bones, The Old Main Drag, Sally
Maclennane, The Town That Never Sleeps, Something Wild, Driving Through the City,
Rainy Night in Soho, Fairytale of New York (1), Fairytale of New York (2), Fairytale of
New York (3), Navigator
Disc Three
The Aria, The Good, the Bad and the Ugly, Haunted, Love Theme from *Sid And Nancy*,
Junk Theme, Glued Up and Speeding, Paris, A Needle for Paddy Garcia, JB 57, Bow-
ery Snax / Spiked, Hot Dogs with Everything, Rince Del Emplacada, The Rake at the
Gates of Hell, Turkish Song of the Damned, If I Should Fall from Grace with God, Bat-

tle March, Lullaby of London, Shanne Bradley, Streets of Sorrow, Thousands are Sailing, The Balinalee, Nicaragua Libré, Japan

Disc Four
Sally Maclennane, A Pair of Brown Eyes, Kitty, Maggie May, Dirty Old Town, The Sickbed of Cuchulainn, Fiesta, If I Should Fall from Grace with God, Johnny Come Lately, Boat Train, Night Train to Lorca, The Mistlethrush, Got a Lot of Livin' to Do, Victoria, Murder (1), Lust for Vomit, The Wake of the Medusa, The Black Dogs Ditch, Aisling, Murder (2), Yeah Yeah Yeah Yeah, Maidrín Rua, Johnny Come Lately,

Disc Five
Johnny Was, Miss Otis Regrets / Just One of Those Things, All the Tears That I Cried, The One and Only, Afro-Cuban Be-Bop, Turkish Song of the Damned, London Calling, I Fought the Law, The Girl from the Wadi-Hammamat, Moving to Moldova, Call My Name, The Sun and the Moon, Living in a World Without Her, Who Said Romance Is Dead?, Sound of the City Night, Four O'Clock in the Morning, The Star of the County Down, White City, Medley: The Recruiting Sergeant / The Rocky Road to Dublin / The Galway Races, The Parting Glass / Lord Santry's Fairest Daughter
Rhino (5144281352) 2008

Shane MacGowan and the Popes

LPs
The Snake
The Church of the Holy Spook, Nancy Whiskey, Song with No Name, Aisling, Roddy McCorley, Victoria, That Woman's Got Me Drinking, You're the One, A Mexican Funeral in Paris, The Rising of the Moon, The Snake with Eyes of Garnet, Haunted, I'll Be Your Handbag, Her Father Didn't Like Me Anyway, Bring Down the Lamp, Donegal Express
ZTT (0630-10402-2) 1995

The Crock of Gold
Paddy Rolling Stone, Rock'n'Roll Paddy, Paddy Public Enemy No. 1, Back in the County Hell, Lonesome Highway, Come to the Bower, Céilídh Cowboy, More Pricks Than Kicks, Truck Drivin' Man, Joey's in America, B & I Ferry, Mother Mo Chroí, Spanish Lady, St. John of Gods, Skipping Rhymes, MacLennane, Wanderin' Star
ZTT (MACG002) 1997

Across the Broad Atlantic
If I Should Fall from Grace with God, Rock 'n' Roll Paddy, Nancy Whisky, A Rainy Night in Soho, Poor Paddy Works on the Railway, The Broad Majestic Shannon, Popes'

Instrumental, Dirty Old Town, Mother Mo Chroi, Body of an American, Granuaille,
More Pricks Than Kicks, Aisling, A Pair of Brown Eyes, Streams of Whisky, Lonesome
Highway, Angel of Death, Sick Bed of Cuchulain, The Irish Rover, Fairytale of
New York
Eagle Records (WK57068) 2002

The Rare Auld Stuff
You're the One, The Song with No Name, Nancy Whiskey, Roddy McCorley, Rock
'n' Roll Paddy, Christmas Lullaby, Danny Boy, Minstrel Boy, Rake at the Gates of
Hell, Victoria, Donegal Express, Ceilidh Cowboy, Paddy Rolling Stone, Paddy Public
Enemy No. 1, Back in Country Hell, The Snake with Eyes of Garnet, Cracklin' Rosie,
Aisling, Spanish Lady, Come to the Bower, St. John of Gods
ZTT 2005

BIBLIOGRAPHY

Barry, Tom, *Guerilla Days in Ireland* (Devin-Adair Company, 1956)

Behan, Brendan, *The Complete Plays* (Grove Press, New York, NY, 1978)

Behan, Dominic, *Ireland Sings: An anthology of Irish songs and ballads* (Vicks Lithograph and Printing Corporation, New York, NY, 1973)

Behan, Dominic, *My Brother Brendan* (Simon and Schuster, New York, NY, 1965)

Boot, Adrian and Salewicz, Chris, *Punk: The illustrated history of a music revolution* (Penguin, New York, NY, 1997)

Bradford, Tim, *Is Shane MacGowan Still Alive?* (Flamingo, London, England, 2000)

Breen, Dan, *My Fight for Irish Freedom* (Anvil Books Limited, Dublin, Ireland, 1981)

Bockris, Victor and Bayley, Roberta, *Patti Smith: An unauthorized biography* (Simon & Schuster, New York, NY, 1999)

Clarke, Victoria Mary, *Angel in DisGuise?* (Collins Press, Cork, Ireland, 2007)

Clarke, Victoria Mary, *A Drink with Shane MacGowan* (Sidgwick & Jackson, London, England, 2001)

Clerk, Carol, *Pogue Mahone, Kiss My Arse: The story of the Pogues* (Omnibus Press, London, England, 2006)

Collins, Michael, *A Path to Freedom* (Nu Vision Publications, Sioux Falls, SD, 2005)

Coogan, Tim Pat, *Eamon De Valera: The man who was Ireland* (Harper Collins, New York, NY 1993)

Coogan, Tim Pat, *The IRA* (Palgrave, New York, NY 2002)

Coogan, Tim Pat and Morrison, George, *The Irish Civil War* (Roberts Rinehart Publishers, Boulder, CO, 2001)

Coogan, Tim Pat, *Michael Collins: The man who made Ireland* (Palgrave, New York, NY 2002)

Coogan, Tim Pat, *On the Blanket* (Palgrave, New York, NY, 2002)

Coogan, Tim Pat, *Wherever the Green Is Worn: The story of the Irish Diaspora* (Palgrave, New York, NY, 2000)

Cronin, Sean, *The Story of Kevin Barry* (National Publications Committee, Cork, Ireland, 1965)

Deasy, Liam, *Brother Against Brother* (Mercier Press, Cork, 1998)

Deasy, Liam, *Towards Ireland Free* (Royal Carberry Books, Cork, 1973)

De Rosa, Peter, *Rebels: The Irish Rising of 1916* (Doubleday, New York, NY, 1990)

Donleavy, J.P., *Fairytale of New York* (Atlantic Monthly Press, New York, NY, 1989)

Donleavy, J.P., *The Ginger Man* (Dell Publishing, New York, NY, 1965)

Dylan, Bob, *Chronicles: Volume one* (Simon & Schuster, New York, NY, 2004)

Fearnley, James, *Tour Diary* (retrieved from www.pogues.com)

Gray, Marcus, *Last Gang in Town: The story and myth of the Clash* (Henry Holt and Company, New York, NY, 1995)

Haverty, Anne, *Constance Markievicz: Irish Revolutionary* (Pandora, London, 1988)

Irwin, Colvin, *In Search of the Craic: One man's pub crawl through Irish music* (Andre Deutsch, London, England, 2004)

Lydon, John, *Rotten: No Irish, no blacks, no dogs* (St. Martin's Press, New York, NY, 1994)

Matlock, Glen with Silverton, Pete, *I Was a Teenage Sex Pistol* (Omnibus Press, London, England, 1990)

McNeil, Legs and McCain, Gillian, *Please Kill Me: The uncensored oral history of punk* (Grove Press, New York, NY, 1996)

Merrick, Joe, *London Irish Punk Life & Music...Shane MacGowan* (Omnibus Press, London, England, 2001)

O'Conner, Ulick, *Michael Collins and the Troubles: The struggle for Irish freedom 1912-1922* (W.W. Norton & Company, New York, NY, 1996)

O'Doherty, Ian, *Shane MacGowan: Last of the Celtic soul rebels* (Blackwater Press, Dublin, Ireland, 1994)

O'Malley, Ernie, *Army without Banners* (Houghton Mifflin Company, Boston, MA, 1937)

O'Malley, Ernie, *Raids and Rallies* (Anvil Books, Dublin, 1982)

Pelling, Rowan (ed.), *The Decadent Handbook: For the modern libertine* (Dedalus, Cambridgeshire, England, 2006)

Po-tuan, Chang, *The Inner Teachings of Taoism* (Shambhala, Boston, MA, 2001)

Purdon, Edward, *The Civil War: 1922-23* (Mercier Press, Cork, Ireland, 2000)

Roddy, Martin, *A Man You Don't Meet Everyday: Shane Macgowan, Christmas 2006* (Friends of Shane Website, 2007)

Roesgen, Jeffrey T., *33 1/3: Rum, Sodomy & the Lash* (Continuum International, New York, NY 2008)

Rotolo, Suze, *A Freewheelin' Time: A memoir of Greenwich Village in the Sixties* (Broadway, New York, NY, 2009)

Scanlon, Ann, *Lost Decade: The story of the Pogues* (Omnibus Press, London, England, 1988)

Smith, Huston, *The Religions of Man* (Harper and Row, New York, NY, 1965)

Tri-colorred Ribbon: Rebel songs of Ireland (Walton's Publications, Dublin, Ireland, 1969)

Zimmerman, Georges Denis, *Songs of Irish Rebellion: Irish political street ballads and rebel songs, 1780-1900* (Four Courts Press, Dublin, Ireland 2002)

Articles from the following sources (many of which cease to exist) were also referenced while researching this book:

Asbury Park Press, Austin American Statesman, Austin Chronicle, Band Magazine, BBC Folk and Acoustic, BBC News Online, Beat, Belfast Telegraph, Billboard, Book Magazine, Boston Globe, Boston Herald, Boston Irish Reporter, Boston Phoenix, Boston's Weekly Dig, Calgary Her-

ald, Canadian Online Explorer, Channel 3000.com, Chicago Magazine, Chart Attack, Chicago Sun-Times, Chicago Tribune, Christian Science Monitor, CNN.com, *Columbia Spectator, Concert Livewire, Contactmusic.com, Cork Examiner, Courier-Journal, Cumberland News, Daily Californian, Daily Cougar, Daily Mail, Daily Mirror, Daily Record, Daily Telegraph, Daily Yomiuri, Dayton Daily News, Denver Post, Des Moines Register, Dotmusic, The Dreaming Armadillo, Drop D Magazine, The Dubliner,* Dublinks.com, *Embassy of Ireland* website, *Entertainment Magazine, Europe Magazine, Evening Chronicle, Evening Herald, Evening Press, Evening Standard, Good Times, The Guardian, The Herald, The Hollywood Reporter, Hot Press, Illinois Entertainer, The Independent, Irishabroad.com, Irish American Post, Irish Examiner, Irish Mirror, The Irish News, Irish Post, Irish Times, Irish Voice, Irish World, The Island Ear, Jamming Magazine, Jerusalem Post, The Journal News, Justice, LA Weekly, Library Journal, Limerick Leader, Liverpool Echo, Loaded, Los Angeles Times, Maclean's, Manchester Evening News, Manchester Music, Manchester On Line, Melody Maker, Metro Times, The Midnight Sun, Mojo, Montreal Gazette, MTV Online Reviews, Nenagh Guardian, Newark Star Ledger, New Jersey Online, New Musical Express, Newsday, News of the World, New York Post, New York Press, New York Sun, New York Times, The Observer, The Patriot Ledger, People, Philadelphia Inquirer, Philadelphia Weekly, The Phoenix, Playboy, Playlouder, Prague Post, Q Magazine, The Record, Record Collector, Ri-Ra Magazine, RockNet, Rock 'n' Reel, Rolling Stone, RTE Guide, RTE Arts, Culture and Entertainment, Reuters Ltd., Ryko Disc, Salon.com, San Diego Union-Tribune, San Francisco Chronicle, San Jose Mercury News, Santa Fe New Mexican, Santa Rosa Oak Leaf, Scotland on Sunday, The Scotsman, Scripps* Howard News Service, *Seattle Weekly, SonicNet, Sky Showbiz, Sounds, The South Town Star, Spin Magazine, St. Louis Post-Dispatch, The Star, Star Tribune, Stuff Magazine, The Sun, Sunday Business Post, Sunday Independent, Sunday Tribune, Sunday World, The Telegraph,* Thomas Dolby's blog, *Time Out, The Times of London, Toronto Star, Toronto Sun, Tucson Weekly, UK Today, Uncut Magazine, Vancouver Sun, Variety, The Village Voice, Viz Magazine, Vox Magazine, Washington Post, Western Mail, and Wessex Scene Online.*

Printed in Great Britain
by Amazon

34530578R00124